TH
WIDOW
OF
WALCHA

Dad

Happy Birthday!

Love you so much

hope you enjoy this

book

xxx April

x

A TRUE STORY OF LOVE, LIES AND
MURDER IN A SMALL COUNTRY TOWN

THE
WIDOW
OF
WALCHA

EMMA
PARTRIDGE

SIMON &
SCHUSTER

London · New York · Sydney · Toronto · New Delhi

THE WIDOW OF WALCHA
First published in Australia in 2022 by
Simon & Schuster (Australia) Pty Limited
Suite 19A, Level 1, Building C, 450 Miller Street, Cammeray, NSW 2062
This edition published in 2024

10 9 8 7 6 5 4 3 2 1

Simon & Schuster: Celebrating 100 Years of Publishing in 2024.
Sydney New York London Toronto New Delhi
Visit our website at www.simonandschuster.com.au

A catalogue record for this
book is available from the
National Library of Australia

ISBN: 9781761424939

Cover design: Luke Causby/Blue Cork
Front cover image: Emma Partridge
Back cover images (from left to right): Facebook, Nathan Edwards / *The Daily
Telegraph*, Facebook
Typeset by Midland Typesetters, Australia
Printed and bound in Australia by Griffin Press

The paper this book is printed on is certified against the
Forest Stewardship Council® Standards. Griffin Press holds
chain of custody certification SCS-COC-001185. FSC®
promotes environmentally responsible, socially beneficial
and economically viable management of the world's forests.

NOTE TO READERS

For authenticity, all sources – including text messages, some internet searches, Facebook conversations, police interviews, transcripts and statements – have been reproduced in their original form, including spelling and grammatical errors. The names of several people have been changed to protect privacy. The accounts of some key witnesses who gave evidence during the NSW Supreme Court trial have not been included in this book, either for legal reasons or to prevent their further suffering.

Trigger warning: Please be advised that this book contains multiple references to suicide, which may distress some readers. The author has not used the phrase 'committed suicide' to avoid the potential negative implications of such usage, unless unavoidable in direct quotes. For more information, go to:

Lifeline: 13 11 14 lifeline.org.au
Suicide Call Back Service: 1300 659 467 suicidecallbackservice.org.au
Beyond Blue: 1300 224 636 beyondblue.org.au
SANE Australia: 1800 18 7263 saneforums.org

CONTENTS

Contents

PROLOGUE

As flocks of sheep huddle beneath trees in a sprawling paddock dusted with frost, blue and red lights flash, illuminating the homestead at Pandora. It's just after 2 am on 2 August 2017; paramedics Colin Crossman and Marion Schaap are first on the scene, responding to a report that grazier Mathew Dunbar is dead. They arrive to find Natasha Beth Darcy doing vigorous chest compressions on the 42-year-old farmer, guided by a triple-0 operator on speaker phone.

Mathew is lying in bed, unresponsive. To the right of his head, a plastic shopping bag is strewn, while a brown gas cylinder – more than a metre tall, the kind used to blow up helium balloons – stands next to his bedside table.

Mathew is dressed only in boxer shorts. He isn't breathing and has no pulse. Above the bed where he lies is a wall decal that says 'Sweet Dreams' in large cursive font surrounded by black butterfly stickers.

Although there are no signs of life, Mathew is still warm, prompting Natasha to ask the paramedics, 'That's a good sign, isn't it?'

Mathew is moved onto the carpet at the foot of the bed before Colin takes over doing compressions, but it's no use. Mathew is pronounced dead at 2.44 am.

Sergeant Anthony Smith, from the local Walcha police, arrives on the scene. A short time later, and with the heaviest of hearts, he declares Pandora a crime scene.

PART ONE

CAPTURING NATASHA DARCY

1
CRAZY EYES

I'm alone, lying in bed in the dark, when I see what she looks like for the first time.

'Oh my God,' I whisper, fingers zooming in on the photo my sister Tess has just texted me.

It's a woman wearing a gold heart-shaped pendant, lying back in a canvas hammock as she poses for a selfie. Her wild stare is penetrating, her dark hazel eyes boring through the lens. My phone beeps again. It's Tess, sending through another photo. This time, the woman is in a white lace top; her head is thrown back mid-laugh and she clutches a bunch of roses. It's haunting.

'Can you believe she's still living in the town?!' Tess writes.

The day before, Tess had called me. She and her husband Tom had just hosted lunch at their home in Newcastle for some of his relatives. During the afternoon, his family explained that there had been a suspicious death of a well-known farmer where they lived in the small town of Walcha, which lies east of Tamworth on the edge of NSW's Northern Tablelands.

Word has it, he'd been found with a plastic bag over his head, hooked up to a tank of helium. Most of the town believed the farmer's girlfriend played a role in his death but, two months on, she was still living free in town, going about her business like nothing had happened.

In the weeks leading up to the farmer's death, his girlfriend had apparently made several attempts to purchase powerful ram sedatives, which quickly raised the suspicions of the local vet because the woman had no legal use for them. The small community of Walcha had lost one of their own, and there was widespread worry a 'black widow' from out of town was living among them. No one knew what to do or how to approach her. Many wanted to know why she hadn't been arrested, and why she was still living out on the farmer's property with her three children.

'Apparently,' says Tess, 'she's already been to jail for trying to kill her ex-husband. He's a paramedic in Walcha, too, and he's the one who found the farmer dead.'

Sounding like a fellow journalist, Tess tells me I should head to Walcha to try and find out what's going on and where the police investigation is up to.

'They reckon it's been made out to look like a suicide, but nobody believes it,' she says.

I'm intrigued, but it's all sounding too strange to be true. Not long after we hang up, I find myself googling the woman's name on the internet and nosediving down a rabbit hole. There are dozens of articles and photographs about her.

'*Woman sentenced over Walcha house fire*,' the headline of a local paper reads. '*Jail time for false evidence*,' says another, followed by '*"Big spender" stabbed in jail*' and '*Woman guilty of fraud*'.

Her past is chequered, there's no doubt about it, but that doesn't automatically mean she's a killer. I wonder if she's a murderer or the victim of the town's rumour mill.

I've been a crime and court reporter for more than a decade, so I've reported on a lot of stories that seem hard to believe. During my time at *The Sydney Morning Herald*, I covered unimaginable and horrific crimes. One of the most harrowing was the murder of Stephanie Scott, the bright and bubbly schoolteacher killed by a cleaner on school grounds, just days before she was due to marry the love of her life in Leeton, a small town in the state's Riverina.

Just an hour south of Leeton, I'd spent more than a week in the town of Lockhart, after farmer Geoff Hunt shot and killed his wife and three young children on their family property. He then walked into a dam and shot himself dead. While some labelled him a 'monster' and others 'a good bloke', the horrific deaths of an entire family tragically highlighted the lack of mental health services available to people on the land. I remember sitting in the back of a helicopter hovering over the property, when I'd noticed tyre tracks snaking through a bright yellow canola field in front of the homestead. The tracks stopped at a ute parked next to a dam. I pressed my face against the glass to get a closer look, then wished I hadn't. We flew over just as police divers pulled Geoff Hunt's body from the water.

A few years later, I was in another small township, Lake Cathie, just south of Port Macquarie on NSW's Mid North Coast, trying to swallow the sick rising in my throat. As I watched on, police emptied a septic tank during their search for missing three-year-old William Tyrrell.

Bad things happen everywhere, but when they happen in small towns, where everyone knows everyone, the sense of loss and shock seems to hit harder.

Even when you see, hear and write about the unthinkable, it's still difficult to imagine how anyone gets to the point where death is the only option. I often wonder, what has happened to this person? What has gone so wrong? What events have they been through in the lead-up to them making the decision to take someone else's life?

So, although murders in small towns are sadly familiar to me, for some reason I'm struggling to believe the story my sister is telling me. It smells like small-town gossip. It's hard to believe it could be true.

I turn to my phone and follow a link to local articles about the death of farmer Mathew Dunbar. An article from the *Armidale Express* on 16 August 2017 reads:

Vale Mathew John Dunbar

Oxley Police say that a forensic autopsy has been completed and investigation into the circumstances surrounding Mathew Dunbar's death continues.

Mr Dunbar was found dead at his property Pandora off Thunderbolts Way, just out of Walcha, in the early hours of Wednesday, August 2.

On Thursday August 17 friends and family paid tribute to the man everyone described as genuine, generous and gentle at a poignant service in Saint Patrick's Church in Walcha.

The article then reveals that Mathew's partner of three years – Natasha Darcy – gave the eulogy, remembering him as 'beautiful, loving, caring, generous, kind and sweet'.

'I fell in love with him because he loved me when I couldn't even love myself,' Natasha said in her tribute.

Before I know it, I'm onto Natasha's Facebook page. Her Facebook status: 'Widowed'.

Just a day after Mathew was supposedly discovered dead, she'd written a public tribute to him, accompanied by photos of him with her and her three children.

'Yesterday (sic) we lost the sweetest man in the world. He was gentle, kind and the best stepfather any mother could want for her kids. My heart aches for you Mathew Dunbar but the pain is worth having had you in my life,' she wrote in a public post, with the account name of Natasha Darcy-Crossman.

In one picture, she has an arm around Mathew, who's wearing a Santa hat in front of a Christmas tree. Other photos show Mathew with his beloved border collies while, in another, he sits with one of Natasha's sons, both donning paper crowns from freshly cracked Christmas bon-bons.

Thoughts swirl through my head. Maybe Mathew had suicided, and the town was fanning a fire in the wrong direction? But then, the articles pop back into my mind about the house fire, fraud, false evidence and everything Tom's family had said.

Perhaps the suspicions of those living in Walcha are true.

2

LUCKY BREAK

Oblivious to the gale force winds outside, I stare at a grey wall inside a bunker hidden on the ground floor of the NSW Supreme Court. It's a room with no windows or air-conditioning; 12 desks are crammed into an area no bigger than a generous-sized bathroom. It's to here that reporters from all the major media outlets descend from the courts above, to file stories on the cases they've covered that day. Or to avoid going back to their respective newsrooms across Sydney.

Despite the cramped space and lack of light, over the years the journalists who've worked here have added splashes of life to the place. Lining some of the walls are court sketches of offenders and judges, while newspaper clippings and photographs are sticky-taped to random spots. They remind us of the big moments we've been honoured to witness and report on.

Technically, we're all competitors, but the room is mostly filled with laughter and never-ending tales of the day's events, a gossip room where we let our thoughts loose about the cases, judges, barristers, witnesses and subjects of our stories.

About 4 pm each day, the room is usually a hot-box of stress, as we all scurry to squeeze the day's events into a 400-word story, 30-second radio file or two-minute TV package. Journalists fly in and out of the room, calling their chiefs of staff or editors but, after the stress of the deadline passes, the chatter resumes, as we all settle in for the dreaded task of trawling the online court lists in search of what we'll cover the following day.

Today, I'm the only journalist in the court bunker; I've lost track of how long I've been staring at the wall. There are 23 floors of courtrooms above me and, although I've wandered in and out of a few cases already, I can't concentrate. I can't stop thinking about the death of farmer Mathew Dunbar, the haunting image of Natasha Darcy my sister had texted me, and all the wild stories I'd read about her.

My gut tells me there's far more to this story. I want to know more. A familiar anxiety fills my chest. It's hard to concentrate on anything else; my mind is overrun with niggling questions coupled with the fear other media might beat me to finding out the answers. I bite the bullet and make a few calls.

My first port of call is the NSW Police media unit. They are the gatekeepers of many stories, helpful but sometimes oppressive to crime reporters. Almost gone are the days when journalists got their scoops over beers at the pub with the cops. The media unit collects information from police about all ongoing investigations and incidents, from car crashes and organised crime to missing person searches, robberies and murders. In turn, they email journalists with media releases, sometimes up to 20 on any given day. The information is helpful, usually accurate and an effective way of reaching all media outlets, but it doesn't leave much room for journalists to do their own digging, or work on a story by themselves. It allows police to set the news agenda and – combined with ever-shrinking newsrooms – the media releases they issue often dictate many stories that go to air in the evening bulletins or are published in the next day's paper.

While it's a love–hate relationship, police and journalists need each other. Police often use the media as an investigative tool – releasing images, security footage or certain information publicly to rattle cages or move a case along. The media need police to feed them with information they can't necessarily get from doorknocking, interviews and internet stalking.

My philosophy – where possible – is to tell the investigating police what I know to get confirmation the information I have is correct. Also, in the hope the police will explain the background of a case to me – not necessarily for me to report, but so I have a better understanding of what they're trying to achieve and what the sensitivities are.

It's also helpful for police to be open because they can ask journalists not to report on certain information, which may impact their investigation. Especially with homicides, detectives need to keep some cards close to their chests. Sometimes, they don't want to spook the suspect they're homing in on, or let them know how much they know. Other times, they need to have fresh information up their sleeves, which they can release down the track during public appeals if they come to a dead end. Often, journalists may find out what type of weapon was used in a homicide but exclude this information in their reports at the request of police. If an 'iron bar' has never been mentioned publicly, for instance, how did the girlfriend of John Smith know he was bludgeoned to death with one?

Sometimes, the omission of certain facts is more of a moral call, such as if police have been unable to contact the family of a person who has just been killed. Journalists are often asked to refrain from reporting certain details or a victim's identity until the next of kin is informed. It's something many reporters respect, but asking an editor or chief of staff to remember the feelings of fellow humans can sometimes be an uphill battle.

Most days, it feels like walking a tightrope – trying to maintain a balance of reporting the facts and doing the right, human thing. It's certainly not sunshine and rainbows. I've lost count of how many times I've cried during my dealings with police and over highly sensitive, and often horrific, cases. For the most part, however, the relationship seems to work in its strange way. Over the years, I've come to know and respect many great police, and even call some of them friends. The same goes with police media officers. I've no doubt some hate me – and vice versa – but there are others I trust and who trust me.

Still sitting in the court bunker, I call someone I trust in the media unit, hoping to find out if there is some truth to these Walcha whispers. I'm completely honest about what my sister has told me and what we've found online before asking them point-blank: 'Is there really some crazy black widow, who's killed a local farmer in Walcha and is still running around the town?'

Off the record, I'm told the farmer Mathew Dunbar's partner is in the frame but, at this stage, the local detectives are still investigating. Shortly after hanging up the phone, I'm emailed an official response, which says:

> Investigations are continuing into the death of a man in the Northern Tablelands two months ago.
>
> Emergency services responded to reports of an unresponsive man at a home on Thunderbolts Way, Walcha, about 2am on Wednesday 2 August 2017.
>
> Despite the efforts of NSW Ambulance paramedics, the 42-year-old man died at the scene.
>
> Strike Force Ballin was established by detectives from the State Crime Command's Homicide Squad and Oxley Local Area Command to investigate the circumstances surrounding the man's death.
>
> As the investigation is ongoing, no further information is available at this time.

A word in the fourth paragraph prompts me to raise my eyebrows: 'homicide'. If police thought Mathew Dunbar's death was a suicide, there's no way the homicide squad would be working on the case two months down the track.

For a brief moment, I'm at a loss. I don't know who else to call because I don't know many detectives or officers who work in the

Tamworth area. I walk out through the court security doors and into the cyclonic wind, to have a ciggie and think. Pacing back and forth in front of the court, I take a stab in the dark. I call a senior police officer I know, hoping he may know someone who may know something. Anything. After a few rings, he picks up. I ask him if he has five minutes to listen while I explain 'a wild but probably not true' story. He listens patiently to my excitable, verbal diarrhoea.

When I finally pause to take a breath, he chimes in.

'My God, sounds like the people of Walcha are really onto something,' he says, a note of mischief in his voice.

'What? It's true? You have to be joking?' I ask, my brain spinning.

There are 17,000 cops in the force, so I'm taken aback that I've managed to call someone who knows about this case. 'You're pretty bang on, it's true, but there are far more twists and turns than you think. I can't go into the whole thing now, but it's quite the story. Even you'll be shocked.'

'So, the helium, the ex-hubby, the ram sedatives, the farmer killed – all true?' I ask.

'There's far more to it, but you're on the right track. There's nothing stopping you from going up there and having a dig around for yourself.'

I ask if I'd be jeopardising anything if I approached Natasha to see what she had to say.

'If the whole town knows what's going on, I don't see the harm in you asking a few questions,' he said, before suggesting I try to speak to Natasha myself. That's what he'd do if he were a journalist.

As far as he can tell, the police officer says, the local detectives have all but finished the investigation and are 'crossing their T's and dotting their I's'.

Itching to get to Walcha, I text the *Daily Telegraph*'s editor Chris Dore, explaining I'll be back in the office soon and need to talk to him. I've been working at the *Tele* for almost a year as their chief court reporter but, every couple of months, I pitch a crime yarn.

Traditionally, crime reporters cover cases from the time they occur through to the point where there is an arrest. After that, the court reporter usually takes over and follows the case through until there is a resolution. If an accused pleads guilty or the charges are dropped, this can happen quickly but, if the case ends up going to trial in the Supreme Court, it can take another two or three years. There is a mind-boggling amount of administration involved in keeping track of hundreds, if not thousands, of cases throughout the state – chasing up dates, tracking where each matter is up to and staying across ongoing trials.

Aside from reporting, my role is to decide which cases the *Tele* should cover each day, which may send three or four journalists to different courts across Sydney. If you're being thorough, it's a two-hour job at the end of each day and, if you miss something other media have turned up to, it's your head on the line.

I'm hoping Dore will allow me to abandon the courts – and all the dreaded administration – for a few days so I can head to Walcha. Our conversation lasts less than five minutes.

'Yes. Love it. Go,' he says from his glass office, overlooking the Surry Hills newsroom.

In light of the scant details I gave him, and after explaining there was every chance I'd come back with nothing, his enthusiasm surprised me.

'What do you need? You don't need to tell the picture desk all the details, but get them to hook you up with a photographer and I'll leave you to sort the rest out.'

3
MAD DASH

'Call me,' reads a text from a police contact.

It's two weeks since my request to head to Walcha. I'm sitting at the back of a courtroom during the first day of a murder trial in Newcastle. I stare at the text for a minute, wondering what's wrong or if I'm in trouble. My mind always ventures to worst-case scenarios, flicking through a Filofax of cases and stories I've covered, wondering what could possibly be wrong. In the past, I've received abuse and criticism I haven't seen coming, so my default position, when I see a missed call or text about something that isn't fully explained, is to worry.

Writing about death – whether it's an accident, murder or coronial inquest – creates so many opportunities to upset people or cause distress (unwittingly), whether it's a lawyer representing a client, a judge, the police, an advocacy group or, worse, the family or friends of a victim.

When covering trials or writing about death, I try to keep in my mind the family and friends of a victim or the person who had died. The test is this: can I look them in the eye after writing this? Of course, it's impossible to omit all upsetting details and facts, but thinking about who might read the story helps me to write with more sensitivity.

A former colleague of mine, journalist Damien Murphy, taught me how important it is to do this when I was a young and green crime reporter, not long after landing my dream role at *The Sydney Morning Herald*.

In December 2013, I was sent out to Rouse Hill, a suburb in Sydney's north-west, to report on the horrific death of a woman, who died after she was set alight with petrol. At the bottom of her driveway, the grass was singed black, marking the place where the woman had collapsed in agony. Neighbours heard her screams, and several described the horror of smelling burning human flesh.

Their accounts saddened and sickened me but, for some reason, I went on to write an article without giving her family a second thought. Perhaps I was going for shock factor when I started my article with the gruesome fact that neighbours had smelled the woman burning alive.

After the story was published, Damien wandered over to my desk in the newsroom.

'How do you think her family might feel reading this?' he asked gently. He wasn't being antagonistic in any way, but genuinely wanted me to think about it.

Heat crawled up my neck, turning my face tomato-red. My stomach lurched. Welling tears threatened to overflow, but I kept them at bay as I listened to the advice of a seasoned journo.

I'd been so caught up in the horror of what I had seen and heard, and the pressure of filing a crime report in a new job, that I hadn't given any thought about how the story might have made other people feel. I still fall back on that moment to this day. I know I don't always get it right but when writing – particularly about death – I try to remember that I'm writing about a person and think of the potential impact my words may have on their loved ones.

Now, still sitting in the courtroom, I look back to the message from the police contact on my phone, but I can't call back straight away.

The Crown prosecutor is halfway through his opening address in the trial of two people charged with the murder of retired architect and much-loved surfer Leslie Wallace. The 65-year-old man was in the process of moving into a Terrigal unit, on NSW's Central Coast, when he was killed during a violent home invasion in a case of mistaken identity.

After the prosecutor finishes his address to the jury, I hastily stand up, bow in the direction of the judge (a court formality) and walk out the door, carefully closing it behind so as not to make any noise.

Unlike many older courthouses, the modern Newcastle Court complex, on Hunter Street in the middle of the CBD, is flooded with natural light. The building's glass panelling allows you to see as far as the lighthouse on the headlands at Nobby Beach and, to the left, the port of Newcastle.

I walk over to a seat near the window and, taking a deep breath, call the police contact who had texted me. To my relief, the phone call is just a friendly heads-up. My contact, one of several I'd confided in about my plans to head to Walcha, tells me other journalists are looking into Mathew Dunbar's death and Natasha's potential involvement in it. They suggest that, if I was ever going to head to Walcha, now would be the time.

I'm kicking myself for not going sooner but, after talking to the *Tele*'s editor, I'd decided there was enough time for me to cover this murder trial in Newcastle before heading to Walcha.

I hang up the phone and bolt towards the lifts, hitting the button repeatedly until the doors open. Once out of the building, I jog to my car, which is parked further down Hunter Street, thinking about who I need to call and how quickly I can get to Walcha. There's already a suitcase packed on the backseat of my car, because I had planned on heading straight to Walcha at the end of the trial I've just walked out of.

For the next five hours, I drive, smoke and talk on the phone – except where reception doesn't allow. I call the *Tele*'s chief of staff to explain I'm heading to Walcha. Now. Next, I touch base with picture editor Nic Gibson and ask if photographer Nathan Edwards is free to meet me at Walcha first thing in the morning. Nathan is a gun photographer who lives at Port Macquarie, about a two-and-a-half-hour drive from Walcha. We work well together and I'm ecstatic to hear he's free to meet me there.

The following call is to an in-house lawyer, flagging the possibility of a story about Mathew's death and the potential involvement of his partner. He barks at me in a raised voice for the best part of half an hour.

'Listen, honeeeeyyyy . . . you're living in la-la land,' he says, turning my cheeks pink with rage.

Apparently, from a legal standpoint, the only way I could write this story is if I manage to find Natasha and allow her the opportunity to tell her side of it. He also tells me that, if Natasha isn't arrested, we will surely be sued for defamation. He's even less thrilled with the news that no police will go on the record, something that could help to save us if we ended up landing in court.

The only way to get the story over the line, he says, is for me to approach Natasha myself and speak to her. She must be given an opportunity to tell her side of the story. I begin to worry about her potential reaction to me lobbing up at her home to ask questions.

There's limited time, too. If she's charged before I write a story, I won't be able to delve into her criminal past, including the detail about her previously being charged with the attempted murder of her ex-husband Colin Crossman.

Media lawyers are wary about publishing a person's previous convictions once they are charged with another crime, for fear it could prejudice their trial before a jury. But sometimes you can make use of a sweet spot, publishing a person's criminal history when they're arrested, but taking the story down online once they're officially charged. Or, when you know their arrest is imminent.

It's now the golden hour. The sun is quickly vanishing when I realise I haven't been taking any notice of the direction I'm driving. Because I was so engrossed on the phone, I've been travelling in the wrong direction. I'm heading north from Newcastle up the Pacific Highway, instead of taking a much quicker inland road, adding an extra two hours to what should have been a three-and-a-half-hour trip. Just south of Port Macquarie, I turn left onto the Oxley Highway, which will lead me all the way to Walcha.

4

WALCHA WHISPERS

Walcha is a cool and misty town, surrounded by rich agricultural land, which is home to some 3000 people. The Apsley River flows through town and into the Oxley Wild Rivers National Park, where it falls off two steep cliffs into the Apsley Gorge. It's also a wealthy farming community; there's no shortage of Range Rovers, Ralph Lauren Polo shirts (worn with a popped collar) and RM Williams boots. There's also an eclectic mix of townspeople: blue-collar workers, artists and retirees.

About five hours' drive north of Sydney, Walcha is at the inter-section of two main roads – the Oxley Highway and Thunderbolts Way. Breathtaking countryside and bushland line both roads on the way in, making it a popular stopover for bikers and car enthusiasts.

Walcha is the oldest settlement in the New England region; the original facades of many historic buildings – the pubs, churches, theatre and bank – remain intact. It's easy to imagine horse-drawn carriages ferrying goods down the main drag. More than 50 outdoor sculptures are dotted along the streets and river, which make its enchanting sense of history all the more visible. This collection of sculptures and artworks, created by local, national and international artists, form what is known as Walcha's Open-Air Gallery. It also includes about 30 sculpted veranda posts – using mainly local timber – installed in front of shops and small businesses. Of note is *The Whale* made from galvanised steel, breaching out of the grass next to a riverside walking track, as well as a statuesque, timber figure named *True Born Native Man*, welcoming people at the western entrance to town. On the eastern side, it's hard to miss *Song Cycle* – a towering, cylindrical structure positioned on the main roundabout in town, the steel shapes and lines suggesting music on a page.

It's pitch-dark when I first pull into Walcha. No maps are needed to spot the white, illuminated sign for the Walcha Motel, which boasts 'Reverse cycle air conditioning' in large, red font.

After checking in and dumping my bags, I head out in search of a pub in town. It's impossible to miss the Commercial Hotel, a two-storey pub perched on a quiet intersection, painted bright yellow with a dirt-red, corrugated-iron roof. The pub first opened its doors on the Queen's Birthday weekend in 1865, and is still being used for its original purpose. While the horse troughs out front are gone, the facade remains true to its original design.

I walk into the front bar and order a glass of the house shiraz. I cautiously assess a handful of locals sipping on schooners. I'm certain Mathew's death has been discussed in this very place. I wonder what everyone in here knows. Or what they think they know.

It's a small town, so it's possible Natasha could be somewhere in here tonight.

I decide it's best not to give away that I'm a journalist but, if someone asks, I won't lie. It's a tiny town so I don't want everyone to know I'm here, especially the local journalists, who I'm sure know more than I do. I'd prefer to do some quiet digging without attracting a media circus.

'What brings you here to Walcha?' the barman asks.

'Just here for work, hoping to grab some dinner,' I reply, acutely aware my answer is being listened to by everyone seated behind me, maybe five or six people.

'What do you do for work?' he asks.

I wince. I'm a terrible liar, and drown in a whirlpool of guilt if I'm not honest. In my best attempt at being blasé, I tell him I'm a journalist, and just in town for a few days.

'Ahhhhhhh,' he says, filling me a country-size glass of wine, well past the white line and right to the brim. 'You must be here to cover the murder down the road?'

'Murder? Yeah, well, I don't know if it's a murder, but I've heard a few things. I'm just here for a few days to try and chat to a few people,' I say, before explaining I also have a loose family connection to Walcha.

He nods slowly, handing me a menu.

I walk around the bar and into the dining room, a little rattled the subject has been raised so soon.

Despite the awkward conversation and thoughts bubbling in my head, I'm hungry, and the kitchen closes at 8 pm. There's nothing more I love than a good, old-fashioned country pub, except a decent-sized, juicy chicken schnitzel with two gravy boats of pepper sauce. Tonight's dinner is the mother of all schnitzels: the size of a pizza, encased in perfectly fried Panko crumbs and with a generous serving of thick, beer-battered chips. Even better is the information served with it.

The barman plonks the schnitzel on my table and crouches beside me.

'Mate, Mathew was definitely murdered. His girlfriend, she's still out there on the property,' he says, his comment reaffirming my strong belief that the best stories, gossip and information can always be found at the local watering hole.

I ask why he's so certain Mathew was murdered. He explains how almost everyone in Walcha knows that all Mathew ever wanted was to find love and have a family of his own. He'd been open about his loneliness and search for a partner, which many believed Natasha had exploited. With her three children, Natasha offered him an instant family, and she was well versed in the seduction of men, especially when after their money.

It makes me wonder, what does she stand to gain financially from Mathew's death?

I mention to the barman what I'd heard about Natasha serving time for burning down the family home, while her husband Colin Crossman slept inside. The house is just around the corner from the pub, he says, giving me the address.

The barman is keen to keep chatting and I let him. He tells me Natasha has taken advantage of another local man, racking up thousands of dollars on his stolen credit card during an almighty shopping spree in nearby Armidale.

Before he gets back to work, he lowers his voice and says many suspected Natasha was up to something in the lead-up to Mathew's death, but had felt powerless to do anything. Apparently, Natasha had suspiciously tried to buy ram sedatives from the local vet when she had no use for them. My sister had relayed the same thing to me.

'Ask anyone,' he says. 'The vet, the butcher or the girls down the road at the café – everyone will tell you Mathew was murdered.'

He can't understand why the police haven't arrested her. The whole town suspects her. They believe there's a murderer in their midst. Why isn't anything being done about it?

The following morning, I take a walk around town to get my bearings. The grass outside the Walcha Motel is frosted white and mist hovers over the Apsley River. There's something magical about the place. I'm due to meet photographer Nathan Edwards at the local café to nut out a game plan, but first, I call Tamworth Police Station and ask to speak to the crime manager, an officer with a position that oversees all major investigations in the region.

I explain who I am and why I'm in Walcha, then ask if he might be free for me to come and meet him. He makes it clear he's not interested. During our brief conversation, he doesn't give much away, but says the investigation is ongoing and asks me to refrain from approaching Natasha. It's another confirmation she's the woman squarely in the frame.

I ask why talking to her would be problematic, especially because it had been more than two months since Mathew's death. All he says is that his detectives are making good progress and now isn't a good time.

'You might be able to help us down the track,' he says, adding I may have an 'opportunity' to speak to her in future and possibly interview the investigating police. It's a typical blow-off I've heard before. Police often dangle 'opportunities down the track' that never materialise.

Begrudgingly, I agree to stay away from Natasha for now, but not before commenting on the town's collective worry she may never be arrested.

Deflated, I hang up. But there's still a lot I can do without confronting her at this stage.

Later, I find Nathan smiling and smoking outside Café Graze – the best place for coffee and local gossip. He knows the owner of the café, Edwina, so we head inside to grab a coffee.

Nathan is a great person to have on a secret squirrel mission. Earlier in the year, we'd spent a few days together up north in Tweed Heads, travelling with the NSW Police drug squad as they raided cannabis plantations on rural properties and in national parks. Before then, we'd covered the disappearance of three-year-old William Tyrrell, who vanished from Kendall, a town near Port Macquarie. Although, at the time, we were working for opposition newspapers, we've spent many hours chatting over ciggies and coffees (our shared vices) to pass the hours and days spent camped outside crime scenes and the homes of potential suspects.

Inside the café, word spreads quickly about our reason for being in town. We've just missed Natasha's ex-husband Colin Crossman by a few minutes – he was in here having coffee with one of his paramedic colleagues.

Talking in hushed tones, one local mentions how Colin had been one of the first paramedics on the scene after Natasha had reportedly found Mathew dead. Another is quick to tell us Colin often drives Mathew's ute around town, a move that riles up a lot of people.

Another local in the café says he knows Mathew from 'way back', having studied with him at The Armidale School, a private school for boys about 60 kilometres from Walcha.

'Honestly, all the bloke ever wanted was to have a family,' he says, shaking his head.

We learn that Natasha also drops into Café Graze on occasion. Everyone is bewildered to see her smiling and going about her business. 'Larger than life' is a common description people use for her, even in the wake of Mathew's death.

Another local later tells me many parents find it uncomfortable working with Natasha on canteen duty at the local primary school, where two of her children attend.

'It's just so weird, it's bizarre,' she says. 'Nobody knows what to say to her, but we all feel for her kids.'

There is so much talk in this town, so many whispers, but there is one man I need to find. This Walcha farmer knows more than anyone about Mathew. Although he may not know it yet, he's also someone who holds explosive information about a possible motive.

5

ROADSIDE MEETING

Nathan and I are on our way to meet Lance Partridge, Mathew's closest friend, at Lance's property Warren Park, not far from the town's centre.

I already get the sense that Lance is a vital part of Walcha's fabric. We've yet to have a conversation with anyone in town without his name popping up, especially when talking about Mathew. Once crowned Walcha's Australia Day citizen of the year, the well-known grazier is involved in every board, show and club imaginable. He's dedicated 50 years to the Walcha Poultry Club and, throwing aside the stereotype of a stoic farmer, he's also a director, actor and writer for the Walcha Musical Society.

Searching the internet, I learn he recently dedicated one of his musicals to his 'dear friend Mathew', who'd spent hours of his time editing, typing and printing the society's scripts with military precision. This is just one of dozens of community-minded services Mathew did, without asking for or seeking any recognition.

I wonder if we could be related. There are a few Partridges in Walcha and dozens rest in the local cemetery.

After Nathan pulls into Lance's driveway, I hop out and walk over to the front door, knocking lightly. I hope he's home. His wife Trish opens the door with a warm smile. Lance is not home but, after I explain why I wished to talk to him, she tells me we should find him on a nearby road herding cattle. Trish tells me a little bit about Mathew. He was part of their family and often spent Christmases with the Partridges, sharing games of backyard cricket and eating Trish's decadent pavlovas. Mathew always arrived with a truckload of presents, gleefully showering everyone with gifts. Trish hopes the police are still working on the case. She and Lance are finding it hard, not knowing what is going on. It's been a while since they've heard anything.

Nathan and I take off down the road. It's not long before we spot Lance. He's hard to miss in his bright red-and-white flannelette shirt tucked into chocolate-brown work pants, herding about a dozen Angus cattle down the road. Two trusty cattle dogs guard the rear; one of them is a border collie named Rascal, which Mathew had given him.

We pull up just ahead of Lance on the side of the road and wait for him to reach us. After introducing myself as a journalist, and a Partridge, I tell him how sorry I am to learn he's lost his closest friend. I explain my loose connection to Walcha (my brother-in-law's family) and how I'd come to learn about Mathew's death. I also make my intentions clear, explaining that I plan on writing an article about his mysterious death in the hope of shedding more light on what's happened.

Lance listens intently, nodding a few times. He's not really giving much away.

I ask him if he'd be comfortable telling me about Mathew – a little bit about who he was and what he thinks happened. He thinks about this for a few moments and, while he's understandably cautious, he agrees to talk.

What's clear from the get-go is that Lance is no fan of Natasha. He needs to keep the peace with her at the moment, however, because he's helping to run Mathew's property Pandora and overseeing the year's shearing with her. He's doing this out of loyalty to Mathew, but will only help out until the police investigation is finished and the property is officially someone else's. Until then, he doesn't want to rock the boat. For a few seconds, Lance looks down at his hands, struggling to describe how much Mathew meant to him.

'I spent a lot of time with him,' he says, slowly. Finding his voice, Lance speaks about their shared love of the poultry club, chuckling as he explains how devoted Mathew was to the club, despite never owning a chicken. Mathew spent hours of his time doing administration and setting up exhibits for shows, without complaining or asking for thanks.

'He was heavily involved in that – he did all the work. He enjoyed that and he enjoyed the company,' Lance says.

He explains Mathew was close to his father, John Dunbar, who'd left his entire estate to his only son following his death about a decade ago. This includes Pandora, 1200 acres (485.6 ha) of prime agricultural land and Gidley, a 500-acre (202.3 ha) property about 7 kilometres from town. Later, Mathew sold the smaller property to a local dairy for about $1 million, keen to raise capital to maintain and improve Pandora.

Lance begins to frown as he talks about the sale of Gidley, then he catches me off guard as the conversation turns from Mathew's assets to Natasha.

'He went through all of his money in the end and that's that,' he says.

Sensing he has more to say about this, I follow up with a question: 'Was that largely – to an extent – spent on Natasha?'

Lance appears to be carrying some sort of burden that he wants to unload, but is unsure about sharing such private information with me here, on the side of a dirt road. But Lance is a straight shooter and tells it like it is. And he tells me a lot. It's all leading up to something gravely important.

A few months after Mathew and Natasha's relationship began, he explains, Natasha was sent to jail for more than a year for a crime I'd later learn much more about.

Although they hadn't been dating long, Mathew remained dedicated while she did her time. He helped to care for her three children and spent thousands of dollars renovating a granny flat on his property for her eldest child, her daughter. He also helped out financially, despite the children all living with her estranged husband Colin, the local paramedic, who was their legal guardian.

When Natasha got out of jail, Mathew showered her with gifts. He allowed her to buy whatever her heart desired: clothes, a brand-new car and $30,000 horse float, for starters.

'So, you know, the money soon went,' Lance says.

I press a little further. What was the relationship like between Natasha and Mathew, especially in the days and months leading up to his death?

'Well, he didn't get what he was promised. When he first got with Natasha, she promised marriage and a chance to have a family and, anyhow, then she broke her parole and went to jail for 12 months,' Lance says, a slight hint of anger in his voice.

'Natasha promised to get a quick divorce and marry Mathew when she got out of jail. Mathew asked me to be his best man, and I said I would.'

This confirms what so many locals have kept repeating: Mathew was desperate to have a family, and Natasha and her children represented what he'd always been searching for. They were an instant family. He wanted it so badly, he was willing to turn a blind eye to her criminal history. Although he didn't like it one little bit, he also allowed her ex-husband Colin to spend time at Pandora with the children.

'I believe she was married to him and is *still* married to him,' Lance says, referring to Natasha and Colin. 'I don't think they've ever got divorced.' He describes their relationship as 'most unusual'.

The fact Colin has anything to do with Natasha, after nearly burning alive in the house she deliberately torched, seems unusual in itself. Even more odd was that Natasha had hung framed professional family photographs of her, Colin and the children on the walls at Pandora. If the family happy snaps weren't upsetting to Mathew, I can't imagine how he felt passing the picture of just Natasha and Colin, hugging as they pose for the camera. I can't imagine how Mathew put up with this warped situation.

'Col was there all the time, out at Pandora, and none of these promises came true – came to anything – the promises of getting married to him and the chance of him having a family,' Lance says. 'It was like Natasha and Col were a happily married couple. It was most odd.'

Colin's presence caused Mathew great distress, particularly in the final months of his life.

Lance recalls having 'private yarns' with Mathew at Pandora, when (and it happened on several occasions) Colin would walk in unannounced like he owned the place. Apparently, he'd sit in front of them while they were talking, listening, but never saying a word. 'It was most rude.'

What also infuriates Lance is that Colin borrowed money from Mathew while Natasha was in jail. Lance finds it hard to believe Colin had the nerve to ask for a loan. Mathew even contributed to Colin's rent. One time, Mathew complained to Lance, 'I even have to iron Col's shirts.'

Lance tells me he advised Mathew to 'rack Col off' but Mathew wouldn't, too afraid of losing his ready-made family. Because Colin was the children's legal guardian, Mathew saw no other option; he did what he was told and put up with the situation.

'All Mathew wanted was a happy family life and Natasha promised that. He already thought of the kids as his own but, when she came out of jail, that did not happen at all.'

Despite his efforts to keep a happy family, Mathew's relationship with Natasha was crumbling. One day, it reached boiling point. About six weeks before his death, Mathew had taken a firearm from the sheds at Pandora and called Lance in great distress.

'He said, "I've taken a gun. I've had an argument with Natasha. I'm going out and I won't be coming back," before he hung up.' The fight was over money.

Distraught, Lance rang Natasha to see whether Mathew had in fact left the property with a gun.

'She said, "He's left the house, but I wouldn't worry about it."'

When he suggested they ring the police, Natasha is adamant they shouldn't.

'"Oh, don't ring the police. I don't want the police involved in it,"' Lance recalls her saying.

Lance wasn't going to ignore his friend's cry for help. He called the police then rang Mathew's phone repeatedly. After what felt like hours, Mathew picked up.

Mathew told Lance he'd driven out to Gloucester Road with a gun and contemplated his suicide but 'couldn't do it'.

'I don't think Mathew ever could kill himself . . .' Lance says, trailing off.

After getting off the phone, Mathew drove straight to Lance's house. Although he'd hinted at problems he was having at home, he'd never fully opened up about the full extent. Until this day.

Mathew was always fiercely defensive of Natasha, dismissing anyone who brought up her criminal history or said she was a 'con bird', as Lance refers to her. But following his suicide threat, Mathew finally opened up to his closest confidant about the true nature of his relationship with Natasha.

'That's when he said – it's the first time he ever said to me – that Col and Natasha were happily married. It was . . .' Lance can't finish his sentence, thinking about the awful situation Mathew found himself in.

Mathew saw Natasha as his partner but, deep down, he believed she was still romantically linked to Colin. And Natasha's daughter, whom he thought of as his own, wasn't spending any time with him. They'd drifted apart, which distressed him greatly.

Mathew also divulged he was in deep financial trouble. Creditors were chasing money, but he had no means of coming up with any cash until shearing time, later in the year.

'I really think that she worked on him all the time, and she worked on the fact that Mathew liked to say he was sick and liked attention,' Lance says, referring to Mathew being a bit of a hypochondriac.

Until Mathew's suicide attempt, and his subsequent confession about the state of their relationship, Lance had tried to have faith that Natasha was doing the right thing.

'I didn't know things had got that bad,' he says.

There was no shortage of people who told Mathew: 'Don't have anything to do with her'. And although Mathew believed Natasha was deeply interested in Colin, she was 'still the love of his life', he told Lance.

While Lance was one of the few people who supported the relationship, it was only because he wanted to have Mathew's back.

'Like the detective said when I went for my interviews, she is very good at what she does,' he says.

'Which is?' I ask.

'Well, she's taken a lot of people down before, you see.' He then summarises the 2009 house fire, which she lit, and the time she stole another partner's credit card, which landed her back in jail.

These past three months, Lance has been putting on a brave smile but, deep down, he doesn't believe Natasha is truly grieving Mathew's death. For starters, she and Colin took the children to a rugby carnival at Moree just days after Mathew's death.

'When it first happened, she said, "How could Mathew do this to me?" and played her cards very well.'

Leaning on the tray of his ute, Lance pauses for some time, thinking hard about what he wants to say next. 'I honestly . . . well, I know that Mathew would be still here and be quite well if he hadn't got attached with her.'

Regardless of whether Natasha physically killed Mathew, Lance holds her responsible for his death, while Natasha continues to maintain Mathew's death was a suicide.

In the version she spun to Lance, on the night of his death, the pair had stayed up late talking. They were sleeping in separate rooms, but she got up in the middle of the night to check on Mathew.

'Why she would get up at half past one or two o'clock to check on Mathew, I'd have no idea. But she got up and found him with this bag around his head, and he'd gassed himself. She said she tried to revive him with CPR until the ambulance came out. And Col came out. Col was the ambulance officer that came out.'

'Anyhow, she said she tried to bring him around with CPR, and she was sure she had him breathing, and then when the ambulance come, they took over.'

Lance speaks unprompted throughout our conversation, words spilling out of his mouth, leaving me little need to ask questions. He tells us about how, on the night he died, Mathew phoned his neighbour Ross King for a friendly chat. He reckons this was 'most unusual for somebody that's planning to commit suicide later that night', because they weren't great friends. They usually reserved their conversation for farming-related topics such as fencing.

I ask Lance what he would like to say about Mathew if, down the track, I print an article about what's happened.

He's lightning-bolt quick to answer. 'Mathew was a very giving person. He had trouble communicating and thought that his money would buy friends.' He explains further; knowing Lance has a keen eye for photography, Mathew had once bought him a Go-Pro camera. But when Lance tried to give it back, Mathew was devastated.

'Everybody that knew Mathew, liked Mathew, because he would never hurt anybody, he'd always help someone out and he was just a giving, giving fellow.'

'He'd give his heart to somebody, and people would, sort of, they'd take advantage of him, because he was so easy to take advantage of.'

In the event Natasha is ever arrested, I ask him, is there anything he would like to say about her?

First, Lance says, no matter what, he wants to get all of Mathew's sheep shorn. This will be his first shearing season without Mathew, and he needs to focus on getting through it. For Mathew.

'I don't really care what happens to Natasha now. I pretend to be good friends and I like her three kids, but what goes around comes around. And if she is charged and goes to jail, then that's how it should be. If she doesn't and she inherits the place, well, that's how it should be,' he says, taking a philosophical approach.

Lance won't be there to help if she does inherit the farm, however, even though he's spent the past 12 years classing Mathew's wool and helping at Pandora.

'I'm not going to be friends with Natasha, because she didn't do the right thing by Mathew.'

'Would you be surprised if she was charged?' I ask.

'No. I know the detectives are wanting to pin something on her and I think they're right in thinking that way.'

Lance then tells me something that suddenly makes everything much clearer about why the police are focusing their attention on the grieving widow. Natasha and Mathew's romance was brief; they'd been together just shy of three years after meeting in about October 2014. But Natasha had spent about half of their relationship in jail.

Lance tells me that, at some point in 2015 while she was serving time, Mathew changed his will, leaving his entire estate to her.

'That's what she wanted and, when she asked him to do something, he did it,' Lance says, swiping at a fly.

Lance was even privy to a conversation in which Natasha pushed and quizzed Mathew about whether he had officially changed his will with a solicitor. The conversation occurred when Lance and Mathew were driving down to Sydney together. Mathew was on his way to visit Natasha in jail, and Lance was coming along for the ride to keep him company. Mathew often visited her but, this time, he was coming to check if she was okay after reportedly being stabbed in a prison fight.

When Natasha phoned, she was oblivious that she was on loud-speaker. Her tone and words were clear for Lance to hear. She wasn't interested in talking about her injuries, or how Mathew was. Her sole focus was Mathew's will.

'She rang up, wanting to know had he changed the will, made a will in her favour. Oh yes, she was most adamant about it.'

Lance says the conversation washed over him. At the time, he didn't think too much about it, because he was worried about Mathew, who was highly anxious and distressed about Natasha's physical state. The significance of the conversation dawned on him in the days following Mathew's death, when Natasha feigned shock at having been made the sole beneficiary of his estate.

'She said, "Oh, I didn't know that Mathew had made the will over to me." And yet, I was sitting in the car driving down to Sydney to see her in jail when she asked him, had he changed it.' Lance lowers his voice. 'I'm sure she thinks she's got away with it all.'

6

THE MONEY SHOT

Leaving Lance on the side of the road, Nathan and I drive back to Café Graze. Natasha's push to be made the sole beneficiary seems like a possible motive. It's also clear that Mathew was experiencing anguish in the lead-up to his death, as evidenced by his threat of suicide.

Lance is adamant that Mathew would never take his own life, but his suicide attempt six weeks earlier makes me wonder. Perhaps, there were underlying mental health issues that contributed to his suicide threat, or maybe these were a direct result of his deteriorating relationship with Natasha. Before he died, Mathew was also stressed about money, finding himself cash-strapped for the first time in his life, after Natasha and her children moved out to Pandora.

So many questions. I need to find Natasha. Eventually, I'll need to approach her and ask about her side of the story but, for now, Nathan and I need shots of her. This story should be told with words and photographs. If we can't approach her on this trip, at the very least, I'd like to get shots of her in case she's arrested before we return to Walcha.

A quick internet search helps me to map out all the places she could potentially be, including the primary school and Colin's house. If all else fails, we can camp on the main drag for a couple of days and hopefully catch her at the local shops.

We know she's still living at Mathew's property, so this seems like an obvious place to head first.

Nathan and I decide to drive in convoy. We travel down Derby Street to the main roundabout and continue straight. The street turns into Thunderbolts Way, a road stretching another 150 kilometres south to Gloucester, the gateway to the world-heritage-listed Barrington Tops National Park.

After driving for 13 kilometres, we pull up at Pandora. Outside the main gates is a cream mailbox in the shape of a bird box with a faded green roof. Next to it, a bright blue signpost points down the driveway with 'Pandora 13520 Thunderbolts Way' printed in white.

The 1200-acre (485.6 ha) property spans as far as the eye can see, with hundreds of Merinos grazing in the front paddocks. From where we are standing at the entrance to the dirt driveway, we can make out the homestead about a kilometre away, which is painted pale lemon and has a terracotta tiled roof.

I stare at the property for a minute or so. It's horrible to think Mathew was possibly murdered in this postcard-perfect setting. Nathan and I do a U-turn to park on the opposite side of the road, about 50 metres from the front gate. Ideally, we'd prefer to be parked somewhere less conspicuous, but there isn't anywhere else to go while still maintaining a visual of the farmhouse. I hop into Nathan's car and pump the aircon. He takes out a long lens and shows me how far he can zoom in to get a clear shot of the property. There are two cars parked to the left of the house; one looks like Mathew's ute, from the descriptions of the locals.

Nathan figures he can jag a shot of Natasha, regardless of whether she leaves through the front or back door, because she will come into view if she walks across to the cars. Seeing two cars is an encouraging sign. There's every chance she is home; all we have to do is wait for her to leave. We watch and wait. About every half-hour, we bolt upright, thinking we've seen movement, but it's just two border collies running into view from behind the house.

We presume her kids are at school, so hope she will walk into our line of sight by 2.30–3.00 pm to pick them up. Suddenly, the dogs bound across the backyard, heading to the fence where the cars are parked. They are not alone. I can just make out a figure walking behind them, headed the same way.

I can't see properly in the passenger seat, but Nathan is all over it. The camera shutter clicks at a million miles an hour, a promising sound.

'Yep, got her,' Nathan says, taking a look at the preview screen.

I lean over so I can see, itching to find out what she looks like. There she is. Nathan captures Natasha mid-stride, her grey T-shirt barely managing to cover her belly. As she walks towards the cars, wearing sunglasses and denim jeans and with an aqua-coloured handbag over her shoulder, three dogs are in tow. In this frame, it's like she has slowed down and turned left to face us directly. I know there's no way she can see us, but I wonder if she is thinking, why there is a huge, black ute parked opposite the property on the main road?

As she gets into her car, Nathan and I decide we should follow her once she gets out of the driveway. I have terrible nerves for following people. Nathan, on the other hand, is supremely talented. My blood runs hot as we see her coming up the driveway in a ute. I pull the seat lever backwards, trying to lie as flat as I can in the passenger seat. I really don't want her to think anything is up. Or even that we are in town.

Nathan calmly rests his hands on the steering wheel, coolly flicking on his indicator a few seconds after she passes us.

I'm panicked. 'Do you think she's seen us? Has she seen us? Do you think we're too close?'

Nathan drives with purpose and assures me we're fine.

Ten minutes later, just before we reach town, Natasha's brake lights flash ahead of us. She slows down, indicating left then pulling into a driveway.

'Oh my God, you've got to be kidding!' I exclaim to Nathan. 'She's pulling into Colin's house!' I know it's his house, because I'd found out his address and made a mental note of where the property was as we passed it on the drive out to Pandora.

Nathan slows down as we drive by the house. With my face squished up against the glass, I watch Natasha head towards the front of the house before veering around the back.

'What is she doing here?' I wonder aloud.

We chuck a U-turn further down the road, driving back to the property on the opposite side of the road. Colin's house is on the main road in and out of town, but it's on a corner block next to a small side road. We turn right into this road and pull up on a patch of grass, which gives us a great view into Colin's backyard. A few gum trees give us some form of cover but, if Natasha or Colin look our way, we are parked in an odd position.

We watch as Natasha reverses the ute into the backyard. She hops out and chats to Colin, before climbing onto the ute tray. She unclasps a strap tied around a washing machine and starts to push it towards the end of the tray. Through the trees, I can just make out Colin, who is standing on the ground as he helps to unload the machine onto the ground.

Is that Mathew's? Is she giving his washing machine to Colin? Surely not. This is all very strange. Why would Colin even have a conversation with Natasha after she'd been accused of trying to burn him alive?

Although the original attempted murder charges were later downgraded, she still admitted to torching the family home, leaving Colin asleep inside while she escaped with her son. It's weird to see them interacting together, even smiling.

Nathan snaps a few more shots, mostly of Natasha. At one point, she appears to be looking straight at us. He also manages to capture a few frames of Colin, partially obscured by a tree.

We decide not to push our luck. We've got what we wanted, so we aim to avoid detection by moving further down the road while we wait for Natasha to leave.

It's not long before she turns out of the driveway and heads towards the town's centre. At a distance, we begin to follow her again, presuming she's driving to the local primary school to pick up her kids. Suddenly, just past Café Graze, Natasha slams the brakes on. Nathan follows suit. I hold my breath as she reverse-parks into a 45-degree angle spot right in front of us, outside the post office. We decide to park, too.

I'm anxious about being so close but, equally, I'm intrigued to see what she does.

Nathan reckons he can get another shot of her – undetected – but I'm hesitant.

'I really don't want her to see us. But it's a good shot, isn't it?' I ask, hoping Nathan will take the reins and choose the best course of action.

Nathan moves the car again to get a better position, so we can see her clearly when she walks out. He thinks he can shoot through the window without her seeing us.

I'm not so sure. Again, I sink into my seat and wait.

After what feels like hours, but was probably only a few minutes, she emerges. She is smiling from ear to ear, clutching a StarTrack parcel she's just collected. Nathan winds down the window slightly and aims. To me, the sound of the camera snapping is as loud as fireworks; I'm positive she's going to glance our way. She doesn't. Nathan winds up the window as Natasha walks back to her car, none the wiser.

I exhale with relief. We've got her.

7

SUDOKU

Without fail, Mathew would drop past his neighbour's every Sunday morning, just a few kilometres down the road from Pandora. A man of strict ritual, he would arrive an hour before Bill and Di Heazlett went to church, just enough time to have a cup of tea and work through the Sudoku puzzles in the *Sun Herald*.

The Heazletts are family to Mathew. The three of them maintained a close relationship, especially after Mathew's father John passed away more than a decade ago.

The day after photographing Natasha, I drive out to their property Roselee, where I've organised to meet Bill. I turn off Thunderbolts Way and into their driveway, admiring the surrounding gardens before stopping near a towering Japanese maple tree, close to their house.

Bill Heazlett opens the door in a sloppy joe covered in paint stains and faded, navy blue cargo pants; I hadn't expected such homely casualness from Walcha's former mayor. Taking one of my hands in both of his, he thanks me for stopping by and explains wife Di is having a quick nanna-nap.

I'd met Di quickly the day before. Nathan and I had dropped in to introduce ourselves on the way out to Pandora ahead of staking-out

Natasha. Our conversation with Di was eye-opening. After ushering us inside, she led us through a living room into the kitchen, over-looking the back of their property. She made a beeline to the stove and popped the kettle on, talking at a firecracker speed about how 'wicked' Natasha was.

'Poor Mathew never stood chance,' she said.

After shuffling slowly over to the kitchen table with our teas, she motioned towards a green folder on the table, insisting I take a look.

'I'm keeping it for later, in case we need it,' she said, nodding.

It was hard to believe what was inside.

The folder was filled with newspaper clippings in plastic sleeves. All the articles were about Natasha and her criminal past. I was taken aback that someone so close to Mathew went to the trouble of keeping track of Natasha like this. Again, it confirmed that those who knew Mathew were worried about the relationship in the lead-up to his death.

'It was a shock, but no surprise at all,' she said, referring to Mathew's death, as she took a seat at the table.

Although she does not have confirmation from the police, Di's strong belief is that Natasha meticulously planned to kill Mathew, and had even been poisoning him to make him sick. She feared this was coming; her gut feelings were so strong, she'd even rung Mathew's uncle John Schell, a former police officer, to ask him to do something. Warn him. Anything.

'We knew something was going on, but there was nothing we could do,' she said, staring into her teacup.

A day later, Bill and I are sitting at the same kitchen table, sipping tea, as he tells me about Mathew.

'Mathew was the essence of generosity, one of those people who would give you the shirt off his back,' Bill says.

Mathew spent countless hours at their property, doing odd jobs and demonstrating the benefits of new farming machinery, hoping to help the Heazletts improve their property. He also gave many gifts and, at times, his generosity bordered on being too much. If Bill made a throwaway comment about liking a certain type of scotch, Mathew would be back in a few days' time with half a dozen bottles.

'He was just a soul of generosity and very few people are, strangely . . . I think Mathew had that in spades.'

Many Walcha locals have been quick to talk of his generous nature, but hearing it from someone close like Bill – and Lance the previous day – makes Mathew more real to me. He's not just an outline anymore, but a person whose death has deeply affected friends left behind.

'It's a loss to us all, a loss to the community, but a loss to us partic-ularly as friends,' Bill says, a lone tear rolling down his cheek and falling into his lap. It's hard to watch him struggling.

'I found it very sad, personally. As you get older, friendships always take time and, if you're meeting people over longer periods of time, you feel that empathy and deepness . . . and I felt that with Mat.' Bill wipes away a streak glistening on his cheek.

For the past 20 years, he and Mathew drank tea in the same spot every Sunday, chatting and doing Sudoku. Mathew would only need to glance at the puzzle before scribbling numbers in random squares, always with dead accuracy.

'He'd just look at it and figure it out, and I'd think, "How did his brain get there?"' he says with a smile.

Bill says Mathew's brain worked differently to most people. While the term 'simple' was often thrown around, he was far from it. He was highly intelligent, but struggled to see the world in anything but black and white. Expressing his emotions was a constant struggle and he was a real creature of habit, extremely set in his ways.

Bill suspects Mathew was on the autism spectrum, pointing to his freak Sudoku skills and brilliant analytical brain, but also because he struggled to communicate his emotions. Typically, this led to the breakdown of many relationships before he met Natasha.

One time, a woman he was dating travelled from the nearby town of Armidale to spend the weekend at Pandora. Mathew was halfway through a kitchen renovation at the time, when his new flame innocently suggested a different colour scheme to the one he'd chosen. Bill says Mathew told her, rather abruptly, the decision wasn't hers to make. It was his house, so he was truly confused why she would suggest such a thing, when she didn't live there or own it.

'The friendship ended in a week,' Bill says with a chuckle.

Another time, a woman who'd driven from the Hunter Valley to visit Mathew lit up a cigarette a few moments after arriving. Mathew didn't smoke and didn't like it at all. Within 10 minutes of her arrival, they mutually agreed it was best for her to leave.

Despite his setbacks, Bill says Mathew was never going to give up his quest for love and a family of his own. Clearly, he was desperate to settle down. Lance had mentioned this to me several times during our roadside chat, as had almost everyone I'd spoken to in town.

'You could tell he was. The fact he was asking girls out was indicating – like all of us – [he wanted] that companionship. I think he felt that; he was looking for that and was going out of his way to do it.'

Mathew's desperate yearning for a family and string of failed relationships set the stage for Natasha to enter Mathew's life.

'He was searching for a family and then, when he met Tash, and the fact she had three children . . . she just played him like a fiddle,' Bill says.

At some point in 2014, Bill believes Natasha was without a partner – or someone to help fund her lifestyle – when she learned about a lonely single farmer, living just out of town on a multi-million-dollar Merino property.

'I think Tash was looking around and didn't have a partner at the time,' Bill recalls.

He doesn't know exactly how they met, but thinks their relationship started when Natasha befriended the wife of a shearer and had asked if she could come out to the farm, keen to see how sheep were shorn.

'She came strutting in, low-cut top, sparkles on her jeans and went straight for him,' Di said, during our chat the previous day.

Bill agrees with his wife, believing Natasha targeted Mathew and knew how to reel him in. When she went out to watch the shearing, Natasha had showered Mathew with compliments, thanking him profusely for letting her watch the day-to-day running of his farm.

'She more or less indicated to Mathew that she was keen to be involved with him in some way. That was, in a sense, a new experience for him,' Bill says.

All his life, Mathew had done the chasing; he was always the one to make the first move on women he was interested in. Usually after a brief period of courtship, however, they ended their relationship with him.

'Whereas, this girl was saying, "You're wonderful." He thought it was just amazing.'

Bill and Di held grave concerns from the get-go. Natasha arrived on the scene quickly and, when it came to their relationship, Mathew was willing to turn a blind eye to anything. Those closest to him quickly learned he wouldn't tolerate a bad word about her. Those who voiced their opinions were promptly cut out of his life.

The Heazletts were well aware of Natasha's criminal past and felt sick that he'd quickly fallen for a parolee with a violent past. Bill had strong views but, like Lance, he didn't want to push Mathew too hard for fear of pushing him away.

'I think she read him like a book, and she had enough worldly experience to go, "I can see what you need so I am prepared to offer you a bit of affection" and he thought, "This is just the bee's knees."'

As Bill recalls, their relationship began towards the end of 2014. From trawling Natasha's Facebook page, I see their first social media interaction was in October.

In a public post on 16 October, Natasha thanked Mathew for allowing her 'babies' – two sheep named Sugarfoot and Lou Lou – to live on his property: 'Such a sad but happy day today. Sugarfoot and Lou Lou have gone to their forever home. Thank you Mathew Dunbar for taking my babies. They made me cry when they followed the car out of the paddock and up the driveway crying. They are in with lots of mummy and other baby sheep now.'

Later, she again wrote in a public post: 'You should have seen Mat though, most guys would be trying not to laugh at me crying over the lambs but he kept asking me if I was ok. He's probably at home now cracking up!'

It appears Mathew took the bait, replying: 'Just worried about you been (sic) upset. That was my concern.'

By December 2014, Mathew seemed to be truly smitten. Commenting on a picture of Natasha, lying back in a hammock at her parents' house at Culburra on the South Coast (the fateful picture my sister had texted me) Mathew wrote: 'You look nice and relaxed and beautiful xo . . . You might not want to leave. Would have to sell the farm and come down and join you if you allowed. Xo'

By January, his love language was growing in intensity: 'You have the best heart, beautiful,' he commented on one of Natasha's posts.

A few days later, he likened her to a superhuman: 'Yes very close to Wonder woman though. The most amazing beautiful special loving greatest lady I have ever met.'

The honeymoon phase of their relationship ended up being short-lived.

Natasha breached the conditions of her parole by committing a brazen crime against the boyfriend she'd met after separating from Colin and before meeting Mathew. I wouldn't hear the full story of what Natasha did to this man for many years.

Less than six months after she and Mathew began dating, Natasha was sent back to jail in May 2015. She wouldn't get out for another 18 months. Her jail status did not deter Mathew, however, who remained unwaveringly dedicated, talking to her on the phone as much as he could and making frequent trips to Sydney's Silverwater Women's Correctional Centre.

'While she was in jail, she wanted him to change his will. So he said "yes", and he did,' Bill says. This is another confirmation that Natasha instigated the changing of Mathew's will.

Like Lance, Bill recalls Mathew renovating a granny flat for Natasha's daughter, turning it into a teenager's dream. He estimates it cost in excess of $30,000.

Once Natasha got out of jail in October 2016, she and her three children moved to Pandora straightaway.

From the moment she moved in, those close to Mathew noticed an instant change. He became withdrawn; the happy Mat they all knew slowly faded before their eyes.

'He probably did not have the ability and experience which other sorts of people have to handle it well,' Bill says. 'He became much more withdrawn and, in a sense, less talkative; he wouldn't share as much.'

Mathew became a ball of anxiety, his mental health quickly unravelling in the weeks before his death. Usually defensive of Natasha, he started confiding in the Heazletts, telling them about Natasha's spending and how cash-strapped he was. She was out of control; nothing was enough. Although he bought her a new car and a $30,000 horse float, she always wanted more. The financial strain was getting too much. He also felt like he was being used as a childminder.

Bill believes pressure from the bank, which told him he needed to watch how he spent his money, was a wake-up call for Mathew. Suddenly, someone from outside his inner circle was telling him something was wrong. All his other relationships had ended by someone else 'pulling the pin'; now, Mathew found himself in a situation he didn't know how to handle.

Bill says, while he would listen to Mathew, he didn't want to tell him what to do. He thought allowing him to drop in and relax at their place, and share his concerns without too much probing, was the best thing for him.

'You're thinking – he really does need help, but what do you do for him? You're here for him . . . but you could see it. You could see this isn't going well for him.'

Bill's eyes well up as he goes over what he should or shouldn't have done. 'I'm at a loss now. A death, you can't do anything, it's all over . . . should I have done more? I knew that he probably didn't have the capability of handling himself and, as a good friend, I wasn't there for him as I should have been. That's what really hurts me . . . I thought, I missed a chance.'

In the end, however, Mathew did open up, telling the Heazletts his thoughts about ending the relationship and how difficult it would be to break away.

'He said, "It was time to end it," and we said, "We can't do it for you," but in retrospect, I probably should have.'

I ask Bill whether he thinks it was possible that Mathew had suicided. He talks about the time the police had gone to the property and taken his guns away, the same incident Lance had recounted. But Bill, too, doesn't believe suicide was something Mathew would ever go through with, even if he'd threatened it.

'I don't think it was in his nature,' he says, peering into his mug.

Especially not how Mathew was rumoured to have been found, hooked up to a helium tank. I think about how, sadly, so many of the friends and family of those who suicide never see it coming. Often, there are no signs to recognise.

'To rig up something like that, that's so premeditated . . . I don't think he was capable of it, personally,' he says quietly, before pausing for a few seconds.

'No, I don't think he could do it that way.'

After about an hour, we walk to the back of the Heazletts' property. Bill points out all the vegetables growing in his impressive patch. In an act of true country hospitality, he cuts off a large bunch of spinach for me before I leave.

For now, I won't be writing anything about Mathew's death. Local police have asked me to hold off so as not to jeopardise the investigation. I don't see the harm in playing ball, but I won't forever. Several people in town are keen for there to be more media coverage about the investigation, in the hope it might motivate police to move more quickly.

As with Lance, I promise Bill that I'd let them know if and when I was planning to publish a story.

Leaving Roselee, I turn right onto Thunderbolts Way in the direction of Sydney. A few minutes down the road, I pass Pandora and wonder when I'll be back.

It will be a lot sooner than I think.

8

THE LAST PHONE CALL

Three weeks after the trip to Walcha, I'm back at Newcastle courthouse, covering the case of a man charged with being an accessory to the murder of 31-year-old legal secretary Betty Dixon, back in the 1980s. As I'm bashing out a story on my laptop, a police contact calls me with an important update: local officers in Walcha are winding up their investigation and there are plans to arrest Natasha.

I'm not given an exact time frame, but it's likely to be in coming days or weeks. If I want to speak to her, now will be my last chance. I wish I could have spoken to her last time, but I was hamstrung with police asking me to wait. My contact says they don't think there's any issue with me approaching her now.

A familiar panic creeps into my throat. Unless she has the chance to tell her side of the story, we can't publish a story about her and her criminal past. And if she's arrested, we can't mention any of her previous convictions, for fear of prejudicing any trial she may face. So there is only a small window of time for me to report the whole story, a story many of those who knew Mathew want told.

I race back to my sister's house, which is only a short drive from the court, and call the newsdesk. The stars are aligning; Nathan is free to meet me in Walcha the following morning. We plan to leave at first light – me from Newcastle and Nathan from Port Macquarie – and rendezvous in town mid-morning with the goal of finding Natasha. Before we do that, however, there's one last person I really want to find first.

Waterloo station is perched on prime agricultural land just east of Walcha and shares a boundary fence with Mathew's property, Pandora.

Nathan and I head out of town on the Oxley Highway towards the property, in search of farmer and well-known local Ross King. Apart from Natasha, Ross was the last person to speak to Mathew on the night of his death. The two old neighbours shared a rare and light-hearted conversation just a few hours before Natasha phoned triple-0.

I'm keen to hear whether Ross got the sense anything was amiss. Cold calling in at anyone's home is always nerve-racking, especially when you want to ask them about a death or murder. Journalists often approach family and friends of people who have died in suspicious or tragic circumstances, in what is morbidly referred to as a 'death knock'. It's the worst part of the job.

Driving onto someone's land or walking up to their front door unannounced, I often get a sinking feeling in the pit of my stomach, not entirely sure what to say. You always hope – if they don't immediately tell you to bugger off – you aren't causing any more grief and, for some reason, the person you are intruding on might want to talk to you. Surprisingly, some do want to tell their story and, understandably, many don't.

Today, I'm hoping Ross King will trust me enough to tell me about Mathew and what he thinks about his suspicious death. What did they talk about? How did Mathew seem? Did he sense Mathew was in trouble, or was there any indication he was depressed?

Usually, you've only got seconds – a few minutes at best – to introduce yourself, explain clearly what you are asking and somehow convince the person you're trustworthy enough to tell their story.

I often wonder what reaction I'd have to someone lobbing up on my doorstep if, say, my mum or sisters died in a car crash, or someone had murdered them. I know I'd tell them where to go. For starters.

So, I'm filled with a familiar sense of anxiety as we roll down Ross's dirt driveway.

We park behind an old corrugated-iron shed, about 100 metres from the main homestead.

A tanned figure emerges behind an old red ute, lit cigarette in hand, saving us from running the gauntlet to the house. I recognise the man from the Commercial Hotel.

When we'd chatted at the pub, he was friendly enough. I'd explained I was in town investigating Mathew's death. I didn't catch his name, but he seemed to be about my age.

Standing next to Nathan's car, I tell him we're looking for Ross and ask if we're at the right place. He explains Ross is home but working in another paddock, and offers to go and find him before hopping on a tractor and driving off.

A few minutes later, a car approaches us. A man steps out; he's wearing an Akubra and his beige work shirt is neatly tucked into denim jeans. Ross introduces himself, offering us a warm country handshake then inviting us into his home.

In the end, I didn't really need to say too much. The other man had explained why I was here, and Ross must have made up his mind to speak to me before I asked.

Inside the house, his wife Penny also warmly offers us her hand and asks if we would like some tea. Their home is as inviting as they are; it's filled with history, artefacts and art. It's the type of home you'd see featured in *Country Style* magazine, one you'd fork out obscene amounts of money for on Airbnb for an authentic farm homestay.

Ross is the brother of local artist Stephen King, whose sculptures have featured in Bondi's Sculpture by the Sea since its inception in the 1990s. Stephen is one of dozens of artists in Walcha, and often exhibits his work at the Walcha Gallery of Art.

We sit at the dining table and I explain a little more about how I'm working on an article about Mathew and the mystery surrounding his death. Penny tells us they've both been worried about where the police investigation is up to. She gently tells Ross she doesn't think it would hurt to explain how he's been feeling about it, too. Ross almost seems a little relieved to be able to get a few things off his chest.

I can't imagine what it would be like, thinking your neighbour has possibly died in suspicious circumstances and, three months on, still having no answers. Ross had known Mathew for nearly 20 years.

'We were just neighbours,' Ross says, stirring his tea slowly. 'And in the country, neighbours try their hardest to be good to each other, and he was fair and nice beyond all people.' Mathew was reserved and quiet, he adds, but always helped in the community, always volunteered.

Ross embarks on a story about 'how good a guy he was', telling me about the time Mathew found some of Ross's lambs on his property, after they'd got through their shared fence. When Ross went to pick up his wandering lambs, Mathew insisted on giving him an extra three or four lambs, which were his.

'These ones hadn't been tailed – so he was going to give me the ones that hadn't been tailed, but they were his. He was going to give them to me, because he couldn't prove they were his. You could just tell by the look of them, and I said, "No, Mathew, they're yours." That's what he's like – he wouldn't steal from anyone,' Ross says.

So much of what Ross is talking about mirrors what Lance and the Heazletts have already told me. Mathew's generosity is the first thing each of them mentioned. It's almost the first thing anyone who knows him mentions.

'He was a giving person … a lovely kind soul. Unfortunately, everyone pulls out the word "simple" but I just describe him as a quiet, lovely gentleman.' Ross adds sadly that he wasn't in contact with Mathew enough to realise anything was wrong in the lead-up to his death.

Their conversations were few and far between but, on the night Mathew died, they spoke at about 7 pm.

'One of the things that concerned me . . . the phone call was made to me and the police, within the first two weeks, never spoke to me, never rang me up,' Ross says, referring to the time after Mathew's death.

'So, I rang [the police] and said, "Look, I'm pretty sure I would have been the last person to speak to Mathew."'

It troubled him that no one had bothered to get in touch with him, even though police had Mathew's phone records.

'Plus, within a week, the crime scene was opened up and no longer a crime scene. She was back in there – that's no fault of hers, to me,' he says, referring to Natasha moving straight back to Pandora.

On the night of 1 August 2017, Ross called Mathew, after he'd heard through the grapevine Mathew had been having problems with his leg. Having not spoken for a while, he was keen to have a yarn and check-in.

There was no answer, so Ross left a message. Mathew rang back soon afterwards.

'He apologised for not ringing me back straight away, and I said, "How are you going?"'

Mathew told Ross he'd been in hospital and was doing physio, but that he was going to have a limp, probably for the rest of his life.

Having previously undergone an ankle infusion operation himself, Ross joked, '"Well, we can limp together." So, we had a laugh about that.'

Although Mathew had mentioned the potential of a permanent limp, he was positive it would improve with physio.

'So, that in itself meant to me . . . that he was looking at how he was going to be down the track. He was going to do a physio program – is that a clue that he wasn't going to kill himself that night?'

Their conversation then moved to a lighter subject – Lance Partridge and his appearance on the ABC's *Australian Story*. Lance was interviewed as part of a story on a Sudanese refugee, who'd travelled to Walcha to do work experience on Lance's property. The same man also did a bit of work out at Pandora, and Mathew chuckled about the colourful shirt he'd been given as a parting gift.

'He said, "Oh Ross, I can probably give you mine [shirt] because my partner doesn't like mine".' Ross smiles. 'It was a bit of a fun conversation.' Because they didn't speak often, Ross remembers being mindful of making sure they 'spoke for a while' that night.

'Would you be surprised if Mathew had suicided?' I ask.

Ross responds quickly. 'Yeah.'

'Can you think of why anyone would have wanted to kill Mathew?'

'Me? No. No, not at all. Not at all,' Ross says.

9

FARM GATE ENCOUNTER

The pencil pines that line the winding, dirt driveway mean we can't see the farmhouse, leaving us blind as to what awaits us at the end. After spending the best part of the afternoon at Ross King's place, it's now dusk. We finish our cigarettes and hop into Nathan's Mitsubishi Triton.

It feels strange moving past the timber front gates of Pandora, having spent hours parked across the road with a long-lens camera just a few weeks back.

'She could pull a shotgun on us,' Nathan chuckles, as we drive over the cattle grid. Beneath his casual tone, there sounds like a kernel of worry.

I stare straight ahead, both hands on my face. We've got about 300 metres to go.

'What if she does shoot us?' I ask, swinging around to face him, trying to get a read on his face.

'Well, it would make for a great yarn. We'd make front page news, for sure,' he says with a mischievous grin. Black humour is a coping mechanism for all of us.

'Jesus Christ, I guess we would,' I say with a light-hearted laugh, trying to mask the anxiety filling my chest. It's a bit of a worry if

Nathan is worried. He's a seasoned professional, who's seen and done everything throughout his career. He captured the southern World Trade Center tower collapse on 9/11. There's a picture of him covered in thick soot, standing as close as you could get, after hitching a ride in with the first-responding firefighters. He was forced to delete photographs during the 2006 Fijian coup with a gun to his head. He'd also had some hair-raising moments, travelling through Mexico in the heart of El Chapo's Sinaloa cartel-controlled regions with an anti-narcotic police squad. He'd described this as 'the most fun ever – guns, body armour and big bulletproof trucks'.

So seeing him slightly apprehensive, wondering if Natasha may have an extreme reaction to our presence, doesn't fill me with confidence.

Grey storm clouds thicken, rolling in our direction. It's nearly dark. We need to do this now. We edge closer. Halfway down the driveway, it dawns on me that I've never confronted a murderer before. I can't be certain she's a killer but, from what I've been told so far, I think she is. I've written about murderers, watching them in the dock during their trials for weeks on end. I was no stranger to learning about the horrors they'd inflicted on others, and I'd spent considerable time with victims and their families. But I'd never spoken to one face-to-face.

We pull up just to the left of the farmhouse, and Nathan turns the car around.

'Let's keep the car running and park it facing the road, so we can make a quick getaway,' he says as we get out.

A loud noise causes me to jump.

A loud, revving dirt bike screams towards us. A boy wearing a full-face helmet, about six or seven years old, stops and glares.

'Hi. Cool bike,' I say, rolling my eyes at myself. What a lame thing to say. The boy stares again before doing a burnout, which I'm sure is done with the intention of spraying us with dirt. He takes off towards some sheds 50 metres away and, as the dust settles, Natasha Beth Darcy walks towards us.

'Sorry about that,' she says as she gets closer, motioning towards her son on the bike. Wearing light denim jeans and a tight-fitting pink polo top, she flashed us an ear-to-ear smile. She places her hands confidently on her hips.

My heart is beating out of my chest. I begin a bumbling apology about turning up unannounced, but I'm interrupted. Natasha's phone is ringing.

'Sorry,' she says to us, before turning her back to answer it.

We are so close we can hear a male voice on the other end. I can just make out what he is saying: something about the police trying to get in touch with her and leaving a message on her phone. Natasha nods and smiles. She's very happy.

'Excellent. It's good – means the investigation is over,' she says, twirling her ponytail in her fingers. The conversation lasts about a minute.

It's truly unbelievable that we're here to witness this moment. Nathan and I exchange several wide-eyed glances, acknowledging the jackpot timing of our arrival.

After she hangs up, I introduce myself and Nathan as a journalist and photographer from the *Daily Telegraph*. I stumble for a bit, using far too many 'ums' but, eventually, tell her I'm sorry to hear about her partner's passing. I explain I'm in town to write a story because the police are still treating his death as suspicious, three months on.

Natasha jumps in before I can finish my bumbling spiel. 'They've just closed it all now,' she says, elated. 'So they're giving me all my computer stuff back, all Mat's phones and everything. That's what I found out just then.'

My mind is spinning. I know what this means, but I don't have time to process it right now. Where it is safe and practical, instead of handcuffs, sirens and flashing lights, police can opt for a calmer approach to an arrest. Detectives tell the suspect the investigation is over, and ask them to come and get their things. Or tell them to come in and make another statement, or do another interview. It's not always a lie; they just omit the part about arresting and charging the person upon their arrival at the cop shop.

In my bones, I know this is what has just happened. Right in front of us. Natasha has just been told the investigation is over and the smile on her face says everything. She thinks she's in the clear. The trap is set; she's been lulled into a false sense of security.

'That must be a relief?' I ask, surprising myself that any words made it out of my mouth.

'Well, I knew it was going to close eventually. I mean, I was there. I know he killed himself.'

Bingo. She'd just given me everything I was after: her version. Relief floods through me, knowing I should now be able to write about what everyone suspects.

Armed with new confidence, I push a little harder. I ask her what happened on the night Mathew died. Politely, she explains she really can't talk to me without her lawyer present. I try to keep the conversation going and – perhaps buoyed by her newfound confidence – she starts yakking away.

'I know there are a lot of rumours and everything in town, and I don't want to add fuel to anyone's fire. We know what happened. The kids are only just getting over it now and sleeping through the night and things like that.'

She pauses.

I'm desperate to fill the gap. I find silence awkward and uncomfortable, and count backwards in my head from five to stop myself from interrupting. *Don't speak, Emma. be quiet and let her hang herself*, I beg myself silently.

It works. She keeps going, digging herself a deep hole.

'I'm dealing with PTSD because I was the one that found him, and I'm working with the counsellors and I just don't want to . . .' Natasha says, trailing off.

I push again, asking her to expand on exactly what happened on the night Mathew died.

She reverts to the line about not being able to speak without her lawyers.

I need to change tack, fast. I ask her to tell me more about Mathew.

'Mat was gentle, sweet, kind,' she says, wiping a tear from her eye. 'He suffered depression his whole life. Tried to kill himself twice,' she says.

I don't recall Lance, the Heazletts or anyone else mentioning a second attempt. I wonder if this is true, or part of a story to make Mathew sound more depressed than he actually was.

She explains that, shortly before his death, Mathew had spent a few days at a mental health facility near Tamworth, but he insisted on keeping his admission private.

'He hasn't had anything to do with [his mother] in over 20 years. His adopted mother. Mat loved everyone – he was the kindest, sweetest man – but he hated his mother. So, if that tells you anything . . .' she says, raising her eyebrows and nodding.

Several people have mentioned Mathew was estranged from his mother and did his best to avoid her since leaving school. After he graduated from The Armidale School, where he boarded, he moved back out to Pandora and lived with his father John, wanting nothing to do with his mother. But she never stopped loving him from afar.

Natasha also tells me she's sure lots of people are claiming to be Mathew's friends, but he didn't really have many. I don't know if he had dozens of friends, but I get the sense he belonged to a close circle of friends, all people who adored him.

Natasha returns to talking about Mathew's suicide threat, explaining how he took a gun from the farmhouse – just a month or so prior – and called her to say his final goodbye. He never followed through.

'I was shocked. Even Lance, his best friend, he's down the back at the shearing sheds with me,' she says, pointing behind her. 'We both said when he did it the first time, it was a call for help . . . there was no way he would kill himself.'

I feel sick at the mention of Lance's name. And even more sick at the sight of the ute emerging from the sheds and driving in our direction. Is that Lance? I didn't want Natasha to know we'd spoken, and I'm worried he'll let it slip. I also don't want to land him in trouble with Natasha, because I know he's keen to help out on the property – for Mathew's sake – until shearing is over.

The ute slows before turning away from us, across the paddock and out of sight.

As Natasha continues to talk, I grapple with the background commotion and competing worries. There's no stopping her. She needs no prompting.

'After he took the overdose, I had his medication in my handbag so he couldn't do it again. I went through the cupboards and took everything out – I thought I was doing the right thing,' she says, her voice cracking before the floodgates open.

I'm confused. Hadn't she just mentioned he was going to shoot himself? Maybe she was talking about the apparent second suicide attempt. Or had she slipped up and lied to us?

The tears come thick and fast. She makes a show of wiping them away as she explains. The day before his death, Mathew was severely depressed after going to hospital for a medical appointment.

'On that Tuesday, the day before he did it, we went to the doctors and they told him his leg wasn't very good. They thought they were going to have to take his leg off and that really, really depressed him,' she says. This news had come after Mathew battled with a painful and mysterious calf infection a few weeks prior. 'But they realised they weren't going to take his leg off,' she adds, in complete contradiction to what she's just said.

Natasha then says Mathew was distressed about living with a limp for the rest of his life 'and maybe use a walking stick'.

On the night of his death, she thought everything seemed 'okay', but Mathew was worried about the future of the farm if he wasn't able to run it.

'We talked for hours that night, because I knew he was upset and I didn't want him going to bed. I kept saying to him, "We'll be okay."'

My mind drifts back to what the Heazletts and Lance had told me. Mathew was stressed about Natasha's spending and planned to confront her about it, because the debts were piling up.

'Were you in financial trouble? Was he stressed?' I manage to ask.

She vigorously shakes her head. 'No, there are no loans or mortgages on the property or anything like that. No, not at all.'

Conscious of steering her back to the night of Mathew's death, I ask, 'So, you stayed up late chatting with him?'

For a moment, she looks confused, pausing for a few seconds before repeating how concerned Mathew apparently was about 'how was he going to run the farm with his leg'.

'I mentioned selling the farm . . . he just could never do it. He just . . .' she trails off. 'Yeah, it was never going to happen.'

She crossed her arms and smiles. 'Anyways, I stayed up late talking to him. I thought I got through to him, because he started making plans with me. Now, when I look back, he was preparing me for what needed to be done in the next few months.' She stops at this point and looks down. I think she's going to continue but she looks up, only to say, 'But . . . yeah.'

I take a deep breath. This is the moment I've been dreading. It's time to ask her the hardest question: Did she kill Mathew?

Nerves get the better of me. 'Yeah, well, okay. I totally understand if you don't want to go into any more detail, but there are rumours in town and I've read about your criminal history as well. I just thought, um, you might want to address that?'

Things take a real turn. Natasha manages to smile but looks pretty unhappy. 'Hmmmm,' she says.

'Did you want to say anything about your criminal history at all?'

'No,' she says, head shaking. 'No. Nup.'

Not knowing what else to say, I force a smile back, knowing there is so much more I want to ask. Her sudden frostiness is petrifying.

'Okay, well, thank you for your time,' I say.

She walks backwards, keeping her eyes firmly on us. 'Okay, thank you,' she says through clenched teeth.

Nathan and I turn towards the car. Once inside, we unleash a series of synchronised expletives. We can't believe Natasha got that fateful phone call right in front of us. Or how much information she divulged. But I'm kicking myself for buckling under pressure. I didn't ask the most important question: Did you murder Mathew?

10

PEN TO PAPER

As the Socceroos are playing Honduras in a World Cup qualifier on TV, I sit cross-legged on my bed at the Walcha Motel surrounded by a Chinese banquet in takeaway containers.

Leafing through my notes, stained translucent with grease splotches, I read over where we've been and what I have to work with. I'm also cross-checking my notes with the recorded interviews, which I've spent the best part of the day transcribing onto my laptop. My deadline is fast approaching: I have 24 hours.

After Nathan and I left Pandora, I called a couple of police contacts, telling them about the conversation I overheard Natasha having, and that I had the sense her arrest was imminent. I'm assured there's no need for me to rush straight to the police station. Natasha won't be going to 'get her things' from the police station straightaway, but it would only be a matter of days.

After finishing dinner, I set up the computer on a small table, facing an exposed brick wall. For the next three hours, I stare at that wall and a blank Word document on the screen. Starting a story is always the hardest part. Typically, I write and rewrite dozens and dozens of first lines, before deleting them. For me, once the first line is written, the rest flows quickly. Coming up with the perfect first line takes time, however; it's a process of ordering all your thoughts, deciding what to include and how the story should unfold.

By 1 am, I have three paragraphs I can work with. The rest will have to wait until the morning.

After hopping into bed, I toss and turn, staring at the ceiling with growing agitation. The Walcha Motel is full, and there's a mid-week party in the car park. More than a dozen bikies are clinking beer bottles and smoking outside their rooms, and a group of NBN workers are intent on having a wild Wednesday.

The following morning, I'm up before dawn, staring at the computer in my pyjamas. For the next 12 hours, I'm locked in Room 19, only venturing out to buy meals on the main drag.

I talk back and forth all day with the sub-editor, and also call police media to let them know we're printing a story about Mathew's death in tomorrow's paper. They ask me not to include any mention of ram sedatives, or Natasha's attempts to purchase them, for investigative reasons. I have no idea why, but I take it out.

Later that evening, work sends me a proof of the article's layout. They've gone big on it. Once the adrenaline and excitement pass, anxiety sets in. Did I get anything wrong? How will people react? Will this help to speed up Natasha's arrest? I feel sick with nerves. I barely sleep a wink in anticipation of the morning.

There's a sizeable line-up at the Walcha newsagency, with about half a dozen locals clutching copies of the *Daily Telegraph*.

Much to my amusement, the cashier yells out, 'Only two copies per person,' as people approach the counter.

'Why didn't the *Telegraph* tell us there was going to be such a big story in today's paper?' the woman behind the counter asks her colleague, exasperated. 'We could have ordered more papers in from Armidale!'

It's a very in-your-face front page. The top half features a picture of Mathew and his dog. Beneath is a picture of Natasha at Pandora – the shot Nathan had taken about a kilometre from the farmhouse.

In large block font, the headline screams: 'The grazier and the widow of Walcha'.

The subheading, slightly smaller, reads: 'A small NSW town is gripped by the mysterious death of a wealthy farmer'.

While the article doesn't accuse Natasha of killing Mathew straight out, it dances as close to that conclusion as is legally possible.

Lawyers for the *Daily Telegraph* had warned me that, if she wasn't charged, we'd probably be sued for defamation, and Natasha would have a strong case. I'd stuck my neck out on this one, but I trusted the police sources I'd spoken to at length, especially those who had encouraged me to travel to Walcha in the first place.

I could only get the article past the lawyers because I had confronted Natasha and asked for her side of the story. With these thoughts running through my mind, I took my place in the line at the newsagency to pay for my two copies.

Raising her eyebrows above her thick, black-framed glasses, the newsagent leans over the counter. 'It was you, wasn't it? You wrote the story?'

I nod, handing over cash for my two copies.

'Good job,' the woman says with a wry smile, handing me the change.

Several people stand on the pavement outside, leafing through the article. Some talk to each other in hushed tones as I walk past. It's pretty surreal to see people reading the article on the street.

One of my brother-in-law's relatives, who I've spent consider-able time with, tells me local social media has gone into meltdown. 'I've been on the phone all morning. Everyone's talking about it on Facebook.'

A friend of hers says Colin has called the primary school to explain that he won't be coming in for canteen duty.

I walk to my car, holding my two copies of the paper. One is for Mathew's mother, Janet Dunbar.

11
ESTRANGED

Janet Dunbar lives in a single-storey, blond brick house on the northern side of Walcha, overlooking town. In the lead-up to the story being printed, we spoke briefly on the phone, but today will be our first meeting. I rang her at the newsagency to confirm I was on my way, and she is waiting behind her screen door as I climb the stairs to her front porch.

After opening the door, she offers me her hand before ushering me inside.

Her cloudy grey eyes glisten with a deep sadness. She's swimming in pain.

Front and centre in her living room is a gold-framed photograph of Mathew hanging on the wall. He's about preschool age; his hazelnut eyes beam as he rests his chin on his clasped hands, smiling through a gap in his front teeth for a professional photographer. Janet takes it off the wall and traces the outline of his face with her fingers, then leads me into her kitchen.

On a small timber table, I notice a collage of photographs, neatly laid out on a cotton crocheted tablecloth. All Mathew. The pictures capture a happy beginning, and an obvious bond between mother and son when he was young. Mathew and Janet were estranged at the time of his death – he refused to speak to her. While I'm sure he had his reasons, I still want to hear about him from her perspective.

Janet smiles gently. There's a faint quiver in her voice as she explains that all Mathew ever wanted, from a young age, was to give.

She begins to tell his life story, starting at age four. Mathew eagerly watched a small circle of graziers parading their prized sheep at the Walcha Show. As a special treat, Janet opened a small packet of potato chips, and placed them in his outstretched hands. Without dipping his hand into the bag or speaking a word, Mathew walked over to the circle and offered each farmer a chip.

After wandering back to his mum, he presented her with the near empty packet and raised it, silently offering her the final two chips.

'He hadn't been to school. You know, a little fellow, not having any brothers or sisters, living out on the farm where he wasn't mixing with other kids, and that was the very first thing he had done,' Janet says, as her smile melts to a deep frown.

'And that's why he was taken in by this woman. He could see himself in her children, being adopted,' she said, referring to Natasha without any prompting. 'Sadly, I was kept away from him by other people. If I had a chance to get to him, he would have listened to me.'

I remind myself that they haven't spoken in more than 20 years and that Mathew had sided with his father after his parents' divorce. Whatever the state of their relationship was, however, this is still a woman grieving the loss of her son.

Picking up a photo of Mathew as a newborn, lying next to a fluffy blue teddy bear about the same size, she explains Mathew entered the world on 4 November 1974 in Newcastle. She and then-husband John adopted him three weeks later.

'That teddy – he absolutely loved Teddy – he went everywhere with him. He just loved Ted. I caught him one day, sitting on the toilet talking to someone, and I said, "Who are you talking to?" And he said, "Teddy, Mummy!"'

Janet had held on to his much-loved teddy, as well as the outfit Mathew's biological mother had dressed him in on the day of his adoption. 'It was beautiful. It was a little blue-and-white top with little rose buds and a little pair of blue pants. So I put them on Teddy and put them in the coffin.'

Janet grew up in the beachside suburb of Cronulla, in Sydney's south, before marrying Mathew's father, John Dunbar, who was living in the northern suburb of Hornsby.

The pair moved to Walcha and took up residence at Pandora. John had bought the property from his parents in 1969. Janet's table is covered with family snaps but, noticeably, not one photo of John.

One photo shows a grinning Mathew, who is in a green-and-white chequered shirt and orange knitted vest, sitting at the kitchen table. With school friends on either side, he's poised to blow out five blue birthday candles on top of a home-baked sponge cake lined with smarties. Fast forward a few years to when Mathew was aged eight or nine – and nearly as tall as Janet – and there's a photo of him with his arms wrapped around his mum next to a fully bloomed Azalea tree, close to the farmhouse.

Next is a photo of him in khaki military attire, outside The Armidale School, where he boarded from Year 7. Hands behind his back, donning a red sash and military hat, he looks every bit as awkward as he is tall. As we look at this photo, Janet explains how, on Mathew's first day of high school, he'd expressed his deep wish to keep his adoption a secret.

'I don't want anyone to know,' he'd said to Janet, when she asked him what he would like to tell his new schoolmates.

Janet tells me Mathew aspired to have a career in IT. His peers often referred to him as a 'wizard'. Other pastimes included playing guitar and soccer. At some point during high school, Janet left her husband John. Mathew was deeply affected; so much so, the school principal called Janet and expressed his concern. 'He said, "Mathew is blaming himself because you've split up. He's quite upset that you've split up."'

The relationship between Mathew and his mother deteriorated from this point onwards.

'I divorced my husband . . . his attitude was that we would stay in the marriage, have separate bedrooms, and he would go off and do his thing. And I could stay at home and look after the home.'

Like so many divorces, the versions can differ and the truth can be skewed. In the end, Mathew chose to live with his father.

After she and John divorced, Janet says, she often drove to Tamworth to have dinner with Mathew and paid his school fees from Year 10 onwards. She also sporadically deposited money into a St George Bank account for him, which allowed him to buy personal items such as toiletries.

'As soon as he finished school, his father forced him out onto the property, and that was the end of it. I never saw him again.'

One of the last times she'd had a proper conversation with Mathew was on his 21st birthday. They shared a meal at the Walcha Memorial Club, and she baked him a birthday cake.

Over the years, Janet watched her son from afar, sometimes waiting months between catching glimpses of him in town. Mathew was always polite and friendly to her in passing, but refused to have a relationship with her.

'Dunbar [John] had told [friends and family] to keep him away from me. He was very much a resentful person and "I'll pay you back for what you've done", and he knew that keeping Mathew away from me was the thing that would hurt me.'

Mathew's friends have told me there is much more to the breakdown of their relationship. Other things happened in his childhood that led him to distance himself from his mother. They did not reconcile before his death. Their estrangement still causes Janet great distress.

In April, four months prior to Mathew's death, Janet learned she needed to undergo surgery for one of her eyes. She hoped Mathew would agree to drive her to Sydney for it, so they could make a start at mending their relationship on the trip. She wanted to call him at Pandora, but was afraid Natasha would answer. One day, while volunteering at the visitor information centre, she spotted her chance. Mathew and Lance were manning a stall for the poultry club on the main drag.

Janet mustered all her courage and walked towards her son. 'I went up to him and said, "Hello," and said, "Mathew, I've got something to ask you,"' before explaining she needed someone to drive her down to Sydney for an operation and take her home afterwards.

In his abrupt but polite manner, Mathew said, 'I'll think about it.'

'That's just how he spoke. He wasn't rude or nasty, but that was the last time I spoke to him,' Janet says, her eyes brimming with tears.

Even though they'd barely spoken for 20 years, Janet sent Mathew a birthday and Christmas card each year. After his father died, she tried even harder. 'I've written that many letters – it would have amounted to a large book.'

She also kept a room for Mathew and bought a custom-made single bed, long enough for her 'very tall boy'. 'He never, ever got to sleep in it.'

In the room that Mathew never saw – or knew about – his bed remains made up with fresh sheets. And his Year 12 class photograph hangs on the wall opposite the end of the bed. On the other side of his room is a wooden tallboy with a framed acrostic poem. I notice there are two 'Ts' in the name, as opposed to the one in 'Mathew':

M is for Memories of a much loved son are mine to cherish.

A is for Always and forever in my heart is where I hold onto you.

T is for Time will not diminish the unconditional love a mother has for her child.

T is for Trusting and putting your faith in others, being their loyal and true friend was who you were.

H is for Heaven, receiving the blessing as an angel in God's kingdom.

E is for Entered eternal life on 2nd August 2017.

W is for Words are never enough to express how much you
meant to me.

When Janet first heard about Mathew's death out at Pandora, the details were scant. But she says she knew straightaway who was responsible. 'It wouldn't sink in. I just couldn't believe it. To think somebody could take somebody else's life, particularly someone like Mathew, and you wonder how they could do that. After all, all he was doing was helping her out.'

The shock of hearing people say Natasha was responsible for Mathew's death is now wearing off for me. Natasha had not been named publicly as a suspect, but many people in Walcha are adamant she's responsible. 'You could see it at the funeral – so many people said to me outside the church, "What an act she's putting on." And it was.'

Janet says she sat as far away as she could from Natasha, who wept in the front pew of St Patrick's Church. It was a full house but, noticeably, empty seats surrounded Natasha.

People spoke in hushed tones, whispering about the order of service – the front of the booklet featured a photo of Mathew with a horse. Those closest to Mathew knew he hated horses, but tolerated them on his property because it was Natasha's main love. Another person close to Mathew told me she 'put on such a display', even penning a letter to Mathew in the booklet:

Dearest Maty, I fell in love with you because you loved me when I couldn't love myself.

You said having the children and I in your life was the happiest you've ever been but we are so much better for having had you in ours. All my love, Tasha.

In lieu of flowers, Natasha asked guests to donate to the Black Dog Institute, a not-for-profit organisation dedicated to the treatment and prevention of mental illnesses, including depression. Some thought this was in poor taste; others were angry, especially because the results of Mathew's autopsy were still unknown and the police investigation ongoing.

Lance Partridge gave a touching eulogy, highlighting Mathew's dedication as an active member of the National Party, who volunteered his time to sit on the local lands board.

'Mathew was a good sheep and wool man, being his only source of income,' he said, then described how well he looked after workers, even going to the trouble of washing his shearers' towels and singlets in fabric softener so they would be 'fluffy' for the next day's work. 'He was so unselfish. Mathew would give his heart and soul to help a friend. He was generous to the extreme. It was something you had to accept; it was just Mathew, the way he was.'

Towards the end of his tribute, Lance struggled to control the quiver in his voice. 'On a frosty morning, August the second, Walcha family and friends woke to hear of the sad passing of Mathew. We were shocked and stunned . . . you will always be so fondly remembered by so, so many.'

Janet doesn't believe her son took his own life. 'Mathew never struck me as that sort of person, that he would get himself in a situation that he thought the only way out . . . I think he would go and talk to somebody.'

A few months after his death, Janet was helping out at the information centre when she caught herself staring out at the hardware store Mathew used to visit for supplies. 'I thought, "I'll keep an eye out," because I thought I might see Mathew go into Richardson's – the hardware store. And then I caught myself and I said, "Janet, wake-up." . . . I have my moments.'

Despite their estrangement, Janet never stopped loving her son for a minute. 'He was very caring, lovable . . . easy-going. He was just out to help everybody. Whoever he could help, he'd help them. He was just such an easy-going young man, and that was his nature.'

Leaving Janet's house, I think about how tragic it is; a mother setting up a room for her son, who never got to see it. Now, it's a shrine.

I can see Mathew's friends and family are hurting, unable to start healing while stuck in limbo. Everyone is in the dark, waiting for the investigation to be over.

12

CAPTURE

Holding a cigarette out the car window and pinning a mug of instant coffee between my knees, I pull out of the motel driveway at dawn and head towards Walcha Police Station. It's a real struggle to see through the car's frosted windscreen.

Driving towards the station, my heartbeat quickens, wondering when and how it's going to happen. Parking the car opposite the station, I see a familiar grinning face, rubbing his hands together to fight off the cold as he strides in my direction. While I have an ally in town, I'm worried the two of us will attract too much attention.

Having also caught wind of Natasha's impending arrest, Dan Sutton, a senior journalist from Channel 10, has flown up from Sydney the night before.

According to police contacts, the plan is for Natasha to be arrested at the station sometime today, lured under the guise of collecting her belongings seized during the investigation.

But we don't have a time and there's no movement at the station.

We chat about our game plan, talking strategy and throwing up theories about how it will all go down, with cameraman Owen and photographer Marlon, a freelancer the *Daily Telegraph* hired to shoot the arrest.

Journalists often spend hours playing fruitless guessing games that lead nowhere, partly fuelled by the paranoia of missing something but also to pass the boredom that stews after hours, days or sometimes weeks of waiting. This morning, we need to figure out where to position ourselves to get the best shot of Natasha, without spooking her or jeopardising anything the police have planned.

It's unsettling that Nathan isn't here to capture the moment we've both been waiting for, but he's been called back to Port Macquarie for work.

I drive up and down the main street, looking left and right down every cross street for police cars, or any signs of Natasha's red Nissan Navara.

Driving past Café Graze, I see Colin Crossman standing out front – he's in his paramedic uniform – sipping on a takeaway coffee. Is he waiting to meet Natasha before they go to the station together? Or is it just a coincidence?

I arrive back at the station; Dan tells me some officers arrived a few minutes earlier, pulling up in a marked police 4WD and unmarked silver Pajero. I wonder if they're here for Natasha.

We decide it's best to split up. Natasha may walk into the station but it's possible the detectives could change tactics and head out to Pandora to make the arrest.

Dan stays put, as does Marlon with his camera, while I drive towards Pandora, parking on the left-hand side of Thunderbolts Way about a kilometre out of town.

If the police decide to arrest her at the farmhouse, they'll have to drive past me, and if Natasha drives in, I'll see her. Not long after I pull over, my phone beeps.

It's Dan. Police cars are leaving the station.

Moments later, the unmarked silver Pajero speeds past my car with two detectives in white shirts. We're on.

My little Mazda 2 screeches onto Thunderbolts Way, the seatbelt alarm dinging as I struggle to draw the belt across. The pedal is literally on the metal as I race to catch up.

I call Marlon and tell him to head out to Pandora. He tells me he's already en route, following Dan and his cameraman when they took off from the station.

I hold my breath for the next 13 kilometres, fretting we won't make it in time. The silver Pajero indicates left, slowing marginally as it pulls off Thunderbolts Way, then turns sharply past Pandora's letterbox and through the front gate. I pull over about 25 metres from the entrance; seconds later, Dan and Marlon arrive.

Leaving keys in the ignition and the engine running, I race towards the property's barbed-wire fence. We watch the Pajero tearing down the driveway.

Instead of stopping out the front of the house – where the long-lens camera can see – it drives around to the back, out of view from the road.

The hum of an engine alerts us; another car is on the approach.

We spot the marked police 4WD, heading in our direction. We all sprint towards the main gate, panting as we film it pulling into Pandora. After hurtling down the driveway, it too parks behind the house, blocking any view we hoped to have. Five long minutes pass.

We spot the marked 4WD making its way back up the driveway, and hustle into position, trying to guess which side she might be on, cameras and iPhone poised.

'You go one side, I'll go the other and we can share our shots,' I say to Dan, as we take up positions on either side of the main gate.

But the windows are heavily tinted and the police don't slow down. There's no time for Marlon to stick his camera in the window before the car turns right onto the main road and speeds back in the direction of town.

'She's not in there!' I exclaim to Dan, and wonder whether she's in the second car.

About 15 minutes later, the same plain-clothes detectives I'd followed earlier make their way up the dirt driveway. They too turn quickly onto Thunderbolts Way towards Walcha. No sign of Natasha.

Has she left in one of the two cars? She must have been in one of the cars.

A third white 4WD, which I don't remember seeing before, drives away from the farmhouse, stopping a few metres short of the gate.

A detective, wearing a fleece jumper with a popped collar, steps out and walks towards us with a roll of police tape in hand. Silently, he wraps the white-and-blue chequered tape around one fence post but doesn't drag it across the front of the drive. He seems to be waiting for someone else to leave before pulling it across.

After a few more minutes pass, another car flies up the tree-lined drive towards the main road. I'm shocked to see Colin in the driver's seat. He's got Natasha's children in the car.

During all the commotion, running back and forth across the fence line earlier to get a view, I can't recall seeing Colin driving in. But seeing him here now, and not at work, I know it's all over.

Natasha is under arrest. And we missed it.

I take off towards Tamworth with Marlon in tow, assuming she'll be charged at the main station in the region. Sitting in the back of the marked 4WD, Natasha is travelling in the same direction. News of her arrest hits town before she makes it to Tamworth Police Station, 90 kilometres away.

On the third Saturday of every month, the local farmers' market is held in the middle of town. The market is a chance for locals to catch up and buy anything grown, baked or handmade locally – there are no shortages of knitted tea cosies and buckets of honey.

The market is in full swing, with the smell of a sausage sizzle wafting through the stalls, when the news hits. It seems fitting that the Walcha community are together when they hear about the moment they've all been waiting for.

My phone rings; it's one of my brother-in-law's relatives.

'She's been arrested, hasn't she?' she asks, as I'm driving towards Tamworth. She's asking because several locals spotted police cars driving out to Pandora, and there are reports of crime scene tape across the property's front gate.

I'm only halfway to Tamworth when Natasha is driven into the bowels of the police station. Shortly afterwards, the NSW Police media unit issues a release, sent to all journalists and media outlets who subscribe to their emails:

> A woman has been arrested in relation to the suspicious death of Mathew Dunbar in the Northern Tablelands three months ago.
>
> Following extensive inquiries, a 42-year-old woman was arrested and conveyed to Tamworth Police Station about 9.30am today.
>
> She is assisting with inquiries.

As Natasha 'assisted' detectives in Tamworth, forensic officers and more police arrive at Pandora. The place is crawling with police; detectives are in every nook and cranny. Officers even climb onto the roof and peer down the chimney. For several hours, detectives go through every room of the house methodically, before ferrying dozens of brown paper evidence bags from the house into the boots of their cars.

Meanwhile, I'm sitting outside the cop shop, wondering what's going on and if there's any chance Natasha will face court today. Late in the evening of Saturday, 18 November 2017, Natasha is charged with Mathew's murder.

The following Monday, her case is mentioned at Tamworth Local Court. I'm disappointed I can't see her, but she doesn't want to be brought up from the cells and into the courtroom.

'Ms Darcy does not wish to be before the court,' her Legal Aid solicitor Garry Johnston tells the magistrate, during the brief mention of the matter.

The case is adjourned to 24 January, meaning Natasha will spend Christmas behind bars. Her new home: Silverwater Women's Correctional Centre in Sydney, a place she knows well.

Widespread relief floods through Walcha, now that an alleged murderer is no longer in their midst. I think back to many weeks ago, when my sister first rang me about the case. Everything the locals suspected turned out to be correct.

But there is so much more they don't yet know.

13

HOW TO GOOGLE A MURDER

A swag of Sydney journalists jostle for seats in courtroom 11A of the NSW Supreme Court. The courtroom sits within a tower of courts, the main court complex in the city. It's plonked in the middle of an area known as Queens Square, a courtyard in the heart of Sydney's CBD and a stone's throw away from Hyde Park.

It's a busy thoroughfare for judges, solicitors and criminals, as well as plenty of barristers racing through in their grey wigs, formally known as perukes, which are said to bring a sense of solemnity and formality to court proceedings.

It's now January 2019. Natasha's legal team is ready to launch their third and final bid for freedom ahead of her impending trial. During the past 18 months in jail, she's applied unsuccessfully to be released on bail twice.

Despite offering to stump up $75,000 for bail money – and after telling the court she would live with Colin and her three children if released – she was refused bail, first in September 2018 and again two months later in November.

It's now a little more than a year since her arrest. I'm eager to hear the thrust of the prosecution case against her and curious to see how she's faring in jail. The last time she was seen publicly was a few days after her arrest, arriving at Tamworth Airport in a black-and-white striped shirt. Freelance photographer Marlon was there to snap pictures of her as detectives led her across the tarmac in handcuffs to a plane bound for Sydney.

Today, Natasha is not attending court in person; instead, she will be beamed into the NSW Supreme Court via video link. Her face pops up on two large television screens affixed to either side of the courtroom. She sits placidly in a room lined with beige, corrugated-iron walls inside Mary Wade Correctional Centre, a women's prison at Lidcombe, in Sydney's western suburbs.

A thick fringe engulfs most of her forehead, while the rest of her hair is pulled back in a tight bun. The bleach-blonde hair has darkened to a burnt orange, with thick brown roots sprouting from her scalp. Wearing a dark-green, prison-issued T-shirt, Natasha sits upright as Justice Stephen Campbell enters the courtroom. Everyone in the courtroom stands briefly, taking their seats after the judge does, as part of an age-old legal tradition.

Crown prosecutor Kenny Ng rises to his feet. He tells the court that the prosecution case will focus on a series of internet searches Natasha allegedly carried out in the months and days leading up to Mathew's death. If true, the extent of her premeditation is shocking.

While Natasha had thought she'd wiped the contents of her phone, forensic specialists were able to recover most of what she deleted. Ng reads a fraction of the how-to-get-away-with-murder type of Google searches to the court.

In the lead-up to Mathew's death, Natasha is accused of searching 'murder by injection', 'the science of getting away with murder' and '99 undetectable poisons'.

Several journalists in the courtroom exchange wide-eyed glances. You can't make this stuff up. Although I'd learned of the searches in the days following Natasha's arrest, it's still shocking to hear them read aloud in court. It's beyond comprehension that anyone would plan to murder someone, let alone use Google to research it.

It's the prosecution case that Natasha also searched how to delete one's internet history, whether police could track private browsing, and if internet providers kept user history and data, before wiping her phone clean. Again, the searches following Mathew's death are almost too much to believe.

Natasha's internet history shows her phone was used to search 'how long after suicide is there a crime scene?', 'can police see deleted text messages' and 'pleading not guilty to murder'.

In her earlier bail hearing at Tamworth Local Court, Natasha's solicitor Tracey Randall outlined explanations for the incriminating phone searches. One explanation was that Natasha's phone was synced to an Apple account used by everyone in the household at Pandora, so other people could have undertaken the searches. There is also evidence that Mathew and Natasha used each other's phones. There were 'perfectly valid reasons' behind the Google searches, Randall argued.

Back in today's hearing, the court hears that, while Natasha deleted her phone data, Mathew's phone wasn't tampered with. This allowed police to discover a chilling internet search at 12.37 am on the night of his death: 'Does helium show up in an autopsy?'

The prosecution argues this search was carried out while Mathew was already sedated in bed, either just before or right after Natasha allegedly killed him.

His phone is again accessed at 1.14 am, sending a text to someone he deeply disliked: Colin Crossman.

'Tell the police I don't want Tash and the kids to find me,' said the text.

Police allege that it was Natasha who sent the text, with a message designed to make Mathew's death look like a suicide. Having spoken to Lance Partridge and the Heazletts about how strongly Mathew disliked Colin, I can't imagine Mathew sending his final message to the man who'd been such a source of misery for him.

About 45 minutes after the text is sent from Mathew's phone, Natasha rings triple-0 at about 2 am on 2 August 2017, telling the operator she's found her partner with a bag over his head and 'gas or something' going into it.

It's almost too much to take in: the Google searches, chilling helium inquiry and the text to Colin. Just when I think there couldn't possibly be anything more shocking, the court hears details about how Natasha allegedly killed Mathew.

On the night he died, Mathew ingested a cocktail of sedatives blended by Natasha in a Nutribullet. One of the many drugs included a ram sedative known as acepromazine, which Natasha had bought under a false name from a vet in Armidale after several other failed attempts to purchase it.

I think back to my first trip to Walcha. The locals suspected something was amiss when Natasha tried to buy the same powerful sedatives from the Walcha Veterinary Clinic. They'd known, but had been powerless to do anything.

After a brief summary of the prosecution case, Ng tells the judge there is a real risk and great concern that Natasha will interfere with witnesses if granted bail.

She's done it before. He points to an instance when Natasha tried to coerce an ex-boyfriend into changing his evidence by fabricating offences he'd never carried out, while still on parole for burning down the family home in 2009.

'This applicant has a tendency to fabricate evidence and effectively come up with very elaborate schemes to create evidence to support her innocence,' he tells the court, as Natasha visibly purses her lips and shakes her head.

The judge appears worried, too. He believes her previous conviction for perverting the course of justice makes her an 'unacceptable risk' for potentially trying to tamper with witnesses' evidence.

The court hears that Colin, who is caring for her three children, is a witness, as is her mother Maureen, who was communicating with Mathew in the lead-up to his death.

Natasha's lawyer, Edward Anderson, argues that, if Natasha is granted bail, she will agree to live under effective house arrest at her parents' home in Culburra, wear an electronic monitoring bracelet and report to police daily. Her parents – who are retired and live on the state's South Coast – will also put up $350,000 as surety. After running through a list of other bail conditions, he turns to the strength of the case against his client.

'This is an entirely circumstantial case,' Mr Anderson says, talking directly to the judge.

Justice Campbell is quick to respond. 'Just because it's circumstantial, doesn't mean it's weak.'

Mr Anderson says his client 'asserts there is a hypothesis that is consistent with her innocence'.

'That is, the deceased committed suicide?' Justice Campbell asks.

'That's right,' Mr Anderson says. He then delves into the history of Mathew's mental health, outlining how he'd threatened to take his own life in the months before his death.

He tells the court that Mathew retrieved a rifle on 13 June 2017 and threatened to kill himself, but didn't go through with it. After being admitted to a mental health facility, he was prescribed a medication known as Zoloft, a type of antidepressant. Anderson explains this is a drug that can induce suicidal thoughts within the first month or two of taking it.

Mathew first took the medication on 13 June and died on 2 August, 'well within the two-month limit which is outlined by that prescription', Mr Anderson argues.

Anderson also tells the court that Mathew's GP upped his dosage on 7 July, noting that his depressive symptoms had not improved following his suicide threat.

After the suicide attempt, Anderson tells the court that Mathew was later hospitalised for a severe infection on his right leg. Natasha maintains Mathew was depressed and complaining his leg was deteriorating before his death, but this is at odds with the consulting surgeon, who told police that Mathew's leg had responded well to treatment and was improving.

The surgeon's statement seems to align with the views of neighbours Ross King and Lance Partridge, who both said Mathew was happy about the progress of his leg at the time of his death.

The defence moves from Mathew's to Natasha's state of mind, explaining how she now suffers anxiety and post-traumatic stress disorder after finding Mathew dead. The judge asks how he can grant bail, given her history of serious offending; namely, burning down the family home while her husband Colin Crossman was sleeping.

Considerable time has passed since 2009, Anderson argues, adding that Natasha acknowledges the offences she has committed. She's not 'a violent individual', he argues.

'Setting a house alight not a violent act?' asks Justice Campbell.

Anderson hesitates before conceding, 'It might be an untoward act.'

Anderson's attempt to ignore her past is laughable.

Before Justice Campbell hands down his decision, he talks about the strength of the Crown case. He notes that Natasha is the sole beneficiary of Mathew's estate, having asked him to change his will and being well aware he had.

'The property is one of considerable value. At least ordinary folk, not having great personal wealth, would think so,' Justice Campbell says.

Acknowledging Natasha's defence – that she and Mathew used each other's phones – Justice Campbell points to the date of 1 August 2017, the last day of Mathew's life, when Natasha is accused of using her phone to look at a helium cylinder on a website and taking a screenshot of it.

The prosecution argues the screenshot's timestamp was at a time when Natasha had her phone and Mathew was in an appointment with his orthopaedic surgeon at Tamworth Hospital, getting an update on the condition on his leg. Shortly afterwards, the pair drove to Supagas at Tamworth, where Mathew got out of the car to pick up the helium that would later be used to kill him.

The judge acknowledges Natasha's tendency to 'use sedative drugs in the commission of a crime' and 'concoct false evidence in an elaborate manner to maintain innocence' may not necessarily be something the jury will hear in her upcoming trial, but says, 'One cannot ignore the applicant's previous records ... it is of great concern.'

Even if a jury doesn't hear about her previous convictions, the judge says he's convinced the prosecution have put forth a 'strong Crown circumstantial case'. Given the seriousness of the crime of murder, and the strong case against Natasha, he decides he cannot grant her bail.

Natasha stares straight ahead, her lips quivering, as her application for bail is formally refused. The audio-visual link is cut and journalists scurry out to file their stories.

PART TWO

COLIN

14

HISTORY REPEATS ITSELF

Sydney is in lockdown following the first outbreak of COVID-19. I'm sitting alone in the public gallery of the city's King Street court complex. While waiting for Natasha to appear on the television screen affixed to a courtroom wall, I'm anxious to the point where I find myself holding my breath. What does she look like and what will be revealed today?

At today's hearing, both parties will argue what the jury should and shouldn't be allowed to hear. It's been a little more than a year since her failed bid for freedom in the NSW Supreme Court and she's still awaiting trial. Because of the pandemic, most murder trials have been placed on indefinite hold; the courts are unable to ensure the safety of the 12 jurors, who travel to and from the city each day, and keep them socially distanced within the courtroom.

Justice Julia Lonergan walks into the empty courtroom with her fire-red hair, adjusting her thick black-framed glasses, then taking a seat at the bench in her judicial gown. She's a relatively new judge; appointed to the NSW Supreme Court just six months before Mathew's death in August 2017. Previously, she worked as a barrister and counsel assisting the Special Commission of Inquiry into child sex abuse allegations in the Roman Catholic Diocese of Maitland-Newcastle.

The television screen crackles into life. Natasha appears from a small room inside Mary Wade Correctional Centre; her hair is pulled back tightly in a ponytail with her signature thick fringe, which accentuates her deep brown regrowth.

A terrible audio connection prompts Justice Lonergan to briefly adjourn the proceedings, leaving her staff to grapple with the technological issues while she waits in her chambers.

'Don't say anything, just stay quiet,' Natasha's solicitor Tracey Randall says, who's dialled into the courtroom remotely and is also on the screen.

'I understand,' says Natasha in a sickly-sweet tone, flashing a smile.

Also on the screen is Natasha's new defence barrister, Janet Manuell SC. I do a quick Google search, skimming the first few results. Manuell has defended some high-profile killers and is one of three Deputy Senior Public Defenders in NSW. Public defenders are barristers who act in serious criminal matters for people who have been granted Legal Aid, which is taxpayer funded.

If anyone could get Natasha off, this woman – on paper – seems to be someone who very well could. As I imagine Mathew's family and friends reading the same web pages I am right now, my heart sinks. There are mountains of evidence against her but, if Natasha has a good barrister, is there a chance Mathew won't get the justice he deserves? If she got off, would Natasha head back to Walcha? Anything can happen in a jury trial.

Also on the screen is Crown prosecutor Brett Hatfield. I haven't come across him before and silently pray he's a good fighter. It will be his responsibility to present the evidence to the jury and convince them beyond reasonable doubt that Natasha murdered Mathew. Before today, I've asked around about him; his fellow Crown prosecutors tell me he's solid and thorough. He's previously worked for the Commonwealth Director of Public Prosecutions in Darwin before moving to London, taking up a position as a solicitor specialising in banking and litigation matters. After returning to Sydney, he became a Crown prosecutor in 2014 and, more recently, worked on the appeal of convicted murderer and former Sydney property developer Ron Medich, who paid $500,000 for a hitman to take out former business rival Michael McGurk outside his home on Sydney's leafy north shore in 2009. Medich lost his appeal; he will be almost 100 by the time he's eligible for parole.

Once the technology finally plays ball, Hatfield begins to outline the prosecution case.

He argues there is strong 'tendency evidence' that is vital for the jury to hear, but it's up to Justice Lonergan to decide what. Tendency evidence is that which proves a person tends to act in a particular way, or has a particular state of mind, when committing crimes. Natasha's past actions, some violent and well planned, he argues, have a 'strong similarity to the alleged conduct in Mr Dunbar's matter'.

He focuses heavily on Natasha having been previously charged with attempting to murder her estranged husband, Colin Crossman, when she set fire to the family home in 2009. The court hears that, at the time of the fire, Colin was sedated by several drugs he did not knowingly take. I'd read about Colin's sedation in media articles from the time, but it's horrifying to think that Natasha sedated him all those years ago then possibly went on to drug Mathew in a similar way.

While the prosecution ultimately withdrew the attempted murder charge at the time, Hatfield argues that Natasha had carried out several acts with 'an intention to kill Mr Crossman'.

It baffles me that Natasha could somehow strike a deal at the time. She ended up pleading guilty to one count of destroying property by fire, but signed an agreed statement of facts that admitted she poured a jerry can of petrol over the bedroom where Colin slept before leaving him for dead.

During the hearing, Hatfield focuses on another violent incident involving Colin, which also bears similarity to how Mathew was killed. He argues that Natasha had assaulted Colin in the lead-up to the house fire. Apparently, Natasha belted Colin over the head with a hammer while he slept in bed and had 'attempted to poison or sedate' him by feeding him oysters Kilpatrick laced with drugs.

I can't believe what I'm hearing. Natasha had tried to seriously harm Colin not once, but twice. Both times, she was accused of trying to sedate him by spiking his food. I underline 'oysters' and 'tacos' in my notepad, never imagining I'd write these words in a hearing about tendency evidence.

It is highly damaging evidence. Not surprisingly, Natasha's barrister, Janet Manuell SC, doesn't want the jury to hear any of this, telling the court, 'The accused would be at a gross disadvantage being called to answer these allegations in the course of this trial.'

Regarding the oysters, Manuell argues there is 'nothing to suggest they had been poisoned in any way' and explains how oysters are 'notorious' for going off, 'especially if transported to an inland town like Walcha'.

The hearing continues over several days, but is adjourned for Justice Lonergan to make an important decision, which will impact the trial significantly.

A year after the hearing, Justice Julia Lonergan finally hands down her decision about what the jury will and will not hear in January 2021, now just a few months away from the trial. She rules that the jury will be allowed to hear the tendency evidence about Natasha setting fire to her home while Colin slept sedated.

'While the material is clearly prejudicial, it is of significant probative value,' Justice Lonergan writes in her judgement:

There is in my view a high degree of similarity between the tendency evidence sought to be led. The knowledge on the part of the accused of the availability to her of significant sums of money if her partner dies, the mix of sedatives found in both Mr Crossman and Mr Dunbar, the steps taken by her to deliberately inflict serious harm on her partner are specific and peculiar matters.

As for the oysters, Justice Lonergan decides, this is not something she will allow the jury to hear during the trial. While Colin had told police the oysters were 'acrid', Justice Lonergan finds there is not enough evidence to prove Natasha had laced them with drugs or poison:

> 'Acrid' means unpleasantly bitter or pungent. There is no evidence that the 'acrid' nature of the oyster tasted but spat out by Mr Crossman was caused by a poison or drug, or that the accused knew there was anything wrong with the oyster. To that extent, I accept the submissions of senior counsel for the accused that that conduct does not support tendency.

While the jury will not hear about the oysters, I have already discovered much more about the two attacks on Colin and Natasha's shady past. Not long after the tendency hearing, I started digging, and unearthed more than I could possibly imagine.

15

WARNING SIGNS

I'm sitting in a treasure trove, a small room inside the Downing Centre Court Complex in Sydney. It's November 2020, six months since the tendency hearing, and after months of applications and correspondence, I finally have permission to view Natasha's old court files. The files from Armidale Local Court were posted to the Downing Centre, while other files were pulled up from a repository in Sydney.

I'm seated in a cubicle attached to the court's registry on the third floor of the Downing Centre, a room in which I will spend the next few days, scouring through reams of paper containing details of Natasha's previous crimes.

There's a lot of hustle and bustle outside the main counter of the registry, as lawyers and their clients pace back and forth, or rush to Courtroom 3.1 next door. It's arguably the busiest court in Sydney: judges are assigned to cases, trial dates are set, and there's a never-ending line of lawyers seeking adjournments for every reason under the sun. Often, the line spills out of Courtroom 3.1 and finishes outside the glass windows of the registry.

The documents contain dozens of police statements from Walcha locals, but Colin Crossman's statements are of particular interest; they outline the start of his relationship with Natasha right up until the moment he found himself sedated in bed inside his burning house.

Colin lived several different lives before meeting Natasha. His father's work at the Rural Bank of NSW meant he and his six siblings grew up in several regional and rural towns across the state.

By the time he reached high school, his family had settled in Bellingen, a quiet river town on the Mid North Coast, halfway between Brisbane and Sydney.

Here, he could put down some solid roots for the first time, taking on an apprenticeship as a mechanic after finishing high school. For the next 25 years, he worked in Bellingen Shire for various mechanic shops, but also worked in hospitality, jumping between hotels and clubs in nearby Coffs Harbour and Nambucca Heads. A few years out of school, Colin met a girl named Catherine and fell in love. They married, but Catherine was killed a short time later in a car accident.

Midway through his life, Colin made a big change, signing up for the NSW Ambulance Service. He started working as a patient transport officer in Newcastle, his birth town. After studying further, he became a trainee paramedic in 2005; it appears that, during his 12-month probation period at Wyong, he decided to give love another crack. Not long after signing up and creating a profile on Lavalife, an internet dating site, he matched with Natasha Beth Darcy.

For weeks, they wrote to each other online, exchanging numbers and often speaking for long periods of time on the phone. Natasha revealed she was the mother of a three-year-old daughter and six-week-old son. Colin, the fifth of seven children, saw no issue with her having young children.

Biting the bullet, Colin decided to make a move. On a block of days off sometime in August 2005, he drove from the Central Coast to Sydney to meet Natasha. He ended up staying at her Rouse Hill home for four days. It was a quick start, with Colin later telling police in a statement that their 'relationship commenced in earnest'.

He was dedicated to spending time with Natasha and her two kids, driving down to Sydney and staying with them on his days off. After finishing his probation period as a paramedic, however, he was posted to Mungindi, a rural town on the Queensland border.

Natasha visited only once, helping him find somewhere to live when he was first stationed there. For the rest of his time in Mungindi, Colin made the long trip down to Sydney whenever his roster permitted.

Quite early in their relationship, Natasha confided in Colin that she suffered from extreme anxiety and took medication known as Effexor. It was a condition, she told Colin, that had gripped her ever since she'd been gang raped by three Pakistani brothers in Penrith in western Sydney when she was younger.

The men had reeked of bourbon, a smell that continued to haunt Natasha; Colin was forbidden from drinking the spirit in her presence.

She claims she was forced to undergo facial reconstruction because she had been severely beaten during the attack, which left her with a visible scar on her cheek. The details were scant; Colin knew nothing more apart from Natasha telling him all three men were still in jail. He never questioned her story, he later told police, and believed what she had told him.

They continued their long-distance relationship for about a year until Colin was eventually transferred south to Walcha in July 2006.

Natasha moved her young family to be with him within a matter of months. The pair purchased a four-bedroom, blond brick home, nestled on a 2.5-acre (1 ha) block in the middle of town – a perfect place for Natasha to have the horses she'd always dreamed of. They took out a mortgage with the Commonwealth Bank to pay for their new country home, which came with a double garage for Colin's tools and garden shed for Natasha to store the swimming products she sold on a commission basis.

Colin loved Natasha's children as his own and intended one day to formally adopt her son, who had been only a few weeks old when they met.

Enjoying their new life together in the same town, they soon became engaged. In March 2007, they married on Great Keppel Island, where they honeymooned for 10 days.

After moving to Walcha, Natasha quickly ingratiated herself with the local community, joining the Bendemeer Pony Club and picking up work as a general workhand at a horse stud.

Here, Natasha began to sow the seeds of many lies.

Colin was under the impression that Natasha had completed part of a vet science degree, but was unable to finish it after becoming pregnant with her daughter midway through her studies. When she started working four or five days a week for local stud owner Keith[1], Natasha claimed she was a vet.

Keith suspected this wasn't true from the get-go. In a statement, he told police: 'I could tell that she did not have much of an idea about the treatment of horses.'

Her lack of qualifications quickly became apparent when Keith left her to oversee his horses while on a trip to the Gold Coast. Despite claiming to have a vet degree, Natasha misdiagnosed a horse as being severely malnourished, calling Keith frantically to organise a vet from Armidale to take a look. When he returned to Walcha, he found Natasha in the paddock – a stethoscope around her neck – asking how they were going to treat the horse. While that particular horse had no issues, Keith was disturbed to see another mare in the paddock with an obvious injury. A bone was protruding from her hoof and the mare was later put down.

Growing concerned about her abilities and character, Keith cut back her hours to weekends, a move that he said angered Natasha. She promptly quit.

After this, she began spending a lot of time with horse trainers Jack and Rebecca,[2] a couple Keith had introduced her to. They lived in the nearby town of Bendemeer.

---

1   Name has been changed
2   Names have been changed

'I would go to [Jack's] property to check on my horses and she would be there virtually every time. We would acknowledge each other but not really talk.'

Through Jack and Rebecca, Natasha was introduced to horse lovers Julie and Darren,[3] the owners of a retail saddlery store in town. After purporting to be a vet with experience working on websites for veterinary companies, she ended up doing some part-time work on their website.

'I believed Natasha when she said she was a vet. I had no reason not to. I remember one time she said that she had to go and dissect a rabbit . . . I assumed it was veterinary work,' Julie told police in a statement.

When she pulled up to the Bendemeer pony camp in her maroon Pajero and horse float during the school holidays of July 2008, Natasha looked the part. But after falling off a horse, she got chatting to a local named Melissa. During their first conversation, Natasha was quick to say she was a vet but 'not into large animals, just small animals'. She'd completed her degree at the University of Sydney and claimed she was still very much involved in veterinary research.

'A couple of things happened during the week that made me think that she wasn't a vet,' Melissa would later tell police. 'She had been asked a question by some kids about horses and she gave a very odd answer.'

While they'd only just met at the pony camp, Natasha performed several detailed monologues, confiding in Melissa the story behind the noticeable scar on her face. Her story was starkly at odds with the tale she'd told Colin about being gang raped. It all rolled off her tongue so easily. She claimed to be a dressage champion at university, enjoying great success with her Appaloosa – an American horse breed known for its striking spotted coats. She was riding through a skate park, she told Melissa, when she was chased by 'guys on

---

3   Names have been changed

dirt bikes' who spooked the horse. She had fallen, hard, as had the horse.

After being placed in an induced coma for several days, she awoke to terrible news. Her horse had suffered severe injuries, her parents informed Natasha, and they'd decided to have it put down while she had been unconscious in hospital. The scar on her cheek was a constant reminder of her heartbreaking loss.

In reality, the teenage Natasha had been kicked in the face by a horse. She was taken to hospital with concussion and had plastic surgery, but suffered no long-term injuries. The horse was not euthanised.

At some point during the pony camp, Melissa recalls, Colin came to visit Natasha with her son. At the time, Natasha's daughter was visiting her father in Sydney.

'During the camp I thought Natasha was really rude to Colin. There were not many people around and she was very short with him,' Melissa said in her statement.

Despite hardly knowing Melissa, Natasha sidled up to her at the end of one day to reveal more about her personal situation. Her marriage, she explained, was only one of convenience. Colin had married her for the sake of the kids, but they slept in separate bedrooms at either end of the house. There was nothing sexual between them.

Natasha and Colin's financial problems were piling up. Natasha begged Colin to buy a $15,000 horse float – complete with its own kitchen – but he refused. He told her there was 'no way' they were going to buy it, considering their debts. She went ahead and ordered one anyway, telling him her daughter's paternal grandmother would foot the bill for a less expensive one – only $10,000 – without the luxury of a kitchen.

Over several months, Natasha drained $30,000 from their mortgage account. Colin was forced to take out a personal loan for $33,000 to pay off three credit cards Natasha had maxed out. At the time, he was unaware that the $12,000 loan for their wedding, which he believed had been taken out jointly, was solely in his name.

'Oh, look, we do it tough, that's why I had to take out another loan to pay for our credit cards. Tash and [her daughter] have horses and that's a big black hole where money's concerned and we did it – we paid most of the bills, there was no drama with it,' Colin later explained to an insurance investigator after the house fire.

'But we had – I mean, I still maintain we had our rows with her about where she's spending money and how much money she's spending and stuff like that, but it never got to a point for me where I thought, well, "I'm going to have to do something about this, I'm going to have to bloody pull her into line or something." It was just the sort of stuff that I think couples go on with,' he said.

Colin also confided to colleagues and a neighbour about the mounting financial pressure, and Natasha's unwillingness to rein it in. As the bills kept coming in and tensions simmered about spending, Colin found a text message in Natasha's phone that knocked the wind out of him.

Natasha had written to a local horse trainer, Jack, who Colin knew was recovering from a broken leg following a horse-riding accident: 'I'm on my way to Tamworth, do you want anything or just a head job on the way past?'

A few months later, Colin discovered another series of texts, some to Jack and others to two more Walcha locals. He didn't know what to make of them. In one of her many texts to Jack, Natasha had asked him, 'Want a root?'

Colin found a text from another horse trainer linked to the Bendemeer Pony Club, which read: 'I wish you were here in these fresh sheets making love with me'.

In the most startling messages of all, Natasha had sent several texts to yet another man named Paul,[4] also associated with the pony club, indicating that she and Colin had separated: 'I hope your mum and [wife] did not get the wrong impression, maybe it would be a good idea if [your wife] did not know of this message. I don't want them

---

4   Name has been changed.

to get the wrong impression; I wasn't trying to come onto you, since Col's left my minds been racing.'

Colin's mind raced, too. Where was this coming from? Why had she told Paul they'd separated? While giving a statement to police, Colin later recalled other texts she'd sent to Paul.

'Do you get a coffee break at work? I'd like to clear something up, I feel embarrassed since Col left a few days ago. [Jack and Rebecca] are my two closest friends and have been great since Col left,' she wrote.

These texts came after Natasha had informed several members at a pony club meeting that she and Colin had parted ways in December 2008.

She couldn't deny it later; too many people heard her proclaim their separation that night. A month later, she told police she'd been upset with Colin after he'd argued with her for staying too late at the meeting.

'I was really upset with Col, and, you know, it was over as far as I was concerned. I love my husband . . . and I just, you know, it just really upset me,' Natasha said in one of her police interviews.

'We had a rough week that week and, yeah, he did storm off at one stage and I did tell [Paul] that he'd just left, but I think I've sent all of four messages to [Paul], and that was only because I'd been talking to him at the pony club meeting and he asked if I was alright.'

About the same time Natasha started telling locals she was a single mother, she began to pepper Darren[5], the owner of a local store, with texts. Many were sexual in nature, and there were countless offers from Natasha to have coffee. While the store owner never returned her messages, she continued to doggedly pursue him.

'Are you working tomorrow? Come and have a coffee with me. I promise not to bite you or lay a finger on you in any way!' Natasha texted.

By the time he made his statement to police, Darren had deleted most of the texts but remembered one of the messages, which went

---

5 Name has been changed

something along the lines of: 'I love my husband and children, but I need something more.'

He also recalls her texting 'Would you like to see my pussy?' then sending a picture of her cat.

At the time, Natasha was also doing some work on his business's website. She approached Darren in his store. His wife was not in earshot. She was never flirtatious in the shop or in person, but had decided to give it one last crack.

'All I want to do is have a cup of coffee with you,' she said playfully.

Darren shot back quickly: 'I'm not interested.'

Natasha never got in touch with him again.

'There is no doubt in my mind that, if I had pursued the matter, she would have been serious. You can't send that amount of texts with that content and not be a little bit serious. To me, the nature and the amount of texts meant it was not just a joke,' he told police.

Although he caught her out sending sexual texts, Colin was oblivious that she was telling people they'd separated. They remained a couple, caring for both children and living in the same house. He also had no idea she was actively making plans to leave him.

Natasha decided she wanted to buy a 2.5-acre (1 ha) parcel of land owned by Jack and his wife, adjoining their property at Bendemeer. Called New Frontier, the property came with a small cottage; she'd offered them $157,000 to buy it. Colin was not privy to the offer.

She'd even emailed a Tamworth-based removalist company several times, asking for quotes on how much it would cost to move 50 kilometres from Walcha to Bendemeer.

In one of the emails, she explained her plans in great detail: part of the furniture was to be picked up and delivered to the new property, with the rest stored in a container while she and her husband built a new home on the land they'd recently acquired.

She listed all the furniture items she owned under two columns: 'Items to be moved to new shack' and 'Items for storage in container on our property at Bendemeer'. She wanted the move to take place during the week of 21 January 2009. She signed off the email: 'Thanks heaps, Natasha and Colin Crossman'.

Colin later told police he had absolutely no knowledge about the planned move to Bendemeer, until he discovered Natasha's emails with the removalist on her computer.

He knew Jack and Rebecca had bought a small block of land adjoining their property, because Natasha had vaguely mentioned she would have liked to have gone halves with them. He hadn't given it a second thought, however, because they were trying to pay off the house in which they were mortgaged up to their eyeballs.

Colin told police: 'This is all very surprising to me. No such arrangements or anything remotely like this has been discussed ... Natasha and I have never spoken about the possibility of moving to Bendemeer together, or the possible purchase of property in the Bendemeer area. Conditions of my employment with the NSW Ambulance Service requires me to live in or around Walcha.'

While Colin was kept completely in the dark, Natasha excitedly revealed her plans about the move to Bendemeer at pony club meetings between November and December 2008, when she'd also announced her and Colin's separation.

'Before the meeting, I was talking to Natasha. She told me that her marriage had broken up, Col was going to Byron Bay and she did not want to go. They were selling the house in Walcha and she is buying the property "The New Frontier",' Melissa explained, referring to the property owned by Jack and Rebecca at Bendemeer.

Natasha began to pester Colin persistently about the need for them to take out life insurance. Natasha made several enquiries with a company called Asteron – both on the phone and over emails – and had completed lengthy paperwork, which she asked Colin to sign.

The joint application would cover them for $1 million. Natasha would receive $700,000 in the event of Colin's death and he would receive $300,000 should anything ever happen to her. Colin never read any of the paperwork but, in mid-December, Natasha told him the application was more or less approved.

When they applied for the life insurance, they already had insurance through CommInsure for their home, valued at $318,000, and for its contents, valued at $143,000.

But there was a hiccup with the life insurance application.

On the forms, Colin had declared he suffered from sleep apnoea; later, he received a phone call informing him the application was on hold, pending a report from his doctor. He forgot to mention this call to Natasha, who possibly thought the life insurance was in place.

Perhaps things would have gone differently if he had.

16

OYSTERS KILPATRICK

A police officer focused on Colin's face as he videoed his conversation with Detective Senior Constable Craig Dunn at 183W Croudace Street, Walcha, the Crossmans' family home. According to the transcript I'm holding, Dunn asked Colin to cast his mind back to the night of 16 January 2009.

'I believe that's the night . . . she cooked oysters Kilpatrick,' Colin says, sitting in the same chair Natasha had served him the oysters while he watched the cricket. 'She said she was going to be romantic and feed them to me, and I let her put one in my mouth.'

When she also spoke to Dunn, in a boxy interview room at Tamworth Police Station hours later, Natasha's recollection of the night begins in a similar fashion. Her interview was also recorded, but with the caution: anything she said might be used in evidence.

She recalled spotting a seafood truck parked near Café Graze in Walcha on the afternoon of Friday, 16 January. 'I got a dozen oysters from the oyster man . . . I've been saying for ages I'll stop and get some things.'

Sitting across the table from her in the sterile room, Dunn pressed her with half a dozen more questions: Where exactly was the van parked? How much did the oysters cost? Where did she park?

'This is confusing. What are (sic) the oysters got to do with anything?'

'We've got a thousand questions to ask,' Dunn replied.

Stumped, Natasha exhaled, 'Wow . . . okay.'

She fast-forwarded to when Colin came home with the kids, having spent the afternoon at the local pool.

'I printed a recipe for oysters Kilpatrick because I knew a friend that used to love oysters Kilpatrick that I used to work with and heard they were really nice . . . I don't eat seafood, yuck . . . I just can't do it.'

In an apparent labour of love, she sprinkled the oysters with parmesan cheese and bacon bits, before adding a splash of Worcestershire sauce, cooking them, then taking them out to Colin on the couch.

'He said they weren't very nice. He said they were off when he had them so . . .' she trailed off.

In his interview, Colin remembered a little extra detail.

'Um, they were oyster Kilpatrick but, when they came out, they had an orangey, yellowy, golden glaze on them . . . I chewed it for a while, but it was a horrible taste. It was an acrid taste. I tried to eat it but I couldn't, so I went out to the back toilet and spat it down the toilet,' he told Dunn.

After the specially prepared oysters did not go down how Natasha envisaged, she returned to the kitchen to whip up a risotto, returning to the lounge room with a glass of red wine in hand.

In a chatty mood, Colin said she rabbited on about horse-riding and how important it was for her to wear a helmet to protect her head. While the chit-chat wasn't out of the ordinary, things quickly took a strange, ominous turn.

Out of the blue, Natasha seemed fascinated by and fixated with the subject of temples, and whether they were the most fragile part of the skull.

'And she asked me, "How hard would you have to hit the temple to do any damage?"' Colin told Dunn, still struggling to process the conversation fully.

'I said, "I don't know; a slap wouldn't do much, but it would probably do a bit more damage if you hit somebody with your fist" . . . I wouldn't have a clue.'

After watching the end of the cricket, he said he went to bed. He later woke up in agony, screaming as he held himself in the foetal position.

'At some time early in the morning, I was smashed over the head with something while I lay in bed . . . I believe it to be a hammer,' Colin told Dunn.

'I immediately thought that the ceiling fan had come loose and struck me. Whatever it was that hit me, I heard it hit the floor straight after it bounced off my skull.'

Indicating with his hands, Colin was positive he was hit on the left side of his head, from behind. He sensed Natasha was standing at the foot of their bed.

'Turn the light on, turn the light on!' he screamed.

But she wouldn't. 'What's wrong? What's wrong?' she asked, fumbling around on the floor.

Instead of turning on the light, she told Colin to 'just wait a minute' before running out of the bedroom and into the backyard.

Back in her interview with police, Natasha recalled Colin's screams that night. 'I actually thought he jumped up and hit his head on something and he, and he sort of screamed, like, a man-type scream.

'And then I just sort of jumped out of the bed and I sort of saw something run down that way, a shadow.'

She claimed she saw a mysterious figure sprinting down the hallway.

'So I immediately, I panicked and ran after [them], thinking, you know, it looked like it had come from the kid's room . . . I assumed that somebody had one of the children. So I ran after them and I couldn't really see.'

Looking at her cautiously, Dunn asked why she hadn't turned the light on.

'Cause I wouldn't have been able to see. You know, when you turn a light on, like, when you go to the toilet at night and you can't see to start with? It's easier just to do it with the light off,' she said.

Colin also asked Natasha why she refused to turn on the light when he asked her. 'Natasha said, "If I had of turned the light on, it would have blinded me for an instant." I couldn't understand why she didn't turn the light on, and I thought it very weird that Natasha supposedly chased a person through the dark out of our house. She usually jumps at her own shadow. Also, if Natasha really thought someone had one of her children, she would have been frantically screaming her head off.'

During Colin's recorded interview with Dunn, he stood at the sliding doors that open onto the backyard, pointing to where he'd later found Natasha near the trampoline.

'She said, she thought she saw someone, so she chased them out of the house and they jumped the fence into the spare paddock next door.'

After checking on the kids, who were sound asleep in bed, and with a pounding headache, Colin walked back to the bedroom and called triple-0. Waiting for paramedics and police to arrive, he made his way to the front TV room and sat on the couch, bewildered. Had this been a home invasion?

'I had absolutely zero enemies. I actually thought that someone had come into the wrong house. Just a mistaken identity, just clocked me on the head, thinking I was someone else,' he said in one of his interviews.

Paramedic David Lucietto found Colin sitting on the couch with a large swelling on his temple near his left eye and badly damaged skin.

'What's happened? What's going on?' he asked.

'I was asleep in bed, and I woke up after being hit on the head. After I got hit, I heard something fall on the floor,' Colin replied.

Lucietto told police he walked towards the bedroom, with Natasha following close behind, and checked under the bed to see if he could ascertain what Colin had been hit with. Nothing was there.

About this time, Senior Constable Brett Paulson arrived at the house. He immediately checked on Colin before walking to the front of the house to inspect the front door. No signs of forced entry.

Colin drew Paulson's attention to the garage. Oddly, the roller door was all the way up and the light was on.

'Inside my garage, I pointed out to Senior Constable Paulson that my hammer, which is usually kept in my nail belt which hangs above my work bench, was missing,' Colin said, infuriated. 'I could not understand why Natasha kept saying things like, "It could not have been a hammer, it must have been, like a mag torch." No, it was a bloody hammer, I know the difference between being hit by a hammer or torch. It was a hammer or iron bar,' he recalled.

Paulson took Natasha aside to chat.

'I know my pink pyjama top's actually quite showy and I remember Brett, the policeman, came over. And I have, I've got that pink top on and I'm just sort of thinking, how embarrassing, of all nights for me to wear it,' she told Dunn in her interview.

Paulson followed Natasha as she retraced her steps to chase 'a male' out the back door.

'I observed that the furniture and coffee table were not disturbed, and that the direction in which the alleged male ran was quite tight,' Paulson recalled.

Shining a torch on the backyard, Paulson noticed dew on the grass; aside from a series of tracks where the family dog had run, there were no other markings or footprints.

Natasha was adamant the person jumped the fence and ran into the neighbouring property. Paulson was unable to make out any tracks.

'I observed that the grass in the neighbouring property was approximately two to three foot high and did not look like anything had been in it for some time.'

Colin was taken by ambulance to Walcha Hospital, where the doctor who examined him was concerned about the swelling on his temple. Needing to go to Tamworth for a CAT scan, he and Natasha returned home to get changed before heading to hospital.

For some reason, Colin decided to open the dishwasher. Inside, he discovered several oyster shells, freshly cleaned. Finding it odd, he asked Natasha why she had washed the shells. Without batting an eyelid, she said she cleaned them to help her daughter with a school project she needed to do in the school holidays.

Natasha later told police, without being asked about the subject, that her daughter was pestering her to try some of the oysters when she was preparing them for Colin.

'So, I actually cleaned the shells and I was going to make her some the next day.'

'Sorry?' Dunn asked, confused.

'Like, not oysters of course, something else I was going to put in it, so it looked like that.'

'Parmesan, Worcestershire sauce and what was the other stuff? Bacon?'

'Yes.'

Dunn then asked her where exactly had she put the shells after Colin had eaten one of the oysters and spat it down the toilet.

'In the dishwasher. I know it's stupid, but I wanted to do something for my daughter the next day.'

'And was that all the shells?' he asked, sensing something amiss.

'I think so. I ended up throwing them out the next day because they still stank. You couldn't get that fishy smell out of them, so I just put them in the bin.'

So, Natasha put the oyster shells through the dishwasher before throwing them out. Fishy, Dunn thought. His colleague Detective Senior Constable Michael Maloney agreed.

They suspected Natasha laced the oysters with sedatives, but she wasn't going to admit it.

During more than four hours at Tamworth Police Station, Natasha answered more than 1300 questions about the series of events spanning from 15 to 20 January in 2009.

Dunn had a few more loose ends to tie up before revealing all his cards. He asked her to cast her mind back to Colin's hammer. 'Do you remember some conversation about the hammer being missing from Colin's tool belt?'

Natasha had no recollection, but claimed she used the hammer to fix her son's sandpit on the day Colin was attacked by a supposed home invader. 'I actually got it from his bench and I put it back where I put all his tools.'

She often collected Colin's tools left lying around the house, she claimed, storing them in the kitchen cupboard.

Dunn didn't buy it.

Earlier, Colin had explained to police that he'd rifled through the kitchen cupboard the day before the hammer attack, looking for a screwdriver to put batteries in a toy Natasha's daughter had been given for Christmas. The hammer wasn't in the cupboard, and if it had been, he would have remembered it.

'Colin says that it was earlier in the week you were trying to fix the sandpit,' Dunn said, stepping up the heat.

Natasha vehemently denied this. 'No, no, it wasn't.'

'No?'

'No. I don't understand why he's doing this?' Natasha asked, referring to Colin.

Dunn didn't answer but began to ask a series of questions about an event three nights after the hammer attack, a far worse crime. He asked harder questions, which Natasha found far more difficult and distressing to answer.

It was hard for close mate and fellow paramedic Mark Doran to ignore the black swelling on Colin's face, as the pair chatted at his house just a few hours after his release from hospital. He remembers Colin telling him he thought he was attacked by a home invader, but couldn't make any sense of it. Trying to lighten the mood, Doran asked if Colin enjoyed the oysters Kilpatrick he'd mentioned Natasha was making the night before. It wasn't much of a mood booster.

The oysters were so putrid, Colin told Doran, he'd run to the bathroom to spit them out.

'He said something like, "It was awful. I don't know what she put in it,"' Doran recalls, during a phone interview more than a decade after the fact. 'I remember thinking, "How do you fuck that up?" It's bacon and Worcestershire . . . it's not that hard.

'I said to him, "Do you think she's trying to kill you?"' He remembers being shocked by the answer.

'Yes,' Colin said, taking Doran completely by surprise.

'He said, "It's funny that you say that. Last week, I had a vivid dream that somebody was holding a pillow over my face. I thought it was a dream but, maybe, it wasn't."'

Colin later told police about the dream, which he was no longer sure was a dream.

He remembered being fast asleep but waking to the feeling of someone pinching his nose. Next minute, there was a pillow on his face and someone was pushing down. It was hard to breathe. He felt like he was being smothered.

'Keep your fucking hands away from my face!' he remembered screaming, before sitting up in bed to see Natasha next to him. She didn't say a word and neither did he.

At the time, he thought perhaps she was just rolling him onto his right side as she usually did. Maybe it had been a bad dream.

Sitting with his mate Doran, however, he wasn't so sure.

17

FIRE

It's not hard to find Natasha and Colin's old family home, near the Walcha lawn bowls club; the house still bears black scars from the night it went up in flames. From the road, I can see the right-hand window is still boarded up. The bricks around it are singed black from where fire blew out the glass in the middle of the night. There's still a sizeable hole in the roof above the front bedroom, exposing burnt timber beams where the force of the blaze erupted, spitting out royal blue tiles.

I think about Colin, who'd been sleeping in that room, unable to wake because of a cocktail of drugs in his system. There had been several warning signs, but Colin had not picked up on them until it was too late.

Three days after the hammer attack, Colin and Natasha spent the morning at a joint counselling session in Tamworth; apparently, both were rattled by the supposed home invasion.

The session did little to quell Natasha's reported anxiety, however, which she was very vocal about. Before heading back to Walcha, about an hour's drive away, the pair stopped at Tamworth Hospital, where Natasha asked if she could get some medication to help her sleep, telling the doctor she hadn't slept a wink since the attack.

A doctor prescribed her Kalma, a medication used to treat anxiety. The active ingredient is alprazolam, a short-acting tranquilliser often sold under the brand name Xanax.

Later that afternoon, Natasha and her son headed next door to Peter and Mary Boyd's for some afternoon drinks. She told them she tried to get Colin to come, too, but he wanted to stay at home. Mary offered to go and get him.

'Yes, go and see if he will come over for you,' Natasha said.

Colin accepted Mary's neighbourly invitation, grabbing a six-pack of Four-X Gold stubbies from the garage fridge and walking over.

The Boyds' daughter Corina was visiting with their grandchild, so the group sat around chatting over drinks for about an hour or so. Natasha's daughter was staying the night at a friend's house.

Citing hunger, Natasha left the Boyds' house with her son at about 7.30 pm; Colin stayed behind while she prepared dinner. After a draining and emotional day, Colin didn't feel like staying much longer and left after drinking three beers in total.

When Colin got home, Natasha was in a jolly mood. 'Let's get drunk tonight. You get some bourbon and I'll get some vodka,' Natasha declared, in a thoroughly confusing proposition. Colin wasn't – under any circumstances – allowed to drink bourbon in their house. She also wasn't a big drinker.

'I thought this was very strange because of what Natasha had previously told me about how she felt about bourbon,' Colin told police, explaining how Natasha claimed she was once raped by a group of men.

'The males who allegedly raped her all apparently smelled of bourbon and she has not been able to stand the smell since.'

Colin declined her offer of getting drunk and retreated to their living room to watch TV, while Natasha prepared a Mexican dinner in the kitchen.

She told police that, prior to the next-door drinks, she'd already cooked some taco mince; all she did was reheat the meat before shovelling it into corn shells with some sour cream, lettuce and tomatoes. Natasha took out four tacos to Colin on the couch, and he devoured them.

This was the last thing he remembered.

Natasha told police she went back to the kitchen to eat one taco with her son.

Worried about not being able to sleep, she said, she took one of the tablets the doctor had earlier prescribed her at hospital, before 'fussing doing some housework'.

About half an hour later, she returned to the living room where Colin was still watching television. She claimed to have given him two capsules of Nature's Own Valerian, a herbal remedy, to help him sleep. After giving Colin a quick kiss, she popped another 'Kalma' tablet and decided to try and get some sleep herself.

About 11.30 pm, Natasha said she was woken when Colin hopped into bed. He gave her a kiss and rolled over to get some shut-eye. Later, she said, she got up to check that all the windows and doors were locked, worried about the prospect of another break-in.

After falling asleep, the next thing she recalled was the fire alarm going off. She told police, 'I heard the smoke alarm, I woke up. I remember my eyes being really sore. I remember looking over and it was really smoky over that side of the bedroom where Col was.'

Flames quickly crawled up one side of the bedroom.

'I screamed at Col and sort of shook him and I assumed he was going to be right behind me.'

Natasha says she scooped up a pile of clothes that were obstructing her path to get out of the bedroom and threw them on the fire, which was making its way towards the door.

'And as I was jumping across, that's when I hit the petrol, whatever, the can. It smelled like petrol. But I could smell petrol before that. Like, I was actually wet and our doona was wet. I remember, when I woke up that was the first thing I thought was, "I'm wet," which I thought was really odd, of course.'

In her version, she bolted towards her son's room and scooped him out of bed.

'I could actually hear that; it was like the fire was taking off. It's a horrible sound, a sound I never want to hear again. I ran down the hallway . . . and then I ran next door.'

In a pink floral nightie, Natasha banged on the side of the Boyds' house, screaming as she held her son in her other arm.

'The house is on fire! The house is on fire,' Peter Boyd and his daughter Corina both remembered Natasha yelling. They opened the front door to find Natasha standing at the top of the veranda stairs.

'What, the house is on fire?' Corina asked in a daze. She asked Natasha whether she'd called triple-0. She hadn't.

'Is anyone still in the house?' asked Peter.

'Col is still inside,' Natasha explained.

'Natasha was dressed in her pyjamas; she seemed very alert and coherent,' Corina recalled.

Corina threw a jacket around Natasha's son, called triple-0 and ran to the kitchen to grab a torch. In the meantime, Natasha claimed she went back to the house but returned a minute or so later, still by herself.

'I went back into the house and, as I was coming down the hallway, I heard an explosion of some sort and I panicked, and my first thought was [my son] would follow me back. Because I know Corina had gone to get the phone and I thought, he's come back and the house is exploding,' she told police.

But her son was safe; he was still sitting on the couch in the Boyds' front living room, right where she had left him with Peter.

'Col is still in there,' Natasha explained, leaving her son again and running back towards her burning house with Corina.

'As I ran down our driveway and into the house next door, I saw that the whole right side of Natasha and Colin's house was well ablaze and the windows were smashing . . . exploding,' Corina told police.

Natasha and Corina both screamed Colin's name repeatedly.

Corina ran to the house's side door. Opening the screen door, she found Colin standing inside the doorway, wearing just his boxer shorts. He was wobbly, holding the house phone in his hand in a complete daze.

'Col just came out in a big puff of smoke. It was like he was intoxicated; it was like he was drunk. And we helped him next door onto the veranda and he was quite sick, he was throwing up,' Natasha recalled.

Corina remembered Colin being unsteady on his feet, covered in soot, disoriented and 'not with it'.

She held him with both arms and slowly walked him next door with Natasha in tow.

Inside the Boyds' front room, Colin kept asking where the kids were. Peter Boyd covered his shoulders with a blanket and assured him everyone was accounted for.

Paramedics Mark Doran and Dave Lucietto, who were on call at home, were contacted by the operations centre, telling them to go to a house fire on Croudace Street.

'I got to the roundabout in Walcha and I went "Holy Shit, that's Col's place," and, as I pulled up out the front, she was standing on the footpath in her nightie, screaming and carrying on, flames pouring out the windows,' Lucietto recalls.

Natasha was completely hysterical.

'Oh my God, my house is burning down, my house is burning down. The cats are still inside. I can smell petrol, I can smell petrol,' she repeated over and over again to Doran and Lucietto, who were in disbelief.

'I'm yelling at her, saying, "What have you done now? Where's Col?"' Lucietto says. He'd been called to the house three nights previously, following the hammer attack. He sensed something was terribly wrong.

Doran told a police officer on the scene he 'smells a rat', joining Lucietto in asking Natasha where Colin was.

'I was like, "Oh man, the penny is dropping now,"' Doran says.

Through sobs, Natasha pointed towards the veranda where Colin was now with her son and the Boyds.

'He seemed really spaced out, it was like he was stoned or wasted,' Doran later told police. 'He had a slight slur in his speech and then had a massive vomit. Part of it went over me and over the veranda onto the ground.'

Colin insisted on going to the bathroom to wash himself before heading to hospital. Doran helped to wipe away soot and vomit with toilet paper.

'Have you taken anything?' Doran asked, as they stood in the back bathroom.

'Two sleepers from Tash,' Colin managed to tell him through slurred speech. When Doran made his way to the front of the house, he wasted no time in questioning Natasha.

'What were the "sleepers"?'

'I think they're called Kalma,' he recalls Natasha telling him.

Natasha's recollection of the conversation differed slightly. She maintained she told Doran she gave Colin two natural valerian tablets.

'Are you sure you didn't say he's taken two Kalma pills?' probed Dunn, during Natasha's police interview a week after the fire.

'Goodness, no.'

'Are you sure?'

'I said that I'd taken two Kalma pills, I didn't say . . . that Col had . . . Col doesn't take any sort of medication like that. He's, he's really anti . . . he won't even take a Panadol if he's got a headache.'

Friends say Colin never takes any drugs and, if he had, he would remember it. He's a paramedic.

At the time, Doran told police he was concerned about Colin's state of drowsiness and wasted no time in asking staff at Walcha Hospital to take blood and urine samples to run toxicology checks, as soon he'd transported Colin to hospital.

'I asked Sonya and said, "You've got to get some bloods out of him because he's been given something." Col's not a recreational drug user and he was so out of it, I knew there was something wrong.

'I was really worried for him. My fear was – where is this going to stop?' Doran said.

Nurse Sonya Hughes gave a similar statement to police.

'Mark pulled me aside and said, "Something is not right, please take blood. I've never been more serious in my life."'

One of the other nurses on duty was Mary Boyd. She was surprised to see Colin in hospital, having spent the evening with him, Natasha and her family at her house before starting her shift at 10.30 pm.

'Colin was brought in on the stretcher and Natasha came in carrying [her son]. Colin was black. He was extremely drowsy. It seemed that he could not comprehend what was happening; the side of his hair was singed. There was a strong smell of smoke and there was a smell of something like petrol in the room.'

While her colleague Sonya assessed Colin, with Doran and Lucietto close by, Mary walked over to Natasha to ask her what had happened.

'There's been a fire in the bedroom. I've got petrol on my feet, legs and my clothes; [my son's] got petrol on him,' Natasha said.

'Where did the petrol come from?' Mary asked.

'There was a tin of petrol on the floor in the doorway of our bedroom. I knocked it over and it splashed onto my legs and feet.'

Natasha said she tried to wake up Colin and left the bedroom to fetch her son, only realising Colin wasn't behind her when she ran towards the Boyds' house.

'I thought it strange as I was aware of the layout of the house and when she would have come out of [her son's] bedroom, she would have passed their bedroom to come down the hallway,' Mary told police.

Mary remembered soaking a washer in warm water, using it to wipe the soot and vomit from Colin's face and chest. Although in and out of consciousness, he managed to ask Natasha, 'Are the kids okay?' Natasha assured him they were safe.

Colin had no memory of the fire, his escape or any interactions with anyone until his transfer to Tamworth Hospital: 'I was watching television and Tash gave me a plate with four tacos on it, which I ate. That is the last thing I remember until I awoke in a cubicle at casualty at Tamworth Hospital.'

A few days after Colin's admission to hospital, police were notified of his toxicology results. Their suspicions were confirmed. There was a wide-ranging mix of sedatives and drugs in his system. The first drug of note was alprazolam, the active ingredient in the 'Kalma' medication, which Natasha collected a script for on the day of the fire. Also present was temazepam, used to treat insomnia, along with venlafaxine and oxazepam, medications used to treat anxiety and depression. But the most surprising drug detected was midazolam; this drug is used to induce sleep and can cause memory loss. While the source of some of the drugs remains a mystery, Colin's colleagues later discovered two vials of midazolam missing from the drug bag at Walcha Ambulance Station.

About a week after the fire, Doran went to Colin and Natasha's place to feed their chooks and cats. Colin was staying with his parents in the small town of Quirindi and Natasha told Doran she was staying at Jack's, but later changed her story to 'sleeping in her car'. Her two kids were staying with Natasha's parents down south at Culburra.

Doran opened up a box in their backyard, where all the Dine cat food was stored. He nearly stumbled backwards when he noticed an empty glass vial inside the box, labelled 'midazolam'. He called the police.

During one of his police interviews with Dunn, Colin recalled a disturbing hospital visit from Natasha. Two days after the fire, Colin said Natasha walked into his room, clutching a boomerang pillow. She placed it over his left arm then rested her head on it as she sat next to his bed. Under the pillow, she found Colin's hand, and put her hand on top of his.

Suddenly, Colin felt an uncomfortable sensation in his arm: Natasha was fiddling with the cannula. At first he wasn't too fazed but, as the pain increased, he worried his arm was bleeding. After ripping his arm out from beneath the pillow, he discovered Natasha had somehow screwed the cap off the cannula and was holding it in her hand. Colin then noticed a few drops of clear fluid on his skin.

'What the hell do ya think you're doing?' Colin yelled, rearing backwards in his hospital bed.

'I'm just having a look to see how it works,' Natasha said meekly.

The episode left him shaken.

18

CHOCOLATE ALMONDS

Sifting through the transcripts of Natasha's police interviews, I initially dismiss the first mention of what, on the surface, appears to be something trivial. The more I read, however, the clearer it becomes. It's Natasha's farfetched cover story to explain the drugs found in Colin's system. My eyes glaze over the subject the first few times but, as I turn each page, it's clear she's fixated with the topic. She's itching to raise it again and again, at any opportunity she can, under intense questioning by detectives.

She first brings up the topic nonchalantly but, whether she's forgotten what she's said – or is desperate to hammer it home – she keeps coming back to it.

Detective Senior Constable Matt O'Hehir remembers Natasha first mentioning the chocolate-covered almonds as she sat with him in an examination room at Tamworth Base Hospital.

It was just a few hours after the fire; he was keen to ask her a few questions on the understanding that anything she said or did may be used in evidence. He recorded their conversation. She told O'Hehir she had a clear memory of hearing the fire alarm go off and later tripping over a petrol can, which – despite the panic, smoke and darkness – she easily described.

'I actually tripped over a petrol can, well, it was a petrol tin can, it was so big, two-litre type thing, and it rattled and it definitely smelled of petrol because I felt I was wet,' she told O'Hehir eagerly.

She quickly skipped ahead to finding Colin back at the house, after she'd run to the next-door neighbours thinking he was in tow, describing how sick he was, most likely suffering from carbon monoxide poisoning. She recalled him 'acting strange like he's on narcotics or something', which is why she thought the paramedics asked her if he'd taken any substances before going to bed.

Immediately after raising the subject of Colin's drowsy state, she told O'Hehir she remembered one thing; not that she thought it was in any way related to the house fire. But it could be.

'Last night, I had rang the poisons information because of some bad Cadbury chocolate almonds that we had and they had, like, a white powder on them,' she explained.

She'd eaten a few of the strange-tasting chocolates a couple of nights prior, after buying two boxes at the BP service station near Tamworth.

'And then last night Col had some more and he said, no, I said, "They're a bit strange aren't they?" So I actually put them in a snap lock bag and I rang and left a message with the consumer line – that I was given by the poisons information – and I left them on the kitchen bench,' she said, not pausing for breath.

'So I don't know if they're burned or not. I hope not, 'cause there was something wrong with them, but that's a whole different thing.'

O'Hehir asked what time she and Colin went to bed the night prior.

Natasha said she hopped into bed at about 10.30 pm, while Colin came in about an hour later, mentioning he felt a bit sick before drifting off.

'He said he was feeling a bit funny, which is why I thought, "Those almonds – I've got to look into that", but other than that he was fine.'

Nine days after her initial interview with O'Hehir at the hospital, Natasha came face-to-face with Detective Senior Constable Dunn at

Tamworth Police Station. This was a longer and much more gruelling interview, covering both the hammer attack and the house nearly burning down while Colin was sedated inside.

During her interview, Natasha was obsessed with raising the topic of the chocolate almonds.

'Okay. You made mention of these to Detective O'Hehir on the Tuesday morning? What was wrong with those, that box?' Dunn asked, finally acknowledging the subject following her continual efforts to raise it.

Natasha was quick to answer. 'They had like a white powder on them and they, well, I thought they tasted funny. Col just said that it looks like they're old, you know, like, melted and re-cooled. But I didn't think they were right. They just didn't taste . . . they tasted powdery.'

So worried about the suspect chocolates, Natasha repeated her story about ringing the poisons information line but, this time, Dunn probed her about who she spoke to and what was said.

'I talked to a man, and he said they haven't heard of any problems because I gave him the batch number because I had the box with me.'

After being told there were no other complaints, she says the man gave her a consumer number so she could report the almonds. After leaving a message with the consumer line – the exact name of which she couldn't remember – she claimed to have rung Cadbury and left a voice message with all her details. No one, apparently, ever phoned her back.

After her unsuccessful attempts to get to the bottom of the rotten box of almonds, Natasha told Dunn, just as she had O'Hehir, that she went to bed at about 10.30 pm. When she got up to check the doors were locked, she noticed an empty can of Coke and a half-empty box of almonds. Colin must have eaten them before heading to bed.

'I thought, "Geez, he's eaten a lot of them." And that's when I put them in a ziplock bag because that's what the consumer people had told me to do.' She explained to Dunn that she left them on the kitchen bench and had already asked his colleague, O'Hehir, to collect them during her initial interview at the hospital.

Dunn knew more about the almonds than he let on, but was keen to steer Natasha away from the subject for a short time. He wanted to hear about her plans to move to Bendemeer and her relationship with local horse trainer Jack, among other men.

'How do you know him?'

'He's, he, he's with the pony club and his kids go to the pony club and he's been very helpful.' She explained he was the only person who could tame a wild mare of hers and, through training the horse, they'd become close friends.

Dunn decided to start showing his cards. From this point onwards, he grilled her.

He explained that police were aware of all the texts Colin discovered on her phone, many of which she sent to Jack.

'He tells us the text message said, "I'm on my way to Tamworth, do you want anything or just a head job on the way past?" Is there any truth to that text?' Dunn asked.

Natasha admitted she wrote the text. But it was just something said in jest, one of the many jokes they shared.

Dunn asked her point-blank if she'd been having an affair.

'Definitely not, no. We, how do I explain that? It's just all, we muck around and tease each other. I mean, even his wife knows about all this, She's, you know, she doesn't like sex and he does and I do. Col and I probably have sex once every three months so it's just a big, I don't know,' she said, pausing.

Dunn allowed her to continue talking.

'It's just a joke thing that we do and, yes, I do send messages like that and it; it's just mucking around. He laughs at me; he never replies to them or anything like that.'

Natasha also admitted she sent the text to Jack asking, 'Do you want a root?' before she confessed to sending one or two messages a week, often with some form of sexual connotation.

'Sometimes, they were serious ones like, you know. I always have my kids with me when we went over there, it wasn't like we were having an affair or anything like that. And you can, I mean, you can ask him. It wasn't a sexual thing . . . we were just mucking around.'

Dunn moved to question her about another male local: Karl,[6] an instructor at the Bendemeer Pony Club. Natasha volunteered that she and Karl had once met for a coffee at his house, near Woolworths in Tamworth. She also quickly admitted to sending him 'lots' of messages, the contents of which she was hazy on.

Dunn asked, what sort of text messages did they send each other?

'Mainly in regards to pony club. We were, we were pretty good friends. His girlfriend and him were having quite a few problems and we'd talk, and I actually stopped all conversations with Karl a couple of months ago because he was getting a little bit attached and I thought it was starting to get a bit funny.'

'Colin tells us he's found a text forwarded to you that says, "I wish you were here in these fresh sheets making love with me." Does that sound familiar?'

Natasha squirmed. 'I, I don't recall. I don't know. No. I don't know.' She shook her head, denying the pair ever had an intimate relationship.

Dunn, who had already taken statements from Colin and several others, began to probe Natasha about whether, in the lead-up to the fire, she had told anyone that her relationship with Colin was over.

Perhaps realising Dunn was aware about her declarations at the pony club meeting in December, Natasha came partially clean. Colin had abused her for not being home by 10.30 pm, while she had been at a meeting, she said.

'I was really upset with Col and, you know, it was over as far as I was concerned. You know, he can't, like, I mean I love my husband but he can be very controlling and I just, you know, it just really upset me.'

---

6   Name has been changed.

So yes, she had told people the relationship was over.

Happy with how the interview was going, Dunn turned to the subject of Bendemeer and whether Colin had any idea of Natasha's plans to move onto the property owned by Jack and Rebecca.

While she never had a direct conversation with Colin about moving the family, she admitted to looking at the land, making inquiries with a builder and getting a quote from a removalist.

'I had sort of hinted to him that I really liked this land but, no, I hadn't, we hadn't discussed it as such,' Natasha said.

'So in effect you were forcing Colin's hand more or less . . . coercing him into or just hoping that . . . ?'

'I was hoping but it really didn't bother me either way. Well, I mean, it would have been nice and the land was really nice but, yeah, it was more just me dreaming I think more than anything.'

Dunn pressed harder. 'But do you think it's gone a bit more than a dream? You've actually got on to a building company to build a house.'

'Yeah,' Natasha managed to mumble, unsure of where he was going.

'You've gone a step further and actually had quotes taken from removalists to store furniture or to move you to, however it's going to occur.'

'Uh-huh,' Natasha responded, seemingly lost for words.

'Do you think that's gone a bit further than just a dream?'

'Yeah, sure.'

At this stage, Dunn and Natasha had been going back and forth in the interview room at Tamworth Police Station for more than three hours. Thus far, Detective Senior Constable Michael Maloney had played more of a supportive act. But he was about to get more involved, in the final and most crucial hour of the interview.

'Had you entertained the thought of leaving Colin?' Maloney asked Natasha.

'No. Well . . . no, no.'

Dunn then went in hard. He took Natasha back to 13 January, a couple of nights before the hammer attack. He told her about Colin's vivid dream, in which someone pinched his nose before trying to smother him with a pillow.

'He now doesn't know if it actually did happen or whether you have done something to him,' he said calmly.

Natasha became hysterical.

'I never hurt him. I can't . . . can't kill one of my chooks when it was sick. I . . . I could never hurt Colin!'

In terrible timing, the machine recording their interview started to beep, indicating the disc was nearly full and needed to be changed. Natasha thus got six minutes to compose herself.

When the interview resumed, Dunn moved straight to the night where she served oysters Kilpatrick, the ones Colin spat out in disgust.

After waltzing into the living room with a glass of red wine in hand, did she ask Colin about the temple being the most fragile area of the human skull?

Natasha answered with a firm 'no', but then decided to elaborate.

'We were talking about my horse Cherry, my wild one, how she'd thrown me not long before that and I'd landed there on my head and, like, I hadn't cracked anything. I never asked anything about the temple or anything.'

But Dunn wasn't letting her off the hook. 'He tells us that you said, "How hard would someone have to be hit to the temple to do any damage?"'

'No, I never said that.'

'No?'

'No.'

'Do you remember any conversation like that?'

'No.'

But she did remember staying up late to watch the movie *When Harry Met Sally* on Austar, after Colin went to bed. After that, *The Quick and the Dead* with Sharon Stone came on, but, too tired to watch it all, she called it a night and went straight to sleep. Next thing, she woke to Colin's screams. She chased a dark shadow out of their room.

Her denials left Dunn unfazed. He forged ahead, taking her to the night of the fire; the point in the evening when Natasha served him dinner.

'He states to us that you said you weren't going to cook a big meal and that's when you provided the four tacos he ate.'

'Mmmm.'

'And he next remembers waking up at Tamworth Hospital.'

'Is that what he thinks? I . . .'

'He has no recollection at all from the time you provided him those tacos.'

'Well, he ate the tacos, he watched TV. He ate almonds, he drank a can of Coke, I mean, I don't know.'

Natasha had brought the almonds up again, but Dunn had a fair idea why. 'Why do you keep coming back to the almonds?'

She had no reasonable explanation, so he moved on, asking her if she believed the same perpetrator was responsible for the hammer attack and the suspicious house fire three days later.

She said she assumed the same person was behind both incidents: 'The only thing I can think of is that it was, somebody was after somebody, and they got the wrong house. That's the only thing I can think of, because nobody would want to hurt him. I definitely wouldn't hurt him. I don't know why he would think that. I love my husband and he's such a good dad.'

Upon hearing Natasha's declaration of love for Colin, Dunn flicked through a mountain of paperwork, before taking out a statement made by Jack.

He read a selection of the texts she'd sent him, including: 'I'm horny', 'I want you in me' and 'Do you want me to suck your dick?'

Natasha nodded and mumbled as he read them aloud.

In his statement, Jack told police Natasha often complained of the problems she was having with Colin; he disliked her passion for horses and was hung up on his ex-wife from Bellingen. She'd failed to mention Catherine had died some 18 years previously.

The statement then explained how Natasha claimed she graduated as a vet with honours, but could never practise because of her emotional attachment to animals, leading her to a job in research with Provet, a veterinary supply company. She also told Jack and his wife Rebecca that she and Col had separated, and offered to buy the land adjoining their property at Bendemeer for $157,000. She mentioned being keen to move soon, so her daughter could start school in the area.

Stunned, Natasha said she didn't remember saying any of this to the couple.

Jack also recalled Natasha phoning him, after the house fire, mentioning she believed the recent violent attacks could be linked to a pharmaceutical company in Sydney or perhaps, something to do with Colin's work. She even said that Colin may have 'stumbled across some information they needed and "they're trying to take him out".'

Natasha tried to explain the conversation but was getting confused. 'We were talking about all different things that it could be, like, maybe it's something to do with Col's work, maybe he came across something. None of this—'

Natasha was cut off by Maloney, who asked why on earth would she blame Colin's work for the recent spate of violent incidents?

'We were talking about all different things. I mean, I've even gone and said how Cadbury's hired a hitman and stuff like that, it was just all different things are going around my head ... nothing was serious.'

'Now, I'll just say again. Why would you say that?' Maloney asked, picking up on the mention of Cadbury.

Natasha said she didn't understand, so Maloney asked her again to clarify the comment she made about Cadbury hiring a hitman.

'Because it's unbelievable what's happening and I just, I mean, I just, I've been saying all different things. Sorry. I'm getting really confused ... Why did I just say what I just said?'

'Do you remember the last comment that you just made?' Maloney asked, with increasing infuriation.

Natasha didn't answer, prompting Dunn to step in and repeat the comment she'd made a few seconds earlier: 'Cadbury's hired a hitman.'

'Yeah, because I was just, you know, because of the, the whole situation. I mean, I mean it's just ridiculous, but you come up with these things, trying to work out what's happened and why it's happened.'

In the final minutes of the interview, Dunn and Maloney began to pepper Natasha one after the other, applying pressure as hard as they could in the hope that she'd crack.

Natasha had previously done some part-time work for Jack and Rebecca. Dunn asked Natasha about the last time she used their computer, and whether she remembered carrying out any Google searches.

She didn't, prompting Dunn to reveal a major hand.

'He tells us that he went to do a Google map search and went into a memory search and has found a number of searches, which have included "Ecstasy", "heroin", "poisons", "poisons to kill" and "how mortgage insurance works". Do you have any knowledge about that?'

'No.'

'No?'

'None of those, no. Goodness, no.'

Sensing she wasn't going to admit to any of the searches – or anything – Dunn asked Natasha whether she rang Jack before coming in for her police interview, and if she did, what their conversation entailed.

'I rang him this morning and I asked him if the police had talked to him, because they think we're having an affair.'

Having had enough of going round in circles, Dunn finally laid it all out on the table.

'Yeah. Okay. The other belief we have is that you were responsible for hitting Colin on the head.'

'Oh God,' Natasha said, reeling.

'With what we believe to be his hammer. You'd been out to the shed and picked up the hammer. After it hit the floor, you went around the bed, picked it up and ran out the door,' said Dunn.

'I can't, I couldn't, I couldn't chop my, my chook's head off. I've never hurt . . . I love Col.'

But Dunn wasn't finished. The reason she'd done this, he explained, was because Colin wasn't prepared to move to Bendemeer. He was stopping her from living her dream. When she'd realised this, she tried to suffocate him with the pillow, then hit him over the head with a hammer and, when that didn't work out, she resorted to burning down the family home.

'Physical evidence indicates to us that an amount of fuel or some substance was poured on the ground or the carpet. It is beyond comprehension that you would not wake him up and make sure he's out of bed when the whole bedroom is on fire.'

Despite everything laid bare, Natasha held firm, denying she orchestrated the fire and clinging to her story of trying to save her son.

'I checked my child first. I made sure he was safe first and then I . . . I thought he'd be behind me, honestly, I did.'

Dunn and Maloney had given her ample opportunities to come clean; they could see it wasn't going to happen.

They informed Natasha they'd taken out a provisional apprehended domestic violence order (AVO) against her. This meant she could not assault, harass, threaten or interfere with Colin, or anyone he had a relationship with. She was forbidden from going within 200 metres of where he was staying with his parents in Quirindi, or his work address.

The application for the AVO would be heard in court in three days' time, and the police would present several pages outlining their grounds to seek the order. Dunn handed a copy of the orders they were seeking to Natasha. She was in complete shock.

'We believe you have tried to harm him for various reasons, and that is something we have to do to protect him. Do you understand that?'

'Yeah,' she managed to say.

Dunn explained that several items had been seized from her home as part of the investigation and asked Natasha if she consented to police taking her fingerprints and a sample of her DNA through a buccal swab.

She agreed and Dunn informed her – at this stage – she was not under arrest.

'I know, but you think I tried to kill my husband.'

'Well, certainly at this stage we . . . that is our opinion.'

'And he thinks that, too. Oh God,' she exclaimed.

She was given one final chance to fess up; Maloney asked her, for the last time, if she would like to respond to the allegations.

'I mean, what can I say?' she asked, before saying plenty.

'I love my husband, and things were just starting to go really well with us, you know. I mean, we had our problems and, sure, I've got this whole fantasy world that I've dreamed up at Bendemeer and everything like that, but I love my husband. He's so fantastic with the kids. He just loves them so much and things were just starting to get better. You know, he'd been diagnosed . . . he was always so cranky, and he was getting help and you know, I just, I can't believe any of this. I would especially never hurt him, especially with my son in the house. There's just no way in the world.'

The interview concluded at 11.33 pm. Dunn had revealed some of his cards, but not all.

Natasha had purposefully left something behind at the crime scene, but Dunn was never going to let on that he had found it.

Three days after the fire, Dunn carefully inspected exhibit D519966, labelled 'chocolate coated almonds from kitchen bench', as he stood in the exhibit room at Tamworth Police Station.

He peered into the cardboard box and noticed a small folded note at the bottom. One of his colleagues reached into the box and carefully prised it out. The letter was addressed to Cadbury management:

The workers at Cadbury factories demand a 10% pay increase by 1st January 2009 or 3 poison filled Cadbury almond boxes will be let out into the stores around Australia . . . If our demands are not met there will be casualties!

He arranged for the letter to be photocopied then placed the chocolate almonds back in their original packaging and sealed the evidence bag. He wasted no time in calling Cadbury head office to see whether they knew about the contents of the letter.

They knew all about it. Cadbury received the same letter on 24 December 2009, after it was posted to its head office and factory at Ringwood, on the eastern outskirts of Melbourne.

Alarmed, Cadbury management contacted Victorian police and, because of the safety threat, decided to stop the production of chocolate-coated almonds while an investigation was under way. Dunn would never have imagined that this development would arise during an attempted murder investigation.

Following this, he applied for a search warrant to enter Natasha's family home and seized all electronics and computers. After this, he requested Jack and his wife to hand over their work computer before sending it away for forensic analysis. He was keen to see if there were any other incriminating searches on the couple's computer, which Natasha had used while working for them.

In addition to the searches Jack had informed police of, computer analysts later found other searches, including 'chlorine ingested', 'arsenic and death', 'hydrochloride' and 'Cadbury chocolate'.

Deep in the deleted section of the hard drive, however, was a draft letter to Cadbury management, typed by Natasha.

A forensic examination of Natasha and Colin's family computer revealed she had also carried out several other searches, including 'chocolate treats', 'Cadbury almonds bad', 'triazolam', 'diazepam', 'oysters Kilpatrick' and 'alprazolam'.

The evidence was damning but, two months later, Colin Crossman stumbled on more, completely sealing the case of the mysterious, chocolate-coated almonds.

While cleaning out his Mitsubishi car at the ambulance station, Colin found something odd in the glove box.

'He was at the station cleaning out the car when he found it,' Doran recalls. 'He came in and said, "I just found this letter," and I said, "You better go to the police mate."'

He immediately phoned the police then drove straight to Walcha Police Station.

After greeting Senior Constable Jamie Waugh, Colin opened the passenger door of his car and pointed to the glove box. Inside, Waugh saw a torn-up piece of paper and an envelope. He carefully retrieved the shreds of paper, placing it in an evidence bag and marking it as exhibit DO42868. This, too, was sent off for forensic analysis.

Placing the pieces back together, police could see it was a hand-written draft of the letter that was sent to Cadbury management. Natasha's left thumbprint was later discovered on a torn-up piece of the envelope.

Eventually, Natasha would sign an agreed statement of facts, admitting she had repeatedly raised the subject of the contaminated chocolate almonds to explain the presence of substances found in Colin's system, which he had not knowingly taken on the night of the fire.

Police never found any drugs present in the almonds and Cadbury resumed making them in February 2009.

19

MOTEL MADNESS

After more than a decade of working as a print journalist, I'm offered a job at Nine News Sydney, which I take with great hesitation; being on camera isn't something I'd ever considered. Newspapers will always be my first, great love. My nanna encouraged me to read articles from a young age, keeping precarious towers of yellowed newspapers all over her living room. Although I loved being a print journalist, the offer at Nine is too good an opportunity to pass up. It's a chance to tell stories in a completely different way, using images instead of words.

To ease into my new role, I pitch several stories that I can work on at a slower pace, before being thrown into the insane TV-land machine. An average day involves turning around a story in less than 12 hours – complete with vision, interviews and graphics. In between, you often need to pull a shorter version of the story together for the morning news, then the 4 pm bulletin, and somehow appear as fresh as a daisy for a 6 pm live-cross at the end of a long slog.

For my first story, I travel down to the state's Riverina region to report on the horrific hit-and-run accident of 15-year-old Braydon Worldon, who was left to die on a dark road near his home at Wanta-badgery, near Wagga, on 19 December 2018. It was his birthday.

At the time of writing, his death remains unsolved. Police want to get as much coverage as possible in the hope someone comes forward with information.

During my time down south, I meet the region's crime manager, Andrew Spliet, who I work on another story with two months later. This too is a heartbreaking death. Toddler Kamahl Bamblett – just 14 months old – was reported dead after several members of his family claimed he had been bitten by a spider in January 2019. Police believe he was murdered following sustained abuse, and died from injuries too shocking to report. Despite the dogged determination of detectives, this case also remains unsolved.

I often think about the case, and one afternoon while I'm sitting cross-legged on the floor of my study, it suddenly comes flooding back to me.

I'm poring over dozens of police statements in Natasha's old court files, when I discover one written by a young Andrew Spliet, back when he was a sergeant for the Oxley Local Area Command in Tamworth. Initially, I'm struck by the coincidence of knowing Spliet but, as I read further, I'm taken aback by the contents of his statement. In it, Spliet details a series of truly bizarre events involving Natasha and a Tamworth hotel on the night of 30 January 2009.

Following her marathon interview with Detective Senior Constable Craig Dunn at Tamworth Police Station, Natasha was highly distressed. She now knew she was the prime suspect in both the hammer attack and house fire. The police believed she tried to kill Colin. She was also the subject of an apprehended violence order.

The day after the interview, Dunn was caught off guard by a phone call at 11.30 pm. There had been an incident at the Motabelle Motel on Goonoo Goonoo Road, Tamworth, and Natasha Darcy was involved. Natasha had checked into this motel after driving to Tamworth from her parents' place on the South Coast for her police interview.

Dunn immediately rang his colleague, Sergeant Andrew Spliet, who was on call that night, to see if he could check what all the drama was about.

Two women found Natasha unconscious in only her T-shirt and knickers. She was lying on the ground just outside the door of the motel manager's living quarters. They leaned down to help her, causing Natasha to stir. Through slurred speech, she told them she'd been brutally attacked.

She said she was in her room when a man, claiming to be a police officer, knocked on her door. As soon as she'd opened it, the man forced his way in, throwing her on the bed, grabbing her throat and injecting her with a substance. She said she crawled from her room to the manager's residence next door.

One of the women noticed a scratch on her forehead and pinprick on her right shoulder with a small amount of blood. Her story seemed to add up.

Paramedic Anthony Zwegers also saw the pinprick as he assessed Natasha, who was highly emotional and groggy. He noticed her pupils appeared to be dilated.

Police arrived on the scene and immediately searched her motel room to try and find anything that could have been used to inject her.

Later, as Zwegers transported Natasha to Tamworth Hospital, general duties police spoke to the motel manager and ventured back into her room for another look.

Standing in the bathroom, police noticed the mesh screen covering the window was slashed. It also appeared to have been pushed outwards. They walked out of the room and around to the window on the other side. On the ground beneath, they found a black-handled knife and a syringe containing a clear fluid, which was later found to be a form of horse tranquilliser.

The following morning, Detective Senior Constable Michael Maloney arrived at Tamworth Hospital with a recorder to interview

Natasha. He hadn't expected to see her so soon, having interviewed her with Dunn at Tamworth Police Station less than 48 hours previously.

Natasha told Maloney she thought she was attacked by a man who said he was from NSW Ambulance. She claimed it was the same man who had followed her into the hospital car park after visiting Colin just a week earlier.

Reading her interview, I wonder whether she's trying to insinuate she'd been attacked by the same man who attacked Colin, but it's not clear. Was this story a set-up to throw the heat off her, following her four-hour interview with police?

Natasha claimed the attacker knocked on her door and, after barging his way through, threatened her with a knife before demanding to know where someone called 'Kel' was. He then 'pulled out a syringe and put it in my arm'.

She later gave a much more detailed description of her alleged attacker to the insurance investigator assessing the claim she made following the house fire.

'He was quite tall, he had short dark hair, which is quite receded, and I think it would have been curly had it have been longer. He had really pale skin and he had a really bad, like, either dermatitis or I don't know, but it looked like a rash of some sort around his face.'

The level of detail is astounding.

'I mean, I'll never forget, like, the dermatitis he had around his face because I remember thinking he looked like, you know in those American shows . . . the ice? What do they use? That ice epidemic; I was watching the CI channel, the ice, meth or whatever they use, the drug. And he looked like his face was quite bad.'

Natasha made a formal statement about the apparent attack on her, acknowledging she would be prosecuted if police found she'd fabricated any part of her story.

Two weeks after the apparent attack at the Tamworth motel, Spliet, who was called out to the motel, was on duty at Tamworth Police

Station. Natasha walked up to him at the front desk. She was angry, demanding answers about where the investigation was up to. He took her into a small room adjacent to the front foyer and attempted to get her to lower her voice.

'Am I still being looked at for hurting Col? It's hard because everyone in Walcha thinks I tried to kill my husband.'

Spliet told her the investigation was ongoing. Police still believed she had more knowledge about what happened than she'd been letting on. The investigation would take some time, while detectives waited for the seized computers to be thoroughly examined.

'You won't find anything on my computer, so you can look at it, or [on Jack and Rebecca's] computer. I would never hurt Col.'

Calmly, Spliet told her the computers had not yet been sent to Sydney for examination, causing a dramatic reaction from Natasha.

'Haven't they been examined yet? I just want this to be over. [They] need their computer back to run their business.'

He got the sense she was fishing; anxious to know whether police had found anything incriminating on the computers. Spliet wouldn't divulge anything more, and Natasha eventually walked out of the station with no more clues about what police had found. She didn't ask if police had made any progress in relation to her alleged attack at the Tamworth motel.

A few hours later, Spliet was still at the station when Jack's wife rang. She wanted to know where the investigation was up to. Straight after Natasha left the station, she'd rung Rebecca and told her she'd been cleared of any wrongdoing. This certainly wasn't the case, Spliet told her.

After months of methodical work – including the forensic analysis of dozens of exhibits – Dunn was finally satisfied he had enough evidence to charge Natasha.

On 25 May 2009, he called her into Nowra Police Station, close to where she was staying with her parents at Culburra.

Two days later, she arrived at the station with her son and, curiously, Colin. Dunn ushered her into a room, leaving her family behind in the foyer.

Accompanied by his colleague, Detective Senior Constable Graham Goodwin, Dunn placed her under arrest. Her charges: Colin's attempted murder, regarding the house fire; common assault, for belting him over the head with a hammer; giving false information about a person being in danger, regarding the threatening letter she'd sent to Cadbury; and public mischief, for falsely claiming she was attacked in her motel room.

She was refused bail; the police did not believe she should be on the streets.

After being fingerprinted and her charges formally logged, Natasha was remanded in custody, leaving Dunn and Goodwin at Nowra Police Station to finish piles of paperwork. Neither of them could predict how Natasha's disturbing and violent behaviour would only escalate from this point forward. Especially Goodwin who, years later, ended up dedicating several years of his career to bringing Natasha down.

20
A GOOD DEAL

Much changed in the year after Natasha was charged with Colin's attempted murder.

I am utterly confused, trying to fill the gaps, going back and forth over old media reports and court files. Reading the transcripts from her local court hearing in Armidale, followed by her District Court trial, it's clear that, at some point, Colin started supporting her and was keen to prevent her from going to jail.

It's hard to believe Colin wanted anything to do with the woman charged with his attempted murder. Did Natasha convince him she was innocent? Was he protecting her for the sake of the kids, who he saw as his own?

Perhaps it was about money. If Natasha were found guilty, they wouldn't be insured for the fire damage, which would add to the financial pressure cooker they were already in.

Maybe other things were at play, but only Colin knew what.

Police close to the investigation say that Colin was well and truly on their side, and was happy to cooperate in the months following the hammer attack and house fire. When they presented him with the evidence, he appeared dumbfounded and made statements about another potential attack Natasha carried out.

'I think it was Tuesday night the 13th of January 2009 while I was in bed. I thought that I had a very vivid dream, during which it felt like someone firstly pinched my nose and covered my mouth with a pillow. I later told Mark Doran about this and whether it may have actually really happened or not. I am certain now that it did actually happen and it was Natasha doing this to me,' he said in his police statement on 28 January 2009.

Colin also refuted Natasha's version of the hammer attack, and disclosed the text messages he'd discovered, revealing her flirtatious interactions and potential affairs with other local men. He also described how, when he was in hospital after the house fire, she had fiddled with his cannula.

When he gave his statement, about 10 days after the fire, Colin told police he was staying with his parents in Quirindi, while Natasha and the children were staying with her parents at Culburra Beach. He'd also stated two vials of midazolam were missing from the drug box of ambulance vehicle 891, which he had parked at home on the night of the hammer attack.

What happened after Colin made that statement in January 2009 is unclear, but an officer close to the case believes his position towards Natasha changed after he'd visited her and the children on several occasions.

He theorises Natasha either convinced him she was innocent – and the police were manufacturing a case against her – or perhaps he didn't want to lose his family. 'He had the instant family he'd always wanted, much like Mathew did, and it was all falling apart.'

What is clear, however, is that Colin had well and truly sided with Natasha by August 2010, when she faced a committal hearing for her charges. A committal hearing is where a local magistrate hears an abbreviated version of the case to determine whether there is sufficient evidence for a jury to convict an accused person. If there is, the magistrate commits that person to stand trial.

In the transcripts from Armidale Local Court, Colin gave evidence for the defence, not the prosecution. While victims are rarely called to give evidence at committal hearings, Natasha's lawyer fought for Colin to testify. Magistrate Mark Richardson noted that, compared to his interview with the insurance investigator, Colin's police statements were 'perhaps bordering on being inconsistent'.

'You could say that, on one version, he is saying that the relationship that he has with the accused is fine and, on the other hand, he is making reference to the potential involvement of third parties in romantic interludes and the like with his partner,' Magistrate Richardson told the court.

Colin told the hearing that their relationship was loving, sexual and appeared to be 'fine' in the lead-up to the house fire in January 2009; when police suggested his partner was behind an attack on his life, he'd been blindsided. Colin had taken part in a sting, agreeing for police to record a telephone conversation with Natasha while he was still in hospital. 'They suggested to me that Natasha was responsible for the fire,' he told the court, 'and that I could put it to her, and she could deny or agree. I suppose I wanted to know. Needed to know.'

He was never asked whether he thought Natasha tried to kill him, but said he believed they were in a happy relationship and that neither of them – at the time – had any intention of leaving each other.

The magistrate committed Natasha to stand trial on the attempted murder charge and allowed her bail to continue.

The wheels of justice turn ever so slowly, however, especially when cases reach the NSW District Court. On average, it takes almost two years for an accused to face trial following their initial arrest. In Natasha's case, it was longer. After being charged in May 2009, it wasn't until November 2011 that she faced the first day of her NSW District Court trial before a jury of 12 in Armidale.

The trial was over almost before it started.

While the prosecution had as many as 50 witnesses lined up, most would never be called to give evidence. On the trial's second day, the defence approached the prosecution with an offer for Natasha to plead guilty to a lesser charge.

The following day, after negotiations between the prosecution and defence teams, Natasha struck an unbelievable – and somewhat questionable – deal. If she pleaded guilty to the offence of intentionally or recklessly destroying property by fire, the Director of Public Prosecutions would drop the attempted murder charge.

She took the deal.

As part of this extraordinary deal, Natasha signed an agreed statement of facts, admitting that she set the house on fire, and was responsible for the hammer attack and Cadbury chocolate almond threats. She also confessed to faking the attack at the Tamworth motel.

While Natasha admitted to everything, she was only convicted of this one charge. I struggle to make sense of the deal or why it was struck. Several people I've interviewed say Colin was apparently not as cooperative a witness as the police may have liked, which would have made the case hard to prosecute. I'll never know the full extent of the plea negotiations, but I can only assume Colin's position (clearly a difficult one to be in, given his commitment to Natasha and the children) played a big role.

This was a huge win for Natasha. Up until this point, she was staring down the barrel of a maximum 25 years in jail, if found guilty of attempted murder. Although she wouldn't be convicted of all the other offences she carried out, the judge would take her admissions into account when determining her sentence.

Natasha was given the ultimate gift, but she threw it back in alarming time.

Less than three weeks after pleading guilty to the house fire, and while out on bail ahead of her sentencing, Natasha struck again. She was broke – as was Colin – because the insurance company refused to pay for any damages to their home because Natasha admitted to torching it deliberately.

Still living down south at Culburra Beach, Natasha attached herself to the Budgong pony club, near Kangaroo Valley. While I don't know how heavy her involvement was, court files reveal she had attended the Budgong pony club Christmas party on 10 December 2011.

Whether in a premeditated or spur-of-the-moment decision, Natasha gravitated towards the handbag of a pony club instructor, a woman who had volunteered her time at the club for decades. At the time, local media reported the bag belonging to Shari-lea Hitchcock, the long-time mistress of late cardboard billionaire Richard Pratt, but I later discover it was actually Shari-lea's mother, Shawne.

Natasha swooped quickly and with precision, diving into Mrs Hitchcock's bag, taking her ANZ Bank cheque book and driver's licence. Two days later, she travelled to an ANZ Bank at Warrawong, a suburb of Wollongong. Having seen Mrs Hitchcock's arm bandaged at the Christmas party (she'd had a melanoma removed), Natasha allegedly bandaged her arm before entering the bank. She walked confidently towards the teller, presenting a cheque made out for $6000 cash. The teller asked Natasha for some identification.

Without hesitation, Natasha stated her name as Shawne Hitchcock, handing the teller the stolen driver's licence with the same name. Natasha's face clearly didn't match the card, prompting the already suspicious teller to excuse themselves for a moment, to call the police. Natasha waited for a considerable time but vanished before the police arrived.

Four days before Christmas, police came knocking at the home she was renting. They arrested her and took her back to the station. Initially, she denied the theft but quickly realised there was no escaping this one. Security cameras in the bank had caught her in the act.

Natasha was finally sentenced for the house fire in March the following year. Crown prosecutor John Stanhope told the judge that Natasha committed another crime shortly after pleading guilty to the house fire: 'The Crown submits the offender has already re-offended, that her conduct shows that she is capable of being deceptive, and that prospects of rehabilitation cannot really be determined.'

Her sentence was a maximum of two years and 11 months' jail, but with a non-parole period of nine months. I am gobsmacked. It's not unusual for people to strike deals before their trials, or even on the first day of their trial, but the terms of this deal are hard to believe. Less than a year's jail for the two attacks on Colin.

I can't help but think, if she'd gone down for Colin's attempted murder, would Mathew still be alive today?

Detective Senior Constable Craig Dunn agrees. 'I wonder what would have happened if Colin had died and burned to a crisp in the fire. I wonder how she would have manipulated the town and the stories she would have made up.'

Unable to stop thinking about why Colin supported Natasha after everything she did, I delve back into the box of court documents. Flicking through reams of paper, eventually I find a bombshell buried in one of the court transcripts.

It turns out that, during her committal hearing in August 2010, Natasha was caring for a newborn son – just three weeks old. This means Natasha became pregnant soon after she was arrested and charged with Colin's attempted murder in May 2009. This was when she was living down south at Culburra Beach and Colin was living in Walcha.

Several people, including police, tell me there is evidence that Natasha was working as a prostitute at the time, while claiming to work at a 24-hour vet clinic. She even took out an ad in the local paper:

JOSIE, 30yrs, size 12, blonde, busty, available Nowra Friday and Sunday nights, in/out calls. Phone 0421-507-096. No private numbers.

So, while Colin and Natasha were living separately and far away from each other, she became pregnant.

Colin maintains the baby boy is his. Perhaps Colin decided to support Natasha, after accepting the responsibility of being the baby's father? Or possibly, it was for the sake of all the children, who he saw as his own. Only Colin and Natasha know the answer.

Not even those close to Colin know the answers.

Fellow paramedic Dave Lucietto remembers confronting Colin about the 'mounting evidence' against Natasha.

'We are going, "Col, it's Tash," but Colin wouldn't accept it, saying, "She would never do that, she loves me." He refused to believe it, he said, "No, no, someone is setting us up,"' Lucietto says, adding that Colin was unhappy about the statements he and his colleague Mark Doran had made following the hammer assault and fire. 'We could see it as plain as day.'

Lucietto recalls Colin constantly arguing with Natasha about money, often on the phone while he was at work. When they'd argue, Natasha would use the kids against him, knowing he wouldn't do anything to jeopardise the family he cared so much about.

'You couldn't not overhear a phone conversation. She'd be ringing him and ringing him and carrying on. It was always money, something to do with money, and she used to leverage the kids on him.'

During one argument, Lucietto remembers hearing Natasha say, 'I won't let you see the kids.' Lucietto says Colin could have got a transfer out of Walcha, but refused to leave because of the children. '[He said] "I'm the only father these kids have ever had, and I won't abandon them."'

Lucietto believes the only reason Colin kept driving south to Culburra Beach following the fire was to see the kids. 'To him, [it was] the only thing that mattered. All he ever wanted was a family and some kids, and she walks through the door . . . Col just fell in love with the kids.'

His words send a chill through me. So many have said this about Mathew, too.

Paramedic Mark Doran remembers Colin supporting Natasha throughout her arrest, bail and sentence. 'I really think that Colin wanted Tash to get off when she burnt the house down – he knew that, if she was found guilty, his house wouldn't be insured.'

'I was under the impression he was taking the line she hadn't done it. The police had said he was an uncooperative witness,' he says. But he's not entirely sure.

Doran counts Colin as one of his closest mates and, although perplexed by his decision to support Natasha, he was never going to judge or question him about it. 'I was kind of scared to bring it up. Col was still one of the best friends I ever had, and it was such a tumultuous time, I didn't want to rock the boat. I just wanted to be there for Col. Whatever decision he was making, he had to deal with the consequences. It wasn't up to me to change his mind.'

Doran has strong views about Natasha. He made several statements to police, none of which painted her in a great light. He still believes she tried to kill his best mate.

When Natasha got out on bail, she was less than pleased to learn what Doran had told police in his statements. She wasted no time making her feelings known, sending him a text he felt was threatening in nature, having a go at him for telling the truth.

'She sent a text something along the lines of: "I hope everything is going well for you and your little family."'

Doran took the message straight to the police. 'I just went and showed them the message, and said, "I don't think she should be writing me stuff like this because I'm a witness for the prosecution."'

Subsequently, she was arrested for breaching her bail conditions by approaching a prosecution witness. 'She was out again in a couple of days, and that would have been the last time we ever spoke.'

Doran tried to encourage Colin to take a compassionate transfer with NSW Ambulance, but Colin was adamant about staying in Walcha.

'Col had said, "Why should I? This is where my home is, this is where I live."'

Doran is gobsmacked by the sentence Natasha received for the hammer attack and house fire. 'I was disappointed when she got nine months. She went into so much meticulous planning to carry out this crime. It's an abhorrent crime when you think about it – drugging someone and trying to incinerate them.

'Colin was working hard to provide for them all and she was

treating him like that – it upset me that someone would treat my friend like that.'

Doran is happy to talk, wanting the 'truth to be told' and to defend his mate. He knows many people can't get their heads around Colin's decision to support Natasha over the years, but says it doesn't take anything away from the fact that Colin is the most loyal and honest man he knows.

'I'll defend my friend to the hilt. He's as honest as the day is long,' he says to me on the phone from his home on the Central Coast. 'No one could ever deny how much Col loved those kids. He took a year off without pay to look after the kids while she was in jail and even to this day.'

PART THREE

UNRAVELLING A WEB OF LIES

21

THE TRIAL

It's a crisp, autumn morning in March 2021. There's not a cloud in the sky above Darlinghurst Courthouse, a colonial building with towering sandstone pillars. Access into this judicial oasis is through a black wrought-iron gate amid the thick hedges lining the perimeter. The hedges block the sights and sounds of Oxford Street's busy Taylor Square on the other side. Five separate courtrooms are contained within the majestic structure; all have doors opening onto a common paved courtyard – marble in parts – overlooking a sprawling lawn.

I'm standing in the designated media area, a patch of freshly mowed grass about 30 metres from the entrance of Courtroom 3, two hours before Natasha's trial is due to start. I pace the grounds with a takeaway coffee in hand, anxiously waiting to see if any of Natasha or Mathew's family will turn up. I've asked Channel Nine cameraman Paul Bousfield to shoot every person he sees walking through the main gates on Oxford Street.

I'm flying blind. I haven't contacted anyone in the past year in case they're called as witnesses. The last thing I want to do is muddy anyone's evidence by interviewing or talking to them about their versions of events. My plan is to wait and see what information comes out at the trial and approach people once they're finished giving evidence.

With 10 minutes to go, I take a seat in the back row of wooden pews, the only place in the public gallery where there is a power point. I'm a few metres behind the wooden dock, where I expect Natasha will be brought at any moment.

A group of law students chatter loudly to my left. In front of them are two grey-haired men in black suits; one is the officer in charge of the case, Detective Senior Constable Graham Goodwin. He's a local Tamworth detective who's been on the case since the day of Mathew's death, organising forensic teams and search warrants, and taking witness statements with assistance from the homicide squad, a Sydney-based specialist group of detectives who investigate murders.

Goodwin met Natasha eight years before Mathew's death, when he helped the officer sitting next to him right now – Detective Senior Constable Craig Dunn – charge Natasha with Colin's attempted murder back in 2009.

I wonder how they're both feeling now, Goodwin waiting to see how the case he's built will be presented, and Dunn hoping Natasha will finally face the full wrath of the law.

There's also a group of four people sitting two rows in front of me. They appear to have just met, whispering with great animation as they each explain to each other why they're here. I crane my neck to eavesdrop, but their conversation ends abruptly at the sound of the cell door beneath the court creaking open. Jangling keys echo through the courtroom, replaced by the sound of heavy footsteps as Natasha clomps up the stairs from the cells below, flanked by two prison officers.

Silence falls over the courtroom.

Reaching the top of the stairs, Natasha is led into a rectangular, timber dock. She fusses with her wavy hair, tucking it behind her ears as she turns around to steal a look at who's sitting behind her in the public gallery. Blank-faced, she lays eyes on two people; later, I find out they're Natasha's sister and her husband. It's clear they aren't here to support her. Upon seeing her family, Natasha turns on her heel and stares at the front of the courtroom before sitting on a timber bench.

Moments later, she and everyone else rise to their feet as the judge, Justice Julia Lonergan, enters the courtroom. Natasha sits back down, unfolds a pair of reading glasses and smooths the front page of a fresh notepad.

I boot up my laptop and stretch my hands, ready to type as fast as I can, my palms slippery with sweat. I'm a woeful typist and mentally kick myself for failing three shorthand courses over the years. It will be impossible to get every word down.

Defence barristers Janet Manuell SC and Nicholas Broadbent, along with solicitor Tracey Randall, sit at the timber bar table in the middle of the courtroom, just a few metres in front of Natasha. To their right is Crown prosecutor Brett Hatfield, who adjusts his horse-hair wig while he and two solicitors from the Office of the Director of Public Prosecutions, Andrew Baker and Hugh Buddin, wait for the jury to be brought in.

Baker, a senior solicitor based in Newcastle, is deeply invested in the case. He's worked on it ever since Natasha's arrest in November 2017. Over the past four years, he's pulled the case together from an overwhelming amount of material, especially Natasha's phone records, which Hatfield will now present to the jury.

As the sun creeps through the skylights of the dark mahogany courtroom, Justice Lonergan asks the sheriff to bring in the jury. Five women and seven men file in from a door on the right-hand side of the courtroom, sitting in two rows of benches, which have a side view of Natasha sitting in the dock.

It's a real motley crew: retirees, perhaps one or two students, and three men in polo shirts who I imagine are IT workers.

We are about to hear the Crown prosecutor's opening address: the outline of the case against Natasha. Here, Hatfield will summarise the evidence the jury should expect to hear over the next two months. Then, it will be the defence team's turn to make their opening address.

Following the opening addresses, Hatfield will call a series of prosecution witnesses and question them, building his case. Then the defence is given the opportunity to cross-examine the witnesses, asking them questions to cast doubt on the Crown's case.

After that, the defence can call their own witnesses, including Natasha, which the Crown can then cross-examine. I have no idea if Natasha will give evidence, but hope she does.

Hatfield rises to his feet, carefully arranging his notes on a lectern. He turns to face the jury. In a clear but not overbearing voice, he explains, concisely and with little emotion, how Mathew died.

The jury hears that Mathew John Dunbar – a 42-year-old farmer – died from asphyxiation after a plastic bag was secured over his head with a white strip of elastic. A piece of a shower hose was inserted into the bag; this was connected to a 3.5 cubic metre tank of helium, which was turned on. At the time of Mathew's death, Hatfield argues, he was heavily sedated after drinking a cocktail of drugs Natasha had blended in a Nutribullet. Unbeknown to Mathew, the drink contained clonidine, a drug prescribed to Natasha's son; quetiapine, an antipsychotic also known as Seroquel; temazepam, a sedative; and acepromazine, an animal sedative.

At 1.14 am on 2 August 2017, a text is sent from Mathew's phone to Natasha's estranged husband, Colin Crossman, a local paramedic in town. The text reads: 'Tell police to come to the house. I don't want Tash or kids to find me.' There is no suicide note.

Hatfield tells the jury they will soon hear an audio recording of the triple-0 phone call Natasha made, telling the operator she had found her partner with a bag over his head and 'gas or something' going into it.

'The accused's claim in the triple-0 call was false,' he says. 'Rather than finding the deceased in those circumstances, pursuant to an act of suicide, he was in that position because of a plan implemented by her to sedate him and to kill him. This was not a suicide.'

Hatfield is quick to get on the front foot, telling the court he anticipates the defence will focus heavily on aspects of Mathew's life that caused him difficulty, in their attempt to prove this was a case of suicide. The defence will paint Mathew as a lonely person who struggled to maintain relationships, he warns, a man who was estranged from his mother and was homosexual, with evidence he once had some form of a relationship with a man.

This is news to me. Is it true and, if it is, who knew about it? Had Mathew wanted this to remain private?

Hatfield pushes forward, telling the jury Mathew also had relationships with women and always dreamed of starting a family. Yes, he'd suffered from depression, but Natasha had used this to her advantage.

'There is no issue that the deceased suffered depression. It is the Crown case that it was known to the accused. She exploited this and she killed him in the manner that she did to make it look like a suicide,' Hatfield says, his right hand striking the lectern to emphasise this point.

The motive is clear, he argues. Money. 'This was the primary motive for the accused to murder the deceased – by faking his suicide – as she stood to benefit financially from his death as the beneficiary under his will.'

A significant part of the Crown case relies on hundreds of internet searches, which Natasha carried out on her iPhone 7, the family's Apple computer and Mathew's iPhone 6. There's also evidence of searches which the prosecution alleges Natasha conducted after Mathew's death on a new iPhone 8.

'The nature and extent of the searches is such that the searches are inconsistent with a person considering suicide and strongly indicate that they were undertaken as research into ways in which the deceased could be murdered.'

Although some of these searches were revealed in the previous bail hearings, it's a shock to hear their chilling and calculated nature and, equally, how far back the searches dated.

The sheer volume is almost unfathomable; it takes Hatfield several hours to read through the list of them. It's horrible to think what we're hearing is only a summary of the cache that forensic specialists discovered.

In between the searches, the jury hears Natasha went to great lengths to source drugs, including a ram sedative from an Armidale vet after three knockbacks from other businesses.

The searches kicked off as early as February 2017, just four months after Natasha was released from jail and had moved to Pandora with her three children. Hatfield arms himself with a highlighter, methodically marking off where he is up to, as he reads aloud hundreds and hundreds of searches to the jury.

I jot down as many as I can.

Natasha's iPhone 7 searches, 2017
9 February
- body break down spider venom
- spider venom kidney
- redback kidney
20 February
- poisonous fungi australia
22 February
- small white mushroom australia
- where are death caps
25 February
- ground cover red berry australia
- dangerous bush berries
- dangerous plants
- deadly nightshade

Towards the end of February and into early March, she's accused of using both her phone and the family's Apple computer to search:

- 11 toxic wild plants that look like food
- wild ground cover red berries
- mushroom poisoning

Hatfield reads the searches with conviction and clarity. As he continues, the more sinister the searches become.

Natasha's iPhone 7 searches
21 March
- artery in back
- spinal tap depth of needle
- how far in does lumbar puncture needle go
- air injected spinal cord

By March, perhaps worrying she may be found out, Natasha turns to Google to assess how exposed she is.

23 March
- can police see websutes (sic)
- if police hsve (sic) your mobile can they see websites
- can police see websites you visit
- can police see websites you visit on monile (sic)

10 April
- stabbed in the brain

Hatfield pauses from the marathon reading of searches to drive home the point that, by mid-April, just four months before Mathew's death, it's clear that Natasha switches focus to suicide. He will explore the timing of these searches in forensic detail, he tells the jury; they are all the more shocking when seen in the context of where she was and what she was doing at the time.

In April, the family computer is used for a series of searches about suicide, leaving open the possibility that Mathew could have been behind them.

Apple computer searches
18 April
- how to commit suicide

- food processor recipes
- sedative suicide
- cyanide pill
- ecstasy suicide
- overdose drug
- overdose pain killers
- lethal dose of clonidine
- micrograms

Hatfield moves to reading another group of searches, which I find disturbing. They are eerily reminiscent of when Natasha had probed Colin about the temple, asking whether it was the most vulnerable part of the skull, before she belted him with a hammer.

Natasha's iPhone 7 searches
27 April
- spine meets brain
- spine meets skul (sic)
- spine vuneravle (sic)
- back of head hole
- stab back of head
- how does skull protect

Hatfield gives the jury another heads-up: he anticipates the defence will argue that Mathew was behind some of the searches. This is simply not true, and he can prove it: the timing and location of some searches make it implausible for anyone other than Natasha to have conducted the deathly searches.

In one of the most damning Google searches, Natasha's phone was used to google 'How to commit murder' on 25 June 2017, right before the family computer was used to search the effects of acepromazine, a type of animal sedative commonly used on rams, which was later found in Mathew's system. Natasha had unsuccessfully tried to buy this drug from the vet in Walcha but, eventually, got her hands on it from another vet.

On the evening of 7 July 2017, a series of searches were undertaken on Mathew's phone, but Hatfield argues they were all by Natasha.

Mathew's iPhone 6 searches
- can you inject Valium
- injecting diazepam
- suicide poem

The searches don't stop there. Hatfield argues Natasha used Mathew's phone to look up the best muscles for injections and, more specifically, the calf muscle. After laying a false trail, she switched to using her own phone, again researching the ram sedative acepromazine, typing 'human acepromazine' and 'acepromazine overdose' into Google.

Just days after these searches, on 10 July, Mathew was admitted to Walcha Hospital with a severely infected calf muscle, and would stay there for eight days.

Suddenly, I'm transported back to Di Heazlett's kitchen table during my first trip to Walcha. I see her leafing through her folder filled with articles about Natasha's criminal past, telling me Natasha had been poisoning Mathew before his death. She was adamant that Natasha was responsible for his leg infection, which caused him so much grief in his final days.

Feeling a tinge of guilt for dismissing her beliefs at the time, thinking it was too farfetched, I now wonder whether this might actually be true.

This was the same leg infection Mathew had mentioned to neighbour Ross King, as the pair chatted in what was Mathew's last phone call.

As Hatfield explains to the jury, Mathew's leg infection had come about after he'd apparently gone for a walk around the property on a

Friday afternoon. However, he didn't remember a thing until waking up in bed on the Sunday morning with a terrible pain in his calf.

While Mathew was recovering in hospital, it's the prosecution case that Natasha busied herself, consulting Google about more methods of killing.

Natasha's iPhone 7 searches
17 July
- Oxycontin suicide
- lethal dose of Oxycodone 200 lb male
- Oxycontin murder
- Oxycontin taste
- temazepam taste
- Valium taste
- promethazine lethal dose

23 July
- Oxycontin murder – suspect pleads guilty
- intubating
- feeding tube
- Ritalin suicide overdose
- can you die from taking Ritalin
- lethal dose of Ritalin
- suicide pills
- painless methods suicide

24 July
- stroke murder
- murder by stroke
- murder by inducing heart attack
- 99 undetectable poisons

Four days before Mathew's death, Hatfield explains, Natasha had travelled north to the small town of Dorrigo with her daughter, leaving Mathew and her two sons behind at Pandora.

During her overnight trip, she searched several types of suicide drugs and ways to kill via injection.

28 July
- death by injection
- murder by injection
- suicide by pills
- paliperidone
- acepromazine

On 29 July, while she was still away, her searches included 'how much hydrogen to kill' and 'suicide bag'. She then allegedly browsed various results before stumbling across an article that listed ways to die by suicide. Helium was recommended as the best method.

From this point onwards, Natasha appeared fixated on this option, doing numerous searches about helium, gas bottles and propane. Then came a series of searches looking at ways to cover one's tracks.

Natasha's iPhone 7 searches, 29 July
- delete all webs history
- how long Telstra web history
- suicide house crimescene
- after a suicide is there a crime scene?
- how long after suicide is house crime scene

For the next two days, Natasha's phone is in overdrive, repeatedly searching places that sell helium, with the results bringing up a company called Supagas. Hatfield tells the jury they will be shortly hearing from a witness who will provide proof that Natasha ordered the gas from a Supagas store in Tamworth.

Seeming to grow increasingly paranoid about her plan, Natasha turned to her phone for counsel on 31 July:

- can police see past web history
- can your internet history be tracked by internet provider
- how long do internet providers keep history

The intensity of the Google searches fails to subside, even after Mathew's death.

Natasha's iPhone 7 searches, 6–16 August
- can the police retrieve deleted facebook messages
- how would helium death tested by coroner
- if police have iphone can they see deleted imessages
- suicide investigation procedures
- how long does it take to get autopsy results
- how does a will work
- reading of a will
- autospy toxicology
- acepromazine
- autopsy results asphyxiation helium

Of particular interest for police were the searches relating to acepromazine. Not even the investigating officers knew it was present in Mathew's blood and urine samples until 24 August and, when they did find out, they were careful not to tell anyone about it.

They held back this information from the public to carry out a secret recording of Natasha following her arrest, in which she talked to undercover police about the sedative acepromazine. At this stage, she had not been informed of Mathew's toxicology results. If Natasha had nothing to do with Mathew's death, why was she mentioning an animal sedative found in his system?

The penny drops. Now I understand why local police had asked me to omit any mention of the ram sedatives from my initial article.

Hatfield moves on to a set of searches three months after Mathew's death, illustrating Natasha's anxiety reaching new heights.

Natasha's iPhone 7 searches, October 2017
- wife poisons husband
- murder by arsenic poisoning
- toxicology issues helium deaths
- how long to test for poisins (sic)
- wife killed husband
- average of investigation to arrest
- acepromazine

At this point, Hatfield has been on his feet in the courtroom for nearly three hours, outlining some seriously dense information. It's a lot to take in. I can see some of the jurors are fading already, struggling to concentrate.

Hatfield is saving an extremely damning part of the prosecution case until last, however; the jurors are soon sitting upright in their chairs once again.

While I've read plenty about the previous events involving Colin, each and every one of the jurors' eyes widen as Hatfield describes Natasha's shady past.

This is the tendency evidence that the prosecution and defence argued about in the months preceding the trial. The jury will hear about Natasha's hammer attack and deliberately lit house fire. But they won't hear that, originally, Natasha had been charged with attempted murder or that the prosecution believes she tried to sedate Colin by feeding him dosed oysters Kilpatrick. Or that she searched Google about death and poisons in the lead-up to the attacks on Colin. What they do hear, however, is still a lot to take in.

Hatfield tells them that Natasha signed an agreed set of facts, admitting she once hit her estranged husband Colin Crossman over the head with a hammer as he slept in bed in 2009.

I try to imagine what the jurors must be thinking as Hatfield explains how, three days after the hammer attack, Natasha torched the family home with a jerry can of petrol – leaving Colin in their bedroom, heavily sedated by a cocktail of drugs he doesn't remember taking. The last thing Colin remembers before waking up in hospital was watching cricket and eating tacos Natasha served him. Blood and urine samples revealed he had oxazepam, temazepam, alprazolam, Xanax, Effexor (a drug prescribed to Natasha at the time) and midazolam in his system.

None of the jurors look remotely asleep now.

I think about how temazepam and a drug prescribed to Natasha's son were also found in Mathew's system. I wonder if the jury picks up on these similarities, but there's so much information to take in.

'Mr Crossman did not knowingly take any of those drugs at that time,' Hatfield says.

He explains the jury will hear evidence about Natasha and Colin's financial situation at the time, and the insurance they'd taken out.

'Now, this evidence is relied upon in this matter by the Crown to prove a number of tendencies on behalf of the accused to act in a particular way. Namely, to act with the intention of inflicting serious harm upon a domestic partner and to sedate her partner with prescription drugs, and to do so with the intention of obtaining a financial or other advantage to herself.'

Natasha is accused of sedating Mathew with a cocktail of drugs before gassing him. The jury have just heard how she sedated her ex before burning their house down. On top of that, the prosecution says they can prove she bought ram sedatives and ordered the helium. She pushed to be made the sole beneficiary of Mathew's multimillion dollar sheep farm, and undertook months and months of murderous searches.

I try to think of any doubt the jury could possibly have at this point. Some of the searches could possibly be explained away, if Natasha and Mathew shared phones or were linked under the same Apple account, but some of the most damning searches were made when Mathew had no access to Natasha's phone.

There are two months ahead in this trial, but I can't help but wonder if the jury has already convicted her in their minds.

22

THE DEFENCE

Defence barristers don't always choose to give an opening address. Not locking in their position gives them more leeway to assess the prosecution's case throughout the trial before putting their case forward.

Natasha's barrister, Janet Manuell SC, gives one of the longest defence openings I've heard. Tucking her shoulder-length grey hair behind her ears, Manuell rises to her feet. She adjusts her rectangular-framed glasses as she introduces herself as Natasha's barrister to the jury.

'I suspect you've listened to the Crown's opening this morning and thought to yourselves, "Well, that seems like a pretty clear-cut case" . . . But that would be the wrong approach, because you haven't heard any of the evidence yet,' she says.

She reminds the jury of what Natasha admitted to during her arraignment – a procedure at the start of a trial, in which details of an offence are read aloud in court and the defendant is asked whether they plead guilty or not guilty.

I missed Natasha's arraignment, so I'm completely taken aback when Manuell recounts what happened during it, two days before the trial.

Shortly after the jury was selected, Natasha was asked to stand up enter a 'guilty' or 'not guilty' plea to the single charge of murder. She did neither.

She stood up and said, 'Not guilty to murder, but guilty to aiding and abetting suicide.'

There was a bubbling fury in Hatfield's voice when he too reminded the jury of what Natasha said during her arraignment, just a little earlier in his opening address. Voice raised, Hatfield emphatically told the jury she's charged with murder and no other offence. The prosecution completely rejects her offer to plead guilty to assisting a suicide.

I am shocked by her new defence. While I'm sure it happens, I've never covered a case where someone accused of murder claims it was an assisted suicide. Whereas it's not unusual for people charged with murder to plead guilty to manslaughter, or plead not guilty to murder by reason of mental illness.

I think back to how Natasha had told everyone in Walcha that Mathew had suicided. She'd even told me during our farmgate encounter that Mathew died by suicide, a plan he'd undertaken without her knowledge and which she'd tried to prevent. I remember the crocodile tears. This new defence is directly at odds with what she has maintained for the past four years and the evidence of murderous searches on her phone.

'You've heard Ms Darcy admit she assisted Mr Dunbar to commit suicide,' Manuell tells the jurors, imploring them to bear her 'condition' in mind, which she says there will be much evidence about down the track. I wonder what possible condition could excuse her from helping someone to kill themselves.

'Ms Darcy is innocent,' she says in a deep bellowing tone, then pauses dramatically. She urges the jury to think about what was happening in Mathew's life at the time of his death.

'Who was he?' she asks, offering up a platter of suggestions, many of which paint Mathew as a lonely man who'd struggled with severe depression throughout his life. He was a frivolous spender, who was worried about his finances. He had a debilitating leg injury, which was threatening his farming future. But this was the same leg injury Mathew remained positive about when talking to his neighbour Ross King on the last day of his life.

Manuell focuses heavily on his adoption and sustained grief following his parents' divorce. At the time of his death, she tells the court, he was estranged from his mother, a woman he strongly disliked and wanted nothing to do with.

Manuell also tells the jury that Mathew was homosexual; he struggled with his sexuality while still having relationships with women. As she focuses on this subject, I feel uncomfortable, thinking about how those closest to Mathew might feel when they listen to or read reports from the first day of this trial.

I also think about how unfair it is to Mathew, a strictly private person, who was now having his sexual orientation discussed in public. I can only imagine how mortified he'd be, having his private life dissected in open court. I also wonder whether this is something Natasha has made up and urged her defence to run with.

Manuell concentrates heavily on the fact that Mathew threatened to take his own life and was admitted to the psychiatric ward at Tamworth Base Hospital on 13 June 2017, less than two months before his death. 'He suffered severe depression before he met Ms Darcy.'

She also spends a considerable amount of time focusing on the distress Mathew endured following the suicide of his close friend and neighbour, Craig Hoy, just a few months earlier.

'Mr Hoy was homosexual . . . Mr Dunbar and Mr Hoy were very close friends . . . you might come to think that Mr Dunbar and Mr Hoy were gentle, like-minded souls who found each other in that small town community.

'We say this is a pivotal time . . . a very significant time,' before repeating the date of Mr Hoy's death several times, slowly. 'We'd ask you to use that date when you're considering things that have been said . . . remember April 11.'

Manuell tells the jury they will hear evidence that, for most of the people he knew in Walcha, Mathew hadn't been honest with or open about his struggles with mental health.

'Mr Dunbar was quite selective with what he told ... he told different people different things at different times ... Who really knew what Mr Dunbar was thinking?'

Even if Mathew had taken his own life, what evidence did the defence have to suggest his sexual orientation played a role? Unless there is some type of medical evidence, I can't help but feel this line of defence borders on offensive. This suicide defence seems to create an extraordinary situation in which Mathew stands on trial along with Natasha. It doesn't seem fair.

Towards the end of her address, Manuell concedes that Natasha told many lies in the wake of Mathew's death. 'From the time Ms Darcy was interviewed by the police, she denied any involvement in Mr Dunbar's death. She also denied that she knew he was intending to commit suicide or that he was actively making plans to die, but I anticipate, after you have heard all of the evidence, you won't accept her denials and, especially, you won't accept her denials in light of her admission on Monday that she aided or abetted Mr Dunbar's suicide.

'Now, Ms Darcy obviously thought the police decided very quickly that she had murdered Mr Dunbar, and you might think there is perhaps a connection between the offences of 2009 and Ms Darcy's perception that the police very quickly suspected her of murder. And she obviously thought the small community of Walcha was talking about her and whispering behind her back, pointing the finger at her,' Manuell says.

'But think about it, if Ms Darcy truly had assisted the suicide of Mr Dunbar, if she had known he had suicidal thoughts, if she had helped him search through suicide websites, if she had spoken with him about it, if she had gone with him to buy the helium, if she had not alerted anyone she knew, medical professional or others, to what she thought Mr Dunbar might do with the helium, if she had done all those things . . . don't you think she might feel as though she had something to hide? Maybe she lied to police because she thought they would never believe her.'

She takes an extended pause, then implores the jury again not to make any assumptions.

'Don't just assume she lied because she is guilty. That would be closing your mind to the evidence. Think about the reason why she would lie, and think about what was going on and what had been going on for a very long time.'

23

WALCHA WITNESSES

The acoustics in Courtroom 3 are far from desirable, prompting Justice Lonergan to relocate the case on Day 2 of the trial. There's also a need for a more advanced technological set-up, because dozens of interstate witnesses will be giving evidence via video link. The new courtroom is just around the corner from the main Darlinghurst complex, built as an extension in the early 1960s.

Over the next few days, the prosecution calls a series of witnesses from Walcha to help build their case. Each person is in court to prove a different piece of the jigsaw puzzle.

Sitting outside the courtroom in a three-piece navy suit, Lance Partridge waits for the sheriff to call him in. He fiddles with his tie, which is embroidered with dozens of miniature Merinos, as he chats with Mathew's neighbour Ross King and the officer in charge of the case, Graham Goodwin.

Lance is here to prove a major part in the prosecution's case. It's been a little more than three years since Lance and I spoke on the side of the road, and I fight the urge to go over and say 'hello'. Erring on the side of caution, I decide it's best to speak to him after he's finished giving his evidence.

Following Mathew's death, Natasha told police on numerous

occasions she had no idea she stood to inherit Mathew's estate. Lance is in the witness box to prove that she did.

'Were you present in a car with Mathew when he had a conversation with the accused . . . about the will?' asks Hatfield.

'Yes,' Lance says clearly.

'In which he informed her, she was the beneficiary?'

'Yes.'

'And Pandora was hers if he died?'

'Yes.'

All Crown prosecutors have their own styles; some are theatrical, others more clinical and detached. Hatfield doesn't swell with emotion, but he's methodical, articulate and doesn't muck around. Some prosecutors allow the evidence to flow through the witnesses, letting them answer questions freely, but this comes with a danger: you never know what they are going to say.

Having carefully studied their police statements, and interviewed witnesses prior to the trial, Hatfield extracts their evidence by reading out relevant passages of their accounts and asking them to answer 'yes' or 'no' to confirm the veracity. Initially, I'm itching for Hatfield to let people speak more freely, but he's adopted this style for several reasons. His questioning ensures he gets through the witnesses' evidence economically, pointing them straight to the relevant parts that help the prosecution.

He also needs to avoid witnesses divulging that Natasha went to jail for other offences, which aren't part of the tendency evidence the judge has allowed the jury to hear. While the jury have heard about the assault on Colin and the house fire in 2009, they won't be told about the threats she made to Cadbury, or the faked motel attack. They also won't hear about offences she'd committed against a man she met, after separating from Colin and before meeting Mathew, which landed her in jail for 18 months.

Hatfield bears this in mind as he carefully guides the witnesses through their evidence, to avoid anyone blurting out something they shouldn't. If the jury find out that Natasha has been to jail for other offences, it's likely the trial will be aborted and start all over again.

Hatfield works methodically, extracting the evidence he wants the jury to hear with little fuss. When he's finished questioning a witness, the defence then cross-examines them.

When it's her turn, defence barrister Janet Manuell doggedly asks most witnesses about four subjects: Mathew's spending, his poor relationship with his mother, his 'troubles' with his sexuality and his mental health.

Manuell questions most of the Walcha witnesses about Mathew's generosity, insinuating he was in dire financial straits because he gave too much away. The court hears how Mathew gave money and expensive gifts to friends, tradies and former girlfriends. This was something he had always done to express how he felt about people and it had never caused him any financial strain in the past.

'He would help out anyone,' Lance tells the court.

Joshua Wellings, a carpenter who did renovations at Pandora, was initially embarrassed when Mathew gave him expensive tools and work clothes, but said people in Walcha 'told me that was just Mathew's way of being generous and to accept them graciously'.

Friend and neighbour Bill Heazlett tells the jury that Mathew would often buy him groceries and helped to put a new roof on his garage. 'If you said you liked something, he'd be inclined to give it to you.'

For weeks and weeks, I wait for Manuell to ask questions geared towards Natasha's defence of assisted suicide, but she doesn't. I find it strange the topic is never brought up again – not even in the defence case – because Manuell focused so heavily on it in her opening address. She never returns to it, at least not in front of the jury.

During the trial, the jury is often sent out of the courtroom while the prosecution and defence engage in legal arguments. This often happens when one of the parties objects to something that is said or raised in court. At other times, the defence and prosecution have planned arguments about certain evidence, so the judge can rule on what she will allow the jury to hear.

Throughout the trial, Manuell persistently asks witnesses about Mathew's sexual orientation, attempting to link this to his depression.

She peppers Lance with questions about Mathew's relationships with gay men, even asking him if Mathew was afraid of contracting HIV.

Lance scoffs at the suggestion. 'Mathew only had one relationship with a male, and it wasn't successful. He wasn't gay,' he says with certainty.

At one point, Hatfield objects to the defence trying to introduce a series of text messages Mathew sent to other males, arguing they aren't relevant. 'There has been an attempt to attach depression with sexuality . . . none of the medical evidence has gone so far.'

Without the jury present, Manuell tries to explain why she's constantly raising his sexual orientation. 'It is the defence case that Mr Dunbar committed suicide . . . a very significant part was that Mr Dunbar was troubled by his sexuality, not only by his sexual identity but sexual dysfunction.'

Justice Lonergan says that, even if Mathew was bisexual, 'we are well past the days' when someone's sexual orientation meant they had a medical condition. 'It's an offensive underlying notion . . . highly offensive,' Justice Lonergan says.

This subject also causes great distress to those who knew Mathew, particularly Chloe Hoy; her brother-in-law Craig Hoy took his life a few months before Mathew's death.

The defence argues Mathew had a relationship with Mr Hoy, his neighbour from a nearby property, and that Mr Hoy's suicide contributed significantly to Mathew's depression.

Chloe Hoy, who works at the Walcha pharmacy, has been waiting outside the court to give her evidence, talking with Walcha locals Lance Partridge and Ross King. Under cross-examination, Chloe tells the court that Mr Hoy phoned her in 2014, intoxicated, and spoke about some form of relationship he'd had with Mathew.

'Craig told me it was nice to have a companion that understood him ... he told me that he and Mat had talked ... he told me he had had an intimate relationship with Mat,' she says, hands folded in her lap.

'Did you ask anything more about the relationship?' Manuell asks.

'There was no mention of anything of a sexual nature ... he just expressed how different it was in a small town ... he didn't feel accepted. He and Mathew shared similar struggles, always struggled to fit in [and said it was] nice to have a companion to talk to and not feel judged.'

Another Walcha witness is Mathew's childhood friend, Belinder Wauch. Although she and Mathew weren't close friends at school, she always felt a sense of responsibility for him, and grew to know him well because they caught the school bus into town each day.

Now a successful businesswoman, Belinder lives in Sydney with her partner Nick and their two children, but still travels to Walcha to visit her mother and father, who live 28 kilometres down the road from Mathew's property Pandora on Thunderbolts Way.

Belinder breeds horses and her mother, Helen, often lent some to Natasha and her daughter, who would ride them at pony camp.

During her trips home to visit family, Belinder met Natasha a few times while checking in on the horses she'd borrowed.

Despite them being casual acquaintances, Natasha was keen to establish more of a friendship, and reel in Belinder as an ally, contacting her via Facebook Messenger.

On the night Mathew died, Natasha stayed up late messaging Belinder on Facebook between 11.25 pm on 1 August and 1 am on 2 August 2017.

Natasha was quick to show this conversation to police in the days after Mathew's death in an attempt to prove her innocence.

Belinder and Natasha Facebook messages, 1 August 2017

1 August, 11.25 pm, Belinder Wauch

Honey ... are you okay? Just saw that Mat's in hospital with his leg?

Anything mum, dad or I can do – let me know..

Natasha Darcy

Hi Bel, no, he's home now, again.

Got bad news today though ,

looks like the

Majority of his calf muscle is dead, so he will have to have surgery in 6 months, but his leg will never be ok.

Nothing anybody can do. Spent hours tonight just talking and trying to get him see that he's actually pretty lucky. Nothing anybody can do. He'll come around

Thanks anyway Bel

1 August, 11.58 pm, Belinder Wauch

Shit honey . . . I know what it's like to have to keep pulling someone you love back into living. . .

2 August, 12.14 am

How did his leg injury start? Wanted to spend some time with Mat when we visited during the holidays but mum wanted to come too & there were kids & family everywhere . . . Do you want

nick and I to come up for a weekend and spend some time with you guys? He's a breath of fresh air, he'd be great for Mat x

2 August, 12.31 am, Natasha Darcy

That would be great. I'd love to get to know nick. Maybe when mats feeling better? He didn't want me sleeping with him tonight so I'm on the lounge xxx

2 August, 1 am, Belinder Wauch

Oh god! I wish nick would sleep on the lounge! Lol he's the biggest snorer ever! I'm on the lounge too.. xx hang in there hon. Ring me anytime.

(Natasha likes message)

Computer analysts aren't able to pinpoint the precise time Natasha 'liked' Belinder's message from 1 am. But five minutes after Natasha wrote her last reply at 12.31 am, Mathew's phone was used to google 'is helium traceable autopsy' at 12.36 am. At 1.14 am, his phone was used to message Colin, asking him to call police.

Belinder is burdened with guilt, having supported Natasha in the weeks after Mathew's death. She couldn't fathom Mathew could have died in any other way than how Natasha had told her. She's sickened that Natasha used their Facebook messages to help support an alibi.

'I feel like such an idiot. I supported her and stood up for her,' she tells me over coffee one day after court.

Belinder is a bright, vivacious woman, who manages to watch the trial online almost every single day. When she occasionally pops into court, it's a comfort to see her; her smile is as bright as the colourful coats, scarves and shoes she dresses in. When she's not in court, she's quick to text me her thoughts on the performance of certain witnesses, as well as Hatfield, who she's flagged to be played by Benedict Cumberbatch if someone ever makes a movie of the case.

Despite her bright energy, it's clear she's been affected by how Natasha used her.

Knowing Belinder had lost a close girlfriend to suicide, Natasha played on this, pulling on her emotions and demons to ensure she had an ally.

'I even suggested we set up donations for the Black Dog Institute, in lieu of flowers at the funeral, to raise awareness of male suicide and depression. After it all came out, I felt totally blind-sided, as if everyone else had been suspicious but me.'

At the time, however, she was living in Sydney and wasn't privy to what was being said in Walcha. Belinder detests 'small town gossip' and believes Natasha used that to her advantage.

She and husband Nick only suspected something was amiss after Mathew's funeral. Some locals were openly discussing the town's suspicions at the wake, which Natasha chose not to attend, for reasons that soon became apparent to them.

Offering to drop Natasha's daughter back at Pandora after the wake, because she had no ride home, Belinder was surprised at what happened next.

'Natasha was hysterical that no one had bothered to approach or console her at the funeral, and her mother was telling us that the police had it in for her because of her past record. Then we saw a stack of evidence boxes in the front room labelled "homicide". At that point, we realised something more was going on.'

After detective Graham Goodwin took her police statement at Rose Bay Police Station in Sydney, the penny finally dropped for Belinder.

'I felt like vomiting, to be honest,' she says, adding how she wishes she'd contacted Mathew as soon as she'd learned of his suicide threat.

'Like everyone else, the intention had been there to catch up with him and say, "Hey, we're here, it's okay to be feeling like this," but it was too late.'

Belinder is adamant that Mathew's death should be talked about as a warning: women are as capable of domestic violence as men.

'Mat won't be the last person that this happens to. Her plan was to isolate and manipulate him through the use of her children. People need to be aware that there are women out there, preying on vulnerable lonely men, who take advantage of kindness and treat it as a weakness. It's important for men to be able to notice the warning signs and not feel foolish to speak up about it.'

More than anything, she wants to watch justice happen for Mathew and feels a sense of responsibility to listen to all the evidence.

'Mat was socially awkward, quiet and reserved, but he was also a gentle generous giant, who didn't deserve what happened to him. No one does.'

As he walks from the courtroom, Chris Kleinekathoefer nearly breaks into a sprint, lips quivering, eyes on the ground. As soon as he makes it to the foyer, he can't hold it in anymore; the tears are uncontrollable.

After giving their evidence, Ross King, Chloe Hoy and Belinder Wauch are sitting in court, listening to what Chris had to say as one of Mathew's closest friends.

Sensing his distress by the end of his evidence, they all swiftly file out of the courtroom behind him. Huddling around him, they listen to him through his sobs. He doesn't think he's said enough to do Mathew justice. He feels as though he's failed him, even though this is far from the truth.

Hatfield calls Chris as a witness to prove that, when Natasha claims he took his own life, Mathew was making solid plans with people he knew. Every person being called by the Crown was helping to build a picture. This wasn't a man who was planning his suicide; he had plenty to live for.

Chris tells the jury he met Mathew through his father, John Dunbar, the pair sharing a mutual love of vintage cars, particularly Land Rovers. Chris, a semi-retired farmer and machinery fitter, used to visit Mathew at Pandora about every eight weeks to help on the property and spend time with his mate. After learning Mathew had met Natasha online, Chris was concerned about the fast-paced nature of their relationship.

He'd tried to caution Mathew, but his advice fell on deaf ears. 'I gave him advice,' Chris tells the jury, before explaining Mathew didn't take it.

Chris was shell-shocked to learn about Mathew's suicide threat in June, which he heard about from Natasha when he phoned the farm landline to catch up with Mathew one day.

Crazy eyes: The photo that prompted the author to investigate the mysterious death of grazier Mathew Dunbar. Source: Facebook

Happier times: Farmer Mathew Dunbar and Natasha Beth Darcy, celebrating their first Christmas together. Source: Facebook

Blind love: Mathew hugs Natasha at his property Pandora, on the outskirts of Walcha. Source: Facebook

Best mate: Lance Partridge, Mathew's closest friend. Source: Oliver Clarke

Crime scene: Police begin a forensic search at Pandora, following Natasha's arrest in November 2017. Source: *Northern Daily Leader*

Papped: Natasha is unwittingly photographed clutching a parcel outside the Walcha post office. Source: Nathan Edwards / *Daily Telegraph*

The ex: Natasha's estranged husband and paramedic Colin Crossman. Natasha was charged with his attempted murder in 2009 but ended up pleading guilty to the lesser charge of destroying property by fire. Source: Facebook

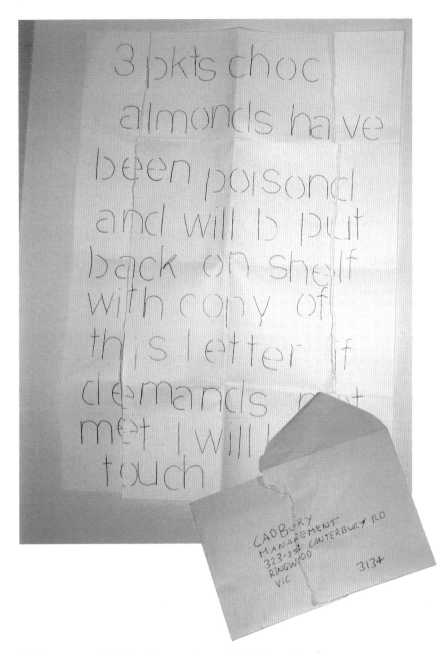

Wild cover story: The ripped-up envelope and draft letter Natasha wrote to Cadbury to explain substances found in Colin Crossman's system the night she burned the house down. She posted a later version to Cadbury's head office in Victoria. Source: Supplied

Blissfully happy: Mathew playing cricket on Christmas Day at Trish and Lance Partridge's property Warren Park. Source: Supplied

Shared passion: Mathew with Lance at the Walcha Poultry Club. Source: Supplied

Blended evidence: The Nutribullet Natasha used to blend a cocktail of drugs (including a ram sedative) to knock out Mathew before she murdered him. Source: NSW Supreme Court

Sickly sweet: Natasha hugs a lamb in a paddock. Source: Facebook

Lucky escape: Natasha stole the credit card of her ex-partner, Fred Nicholson, and went on a spending spree, then falsely accused him of assault when he refused to change his police statement. Source: Oliver Clarke

Facing trial: Natasha leaves the NSW Supreme Court on King Street, Sydney, following a pre-trial hearing a week before her trial starts in March 2021. Source: Nine News

During his conversation with Natasha, he 'found it odd' she kept banging on about the fact she'd taken charge of Mathew's medication. 'Natasha told me ... she's looking after his medication ... she has hidden his medication and that she's administering his medication.'

Chris outlines his last conversation with Mathew, two days before his death, on 31 July 2017. 'I spoke to Mat and I asked him how his leg was. He said it had gone down to about a third of the size ... he sounded sore over the phone, but he was still chirpy Mat.'

He takes a few deep breaths, struggling to swallow the lump in his throat as he tells the court he and Mathew made plans to catch up in a few weeks' time.

'We never missed AgQuip every year. We never missed AgQuip,' Chris tells the jury, pausing often to make himself clear.

'AgQuip is an agricultural ... Gunnedah agricultural show. So I said to him, "Look, I'll arrange to hire a scooter for you ... at least we can go together," and Mathew had agreed he would still go, despite his leg injury.'

Chris is barely managing to hold it together when Hatfield finishes his questioning.

Manuell moves to cross-examine him. She asks him questions about gifts Mathew had bought him. She's trying to make out that he was a spendthrift, that he was irresponsible with money and that his spending, not Natasha's, was the cause of his financial troubles.

It's almost too much for Chris. His voice breaks several times but he manages to keep the tears at bay until he's through the courtroom doors.

24

COLIN'S EVIDENCE

I watch with great interest as Colin Crossman appears on the screen in the NSW Supreme Court. I've only ever seen him from afar, when Nathan took photos of him on our stake-out, as we watched him and Natasha unload a washing machine at his house in Walcha. While I've studied a few grainy Facebook photos, I've never heard him speak.

Wearing a grey sweater over a light pink collared shirt, he's stony-faced as he sits in an interview room at Tamworth, rectangular-framed glasses hanging from a chain around his neck.

The prosecution has called him as a witness to introduce the tendency evidence against Natasha: her tendency to sedate her partners and commit crimes against them to gain financial benefit. He'd also received a text from Mathew's phone on the night of his death at 1.14 am.

As Hatfield reads the agreed statement of facts to the jury, I wonder what's running through Colin's mind. How does he feel about being dragged into this mess again? What's it like hearing what had happened to him again? Now that she's facing trial for murder, is he still supporting Natasha?

Police say that, by the time Natasha faced her attempted murder trial in 2011, Colin was unwilling to cooperate as a witness. I wonder whether he'll cooperate today.

Natasha has been in jail since 2017 and, to this day, he's still caring for her daughter and two sons.

The jury hears an abbreviated version of the facts, which include how Natasha applied for life insurance, which would give her $700,000 in the event of Colin's death, shortly before she burned down the family home in 2009. Also how she'd set fire to the house when Colin was sedated in bed with a cocktail of drugs in his system, which he did not take himself.

'The accused's decision to light the fire was not spontaneous and there was a degree of planning to it,' Hatfield says, arguing Natasha had a tendency 'to act with the intention of inflicting harm and sedating her partner with the intention of obtaining a financial advantage . . . The Crown says the accused had the tendency to act in these ways, which makes it more likely she committed the act of murder on Mr Dunbar.'

As Hatfield outlines what was done to him, Colin crosses his arms and shows little emotion. Hatfield begins to question Colin about his relationship with Natasha and Mathew.

Colin agrees he is still legally married to Natasha.

'Is it your intention to obtain a divorce?' Hatfield asks.

'It is when I have a spare few dollars,' Colin says gruffly, explaining he's been under financial strain since the house fire, which had left him bankrupt.

Hatfield moves his focus to Mathew, asking Colin to confirm the pair were not especially close.

'No, I wouldn't have called him a real friend,' says Colin.

This statement is at complete odds with what Natasha told police.

The jury hears that, at some stage in 2015, Colin had moved into Natasha's home in town to care for her three children while she was 'away'. This is code for the 18 months she spent in jail for the offences against her ex-boyfriend. During the trial, this issue is delicately danced around to keep the jury in the dark about her previous crimes.

Colin agrees Mathew helped to care for the children from time to time, and that Mathew once loaned Colin $2000. 'To help me with financials with the house that was burned down,' he explains.

Colin confirms he often spent time at Pandora to see the children; he was there the weekend before Mathew's death while Natasha and her daughter were away in Dorrigo.

They all shared pizza on the Saturday night, Colin tells the court, saying Mathew spent most of the weekend out and about on the property doing jobs. 'He seemed happy. There didn't seem to be any problems. He didn't seem depressed.'

Colin recalls helping Mathew load a quad bike onto the back of his ute on Monday, 31 July; the same bike Mathew dropped off in Tamworth the following day for repair.

This is the last time Colin remembers seeing Mathew alive.

Colin tells the jury that, at 2.02 am on 2 August 2017, he woke to his phone ringing on his bedside table. It was the operation centre, informing him of an urgent job on Thunderbolts Way. It wasn't until after getting dressed, he says, that he noticed the cryptic message sent at 1.14 am from Mathew's phone, asking him to call the police.

'Tell police to come to house. I don't want Tash or kids to find me,' read the text.

Colin replied with 'What???' and showed the text to his colleague, Marion Schaap, after she picked him up from his home in the ambulance. They sped out to Pandora, arriving at about 2.17 am.

After trying to revive Mathew without success, he recalls Natasha screaming at him and Marion to keep doing CPR.

'I took her into the other room and said, "Nothing else can be done,"' Colin says, explaining Mathew was pronounced dead at 2.44 am, lying on the carpet at the foot of his bed.

Mathew died with Natasha by his side and her ex by hers, a man she'd almost killed, too.

25

MATHEW'S LOVE

As part of their case, the prosecution must prove Natasha had motive to kill.

Hatfield sets out to do this by showing the jury how their relationship began, and the speed at which Natasha convinced Mathew to change his will. He's also armed with a series of text messages, illustrating how Natasha groomed him while he blindly gave her his heart.

The exact origins of their relationship remain a mystery but, after speaking to his friends and trawling though Mathew's Facebook account, they started calling themselves an item towards the end of 2014. I want to know how she managed to lure him with such ease, and what she said and did to earn his trust so quickly. And particularly, how she did this while Colin still appeared to be in her life.

By all accounts, Natasha did the chasing. Mathew confirms this himself in a series of messages to a friend on Facebook, shortly after meeting her: 'And yes, Tash chase me for a month or so but is only 10 mins down the road. And we match so well it is freaky.'

'She chased me which is unusual but we have clicked on so many levels and the kids love me too so yes it has been strange as I feel a sense of belonging though its hard to explain.'

Mathew's own words confirmed what those closest to him maintained all along: he'd fallen in love with the idea of having a family.

Hatfield tells the jury they'd met online; the reality of their meeting was a little less romantic than the story Natasha had spun. In her first interview with detectives, Natasha told them Mathew had found her 'walking in the rain', gallantly offering her a lift. This is just one of the many lies she would tell them.

Lance Partridge recalls Mathew telling him he'd met Natasha on the internet, possibly on Facebook. He first met her when she turned up at Pandora with the wife of a shearer in November 2014.

'Well, after that first occasion, she came out to the wool shed every day during shearing – at one stage I walked over and they were cuddling,' Lance tells the court. But the strong affection between them at the start quickly fizzled out when Natasha moved to Pandora with her children in October 2016, following her 18-month jail stint.

'The relationship changed when Natasha came back from Sydney. They weren't lovey-dovey, but they were friendly,' says Lance, using 'Sydney' as his euphemism for jail. He'd been warned by the prosecution not to mention her jail stint during her relationship with Mathew in front of the jury.

While the evidence of friends during the trial sheds partial light on their relationship, a series of text messages between Mathew and Natasha proves to be the most eye-opening.

I can only imagine how horrified Mathew would be, having his private messages photocopied and handed out to each of the 12 jurors. But they're necessary to show how Natasha targeted and groomed him. They also offer a rare glimpse into Mathew's mind; his words baring his soul, showing a strong love, but one that is very much blind.

Natasha's manipulative messages make for uncomfortable reading. It's clear her focus was on one thing, and it certainly wasn't Mathew.

It was the day before Australia Day in 2015. Natasha was laying it on as thick and fast as she could manage. She was still nursing several self-inflicted wounds from a week prior, when she claimed her ex-boyfriend assaulted her, but had fabricated the attack on herself.

Natasha's performance on the night she faked being attacked confirms that Mathew was well and truly in her corner. Mathew sped to her defence straight from Pandora, then called the police and made a statement in support of her claims.

Despite only knowing each other for less than a few months, Mathew appeared to be deeply in love.

Natasha and Mathew iPhone messages, 25 January 2015
Natasha: We should just get married and move in together, we always want to be with you.
Mathew: Yes agreed. Be up for that anytime. Only prob is you still married to Col. I love you always and forever and ever most beautiful person in the universe. xoxoxoxoxoxoxoxoxo

Three days after this text exchange, police charged Natasha with perverting the course of justice regarding the fake attack. Refused bail, she spent the next four weeks in custody, where she had plenty of time to think about her next move when she got out.

Mathew remained her biggest support, funding her defence and keeping in regular contact with her until she was released from custody on 27 February.

Natasha and Mathew iPhone messages, 13 March 2015
Mathew: Doctors appointment done. He is happy with me. Even did a skin cancer check and blood pressure which I passed with flying colours. So no chance of me dying soon
I love you always beautiful xoxoxoxoxoxo
Natasha: Excellent. Cause I don't want to loos you
Mathew: I don't want to ever loose you either. Your my world along with the kids. I love you so much beautiful xoxoxoxoxoxoxo

Their text messages reveal Natasha had already raised the subject of Mathew's will by the end of March 2015, less than six months after they'd met.

Natasha and Mathew iPhone messages, 22 March 2015
Natasha: Don't forget you need to change your will . . .
. . . and make lance or someone the button presser
Not your mum, she scares me
Mathew: Okay

Aware of her fast-approaching court case for fraud and perverting the course of justice charges – with the high probability of being sent back to jail – Natasha turned up the pressure, pushing and probing Mathew about his will again in April. His thoughts were clearly focused on his feelings for Natasha and, while she inserts sweet messages where necessary, she appeared to be just sugar-coating her sole focus: his will.

Natasha and Mathew iPhone messages, 19 April 2015
9.33 pm, Natasha: Can you promise to do one thing for me this week?
9.37 pm, Mathew: What?
9.44 pm, Natasha: Call solicitor for appointment to sort out your will.
9.50 pm, Natasha: Ok, your silence says it all
10.03 pm, Mathew: Goodnight my love. Sleep well, see you tomorrow xxxx
10.10 pm, Mathew: Sorry was in the shower. Okay will do especially for the enduring guardianship.
10.11 pm, Mathew: Hoping you sleep well and have sweet dreams. I love you so much beautiful xoxoxoxoxoxo
10.12 pm, Natasha: I love you too darling xxx
10.13 pm, Mathew: Miss you heaps. You are beautiful and perfect in every way. I love you always beautiful. xoxoxoxoxoxoxoxoxoxoxoxoxoxo

10.16 pm, Natasha: You say the nicest sweetest things. I want to be your partner for the rest of our lives. I want to Care for you and be the last thing you see at night. I want to die 5 seconds after you so I dont have to live without you

10.19 pm, Mathew: I dont want to live without you either. Closing my eyes at night and then opening my eyes in the morning to the most amazing lady ever makes my heart happy and it always will. You are the best. I love you so much beautiful xoxoxoxoxoxoxoxoxoxoxoxoxoxoxo

After this exchange of messages professing deep love, Natasha was unsatisfied with what Mathew had told her. She was waiting for a response about something more important.

10.23 pm, Natasha: I'm just curious, why do you say especially for the enduring guardianship? What about the rest?

10.36 pm, Mathew: Enduring guardianship is medical. Power of Attorney is financial.

10.36 pm, Natasha: Oh ok, dumb blonde I am

10.37 pm, Mathew: Nope not at all. Beautiful smart and brainy blonde lady

10.38 pm, Natasha: Lol Who are you going to put as both?

10.38 pm, Mathew: The ones you suggested

10.39 pm, Natasha: Which were

10.39 pm, Mathew: Lance and you

10.39 pm, Natasha: Good idea. We work together for your best interest

10.39 pm, Mathew: Yes

10.39 pm, Natasha: What about powerful attorney?

10.40 pm, Mathew: Same

10.45 pm. Natasha: It makes me feel good and proves to me you do love and trust me to legally put me in such an important ro [role]

10.46 pm, Mathew: I want to be the best for you and the kids always

10.46 pm, Natasha: You are. XXXX

10.48 pm, Mathew: I try.

Natasha and Mathew iPhone messages, 4 May 2015
Mathew: Rang solicitor and organised will change. I love you so
much beautiful xoxoxoxoxoxoxoxoxoxo

A few days after Mathew's text, declaring his intention to make
Natasha the sole beneficiary of his estate, Natasha was found guilty
of 12 counts of dishonestly obtaining property by deception at
Armidale Local Court. She was taken into custody. During one of
many recorded jail calls, Mathew spoke to Natasha and explained
he was en route to the solicitors to change his will. The jury were not
told where this conversation was recorded.

Recorded jail phone call, 13 May 2015
Mathew: I've just brought Lance to, ah, Tamworth today . . . We're
gunna go see the solicitors, and sign the Wills and things like that.
So all that goes into effect today.
Natasha: Oh, okay. Are you changing it?
Mathew: Ah no, not at all.
Natasha: Oh.
Mathew: So it'll be still the same as what you have got at home.

The following day, they spoke on the phone again; Mathew
confirmed the will was now legally binding.

Recorded jail phone call, 14 May 2015
Natasha: How was yesterday?
Mathew: Good. Good. Um, yep, got the Will done and the Guard-
ianship and Power of Attorney done, so . . .
Natasha: Uh-huh.
Mathew: You, you now own Pandora if I die.
Natasha: I don't want Pandora, I want you.
Mathew: Yeah, I know, but . . . but that's to protect you as well.
Natasha: Yeah.

A file note written on 4 May 2015 by Mathew's solicitor, Natasha Wood, during the process of changing the will, indicates he very much wanted Natasha to be his life partner:

Mathew is currently in a relationship with Natasha Beth Darcy-Crossman. They are not married but he anticipates they might get married in a few years.

Mathew has no children. Natasha has three children from a [previous] relationship. Natasha's children reside with Mathew and Natasha at Mathew's property in Walcha.

. . .

Mathew instructed me that he would like his estate to be given to Natasha and then to her daughter and then to Natasha's other two children.

Mathew also wrote an accompanying letter to attach to his new will, making it crystal clear he was willing to leave Natasha everything:

I am a sheep farmer with about 2800 sheep I care for. I own the property Pandora which is about 1200 acres [485.6 ha] approximately 12 kms from Walcha. I have recently rewritten my will so Natasha and then [her daughter] get it if I pass away.[7]

Although Mathew finally did what Natasha had asked, it had taken him several months to come around to the idea, discussing it with friends in the lead-up.

Close friend Michelle Bray, in her evidence given via video link from Newcastle, confirms she and Mathew spoke about Natasha, and some of the things she'd said to him about changing his will.

After forming a friendship through the Walcha poultry club, Michelle and Mathew often talked on the phone. In one of their

---

7   Last Will and Testament of Mathew John Dunbar, 13 May 2015.

conversations, Mathew revealed Natasha was asking a lot of questions about what would happen to her and the children if he died. In the event of his death, Natasha asked him if she and the children could live at Pandora for at least six months.

'I told Mathew, a person who makes plans for your death does not love you,' Michelle wrote in her police statement.

She'd also warned Mathew she thought it was a bad idea to change his will, especially after hearing Natasha had pestered him to make her the sole beneficiary of his estate.

The evidence of Mathew's friends and the text messages were key to proving Natasha had a motive to kill, and disproved her claim that she'd had no idea she stood to inherit a thing.

In a Facebook message Natasha wrote to an old high-school friend on 8 August 2017, six days after Mathew's death, she says: 'Mat made us both executors but I never got around to signing before a JP to say I accept. I am the only beneficiary of the Will though so that part should be easy.'

Having read the portion of Mathew's and Natasha's text messages where they discussed his will, Hatfield argues the motive is clear.

'She was without any income herself, dependent on him financially . . . she would have given much thought to his death; she would have given some consideration to her situation should he die,' he tells the jury.

'It was clear, you might think, that her motive for murdering the deceased was what she would obtain or benefit with, from under the will, a property valued between $3.4 to $3.6 million, but you heard from Mr Partridge [that Pandora] eventually sold for $4.6 million. Quite a substantial motive, you might think.'

26

GROUNDWORK

Two corrective service officers bring up Natasha from the cells into the courtroom; she's smiling broadly, donning her signature topknot bun. I strain my ears and lean forward, attempting to eavesdrop on what she's saying to her legal team, but the Perspex box around her makes it difficult to pick up much sound.

I wonder why Natasha is so chirpy this morning.

It's not long before her smile vanishes.

Appearing on the courtroom's video screen is a woman who was the source of a giant row between her and Mathew, which led him to threaten suicide. Soon, the jury will hear there was much more behind Mathew's threat; he was possibly a victim of gaslighting, with Natasha pushing him to his limits on purpose.

Tanya Morley is about to give her evidence from where she lives in Mackay, Queensland. She's clearly nervous, rocking back and forth slightly, and fidgeting with a thick blonde braid draped over her right shoulder.

Tanya dated Mathew back when she was in high school, 17 years ago, but they'd kept in regular phone and Facebook contact ever since. Over the years, Mathew occasionally loaned her money, which she always repaid. The last time he loaned her money was just a few weeks before his death, to help her pay the cost of damages caused by floods in the region.

Shortly before Mathew threatened to take his own life on 13 June 2017, a volcanic argument erupted between Mathew and Natasha. Natasha saw red when she realised Mathew went behind her back with the loan. The proof was right in front of her: a Rabobank internet banking receipt showing the transfer of $1200 to Tanya L Morley.

She used her phone to take a screenshot of her discovery at 2.51 pm and, presumably, confronted Mathew, who later headed out to his shed to retrieve a firearm.

At 3.46 pm, Natasha sent Mathew a text – the contents of which will never be known because, conveniently, it had been deleted by the time police examined her phone. While police could retrieve most deleted data, the iPhone messages she'd wiped were not recoverable.

Whatever she wrote, it was enough to push Mathew to the edge. Perhaps this was her plan all along.

About 15 minutes after sending Mathew a text, Natasha sent another one, indicating their argument was still in full swing.

'Okay, but this is your farm, I have to leave,' Natasha texted Mathew. She also sent Tanya Morley a series of messages, after requesting they connect as friends on Facebook.

Natasha and Tanya Morley Facebook messages, 13 June 2017
Natasha: I hope your husband knows everything that's going on between you and Mathew. I'm giving you [the chance] to tell him. I have every message you guys have shared. And it's not normal
Tanya: There's nothing going on between Mat and I. We have been friends for a very long time. And husband? I don't have a husband. I've never been married so I can't have a husband.
Natasha: We are struggling financially. He's selling stuff so we can make ends meet. And he gives you $1200 we don't have
I think I have every right to be angry

Anyway, he's yours noe

Now

Tanya immediately texted Mathew and explained they needed to talk.

'No because I will be gone,' replied Mathew.

A few minutes later, Mathew called Lance Partridge and told him he was 'leaving Pandora for the last time'.

Lance listened as Mathew explained how Natasha found out about the money he loaned Tanya. She was now accusing him of having an affair. Lance tried to keep him on the phone for as long as possible but, eventually, Mathew hung up.

Lance phoned Natasha straight away, but she didn't sound overly concerned. Quite the opposite. Yes, they had a blue, but she knew nothing about him taking out a gun from the shed. 'It wasn't much of an argument,' Natasha had said, before telling Lance she didn't want to call police about it. She really didn't want to involve them.

Although Lance didn't believe Mathew would go through with his threat, and despite Natasha playing everything down, he called Walcha Police Station to let them know what was going on.

'Mathew could never have killed himself. I was more concerned Mathew had turned to Tanya and gave her help when he had promised not to. And I think he was aware that the situation at Pandora – with his partner – was going to come to nothing,' Lance tells the jury during his evidence.

Not long after Lance's phone call, Senior Constables Tony Souzu and Mick McDonnell arrived at Pandora. Natasha was lingering in the front yard. They informed her that, following Mathew's threat to take his own life, they were concerned for his welfare and wanted to find out where he was.

She laughed it off, explaining they'd had a fight after she found out Mathew had loaned an ex-girlfriend money. She wasn't too worried, despite Mathew sending her the text saying, 'I will not be returning to the property'.

'I didn't think much of the text message. Mathew can be an attention seeker and I just thought he was having one of his poofter hissy fits,' she told the pair.

Taken aback by her callous attitude, and how she described Mathew's state of mind, Souzu asked Natasha if there was anywhere she thought they should check, or any places on the property he could have driven to.

'You are more than welcome to search the property if you think I've buried him somewhere, if that's what you're implying,' she said, defensive.

Although Mathew had taken a gun from the sheds, Natasha told police she was adamant he didn't go anywhere near the sheds where he kept his firearms. It's as if she was trying to play it down and wanted them to go away. They left, perplexed. Driving back towards town, however, Souzu and McDonnell received a welcome phone call. Mathew was safe and at Lance's property.

When they arrived there, Mathew was honest and frank about what happened, apologising for all the fuss. He told them he'd loaded his gun and aimed it at his head, but couldn't go through with pulling the trigger. He willingly handed his firearm back to the officers and they gave him some space to talk to Lance. In his evidence, Lance tells the jury Mathew was distressed about the state of his relationship with Natasha.

'He was very concerned about the relationship with his partner and her husband, and he was generally upset that he wasn't getting the family life he had hoped for. He said Natasha was still happily married to her husband,' Lance says, referring to Colin.

'She promised a quick divorce and Mathew would marry her, and he had even asked me to be best man . . . he was most concerned this hadn't happened.'

Mathew was also stressed about his finances, and the rate at which Natasha was spending his money. He'd loaned a small amount of money to Tanya Morley, but this was nothing compared to some of the big-ticket items Natasha had splashed out on.

'He said one of his main concerns was the cash-flow problem . . . just the fact he had no money to pay his bills at that time, because his partner had spent all the money.'

Lance also tells the court Mathew was 'frightened' of Colin, and worried he would stop him from seeing the children.

While Natasha was in custody for the fraud offences against another ex-boyfriend, Colin moved into the house she was living in to care for the children, but needed Mathew's help when he was working.

'Mathew came in and acted as a nanny, looked after the children. He loved the children,' Lance tells the court. Much to Mathew's distress, however, when Natasha eventually got out of jail and moved to Pandora, Colin continued to hang around, often spending his days off at the property.

Lance could sense Mathew was gravely upset about this as they spoke. 'Mathew didn't like the fact he was there all the time.' Mathew had confided to Lance, it was like Natasha and Colin were still 'happily married'. He was upset Natasha hadn't come good on her promise to get a divorce.

It was a heavy conversation but it allowed Mathew to get a load off his chest. For the first time, he'd confided in his closest friend about the true state of his relationship.

After they finished talking, Souzu and McDonnell drove Mathew to the Banksia Mental Health Unit at Tamworth Hospital, where he was admitted. Either on his way to hospital or shortly after his arrival, Natasha sent him a text after calling him more than a dozen times.

'Mat the kids and I love and miss you. Let me know what's happening please,' she wrote at 7.06 pm, some three hours after Mathew left Pandora.

This text – Hatfield later argues at the trial – was a 'transparently superficial response' to Natasha learning Mathew had been found safe. Her conduct earlier in the afternoon was 'more indicative of her attitude and feelings towards him', he argues, reminding the jury of how Natasha dismissed Mathew's suicide threat as 'one of his poofter hissy fits'.

'When the police come to Pandora, she speaks to them about the deceased in that way that she did. That nasty and callous way she spoke about him at that time, you might think that she was unconcerned for his welfare. Completely unconcerned,' Hatfield says, in his analysis of what happened that day.

'You might find the attitude displayed to police and Mr Partridge entirely consistent with that being unconcerned for him at all.'

Following Mathew's admission to the Banksia Mental Health Unit, he was assessed by a consulting psychiatrist, to whom he truly bared his soul.

As Dr Clive Stanton sits in the witness box, methodically detailing some of the trial's most disturbing evidence, I find myself gasping in parts – as do Mathew's aunt and uncle Elaine and John Schell, who are seated behind me.

I can only imagine how awful it would be for them, as family, to learn what Natasha was saying to Mathew behind closed doors before his suicide threat.

I met Elaine and John on the first day of the trial; I'd noticed them sitting in front of me during the opening addresses. Throughout the trial, we often sit near each other in the public gallery, discussing the evidence in the breaks. We also text each other if one of us hears a juror is sick, because the trial can't run without all 12 of them.

The retired couple, with three children of their own, catch the train to the city from their home in northern Sydney for almost every day of the trial. John, the brother of Mathew's mother Janet, is a former police officer, just as their father had been.

John and Elaine tell me stories about Mathew and the time they spent with him.

It's often just John, Elaine and me in the public gallery, listening as hundreds of lies unravel from Natasha's sticky webs of deception.

Today, we sit in collective shock as Dr Stanton gives evidence about the disturbing conclusions he drew following his consultation with Mathew after his suicide threat.

Clearly, the English-born doctor wants the jury to hear what he thinks really happened to Mathew. He speaks with a deep conviction, explaining a situation Mathew never could.

Medical evidence can have the effect of a sleeping pill on juries – and everyone in the courtroom – with doctors often speaking in clinical tones and jargonistic language that no one understands. Dr Stanton has the opposite effect, however; the jurors all sit a little straighter in their chairs after he's finished.

Referring to his original police statement and medical notes from the time, Dr Stanton outlines what Mathew told him during their 40-minute consultation at Banksia Mental Health Unit, at Tamworth Hospital, in June 2017.

Mathew told Dr Stanton his life changed significantly after his new partner, Natasha, and her three children, moved to Pandora. For the first time in his life, he was stressed about his finances and cash-flow.

It wasn't just the usual day-to-day costs of caring for a family; he was also responsible for paying off Natasha's debts. At the same time, she was burning through his cash, buying big-ticket items, such as a new horse float, for herself and her kids.

'He had never had previous financial problems . . . he was concerned she was spending an awful lot of his money and didn't know how to curb that behaviour,' Dr Stanton tells the jury.

On top of the money problems, Mathew confided, his relationship with Natasha was rapidly deteriorating.

'He said that things have been going downhill at home. He didn't know if he was really wanted at home. He didn't know if he was really wanted for the past two to three weeks.'

Mathew also confided that Natasha had recently bought a separate double bed to sleep in and was continually saying 'cruel things to him which played on his mind'.

'Cruel' doesn't go halfway to describing what the court hears next.

'She also hinted about the rafters in the shed and whether they would be high enough to hang himself,' Dr Stanton says.

It's a sickening revelation. Was this the only time Natasha goaded Mathew to kill himself?

The day prior to his suicide threat, Mathew explained that Natasha threatened to leave him following an argument about an ex-girlfriend. He spoke openly and with insight, Dr Stanton says, explaining how, erratically, he took a gun from the sheds. He thought hard about pulling the trigger.

'Mr Dunbar reported feeling emotionally manipulated by her, and that she had made suggestions to him about killing himself?' Hatfield asks.

'That is right,' Stanton agrees.

'Did he also tell you he took the gun and thought about killing himself, as she had suggested; however, when he spoke to his friend, Lance, he decided not to do it?'

'That is right.'

Mathew felt under extreme strain that afternoon, as Natasha barraged him with messages and 19 phone calls. In one of the texts, she told Mathew he was 'doing this for attention'.

'Mr Dunbar was relating to me his distress at receiving a number of text messages, which he relayed to me ... [they] seemed to be insinuating for him to take his own life or, certainly I guess, taking the Michael out of him or embarrassing him,' Dr Stanton says.

He says he formed the clinical opinion that Mathew was not suicidal or depressed, but a vulnerable man who had been emotionally exploited by his partner.

'I don't know if the jury are familiar with the term "gaslighting" but my view is that Natasha Darcy was manipulating Mr Dunbar and she was using the relationship with him to manipulate him, you know, threatening to leave him.' He pauses briefly.

'He didn't want her to leave because there were many good

things about the relationship, the children in particular. He loved the children, he enjoyed spending time with the children.' He then adds that Mathew had formed a strong bond with her children while helping to care for them during the 18 months she'd been 'away' (referring to her jail stint).

'When she returned, things seemed to deteriorate and she started to manipulate him and make him feel, you know, wondering whether he was wanted in the relationship, whether he was loved. I think he was stuck, he couldn't do with her, he couldn't do without her. I was concerned,' Dr Stanton says.

Mathew was also upset that Natasha's daughter had distanced herself from him, with Dr Stanton noting, 'The older daughter has not been very nice to him recently.'

'He appears to be a vulnerable isolated man that is in a relationship which is "particularly" exploitative, and I think he feels stuck. Without his partner, I suspect he feels that he has little point to life,' Dr Stanton wrote in his medical notes.

While Mathew was having his consultation with Dr Stanton, Natasha relayed quite a different story over the phone to another doctor in the Mental Health Unit.

Medical notes recorded that Natasha had 'grave concerns' for Mathew and that he'd previously harboured suicidal ideations. But Mathew never mentions previous thoughts of suicide to Dr Stanton, who believes Mathew was as honest as he could possibly be.

Over the phone, Natasha told the doctor Mathew had become withdrawn, and had also been on and off antidepressants since 2014.

'[She said] there were lots of problems with him. He can't have sex, doesn't relate to people, he has a visual disturbance and can't close his left eye, and says she has concerns about discharge.'

After overexaggerating Mathew's state of mental health, Natasha agreed to come in for a meeting with Mathew and his doctors the following day.

She does some research first.

At 8.30 pm that night, as Mathew lay in his hospital bed for a second night, Natasha sat down at the family's Apple computer and began another series of searches, looking up ways to 'overdose' and the drug 'sertraline' – a drug she knew Mathew was prescribed after being admitted to hospital. She also searched for 'Seroquel' – an antipsychotic drug that Natasha would later go to great lengths to find.

Apple computer searches, 14 June
- antidepressant types
- sertraline
- sertraline overdose
- Seroquel
- Seroquel suicide
- Seroquel overdose
- Seroquel overdose with alcohol
- taking Seroquel after drinking

After a late night of googling, Natasha drove to Tamworth the following day to meet Dr Stanton. He didn't mince his words as he explained his belief: her relationship with Mathew was the cause of his rapidly deteriorating mental state.

'I told her that I thought she was the cause of the problems and that she needed to stop manipulating Mr Dunbar in the way that she was,' he tells the jury.

Natasha repeated her 'grave fears' for Mathew to Dr Stanton, saying how he was 'extremely suicidal'.

'I formed the opinion that she was trying to exonerate herself for any responsibility for Mr Dunbar's recent deterioration and mental state. Her story didn't match the story Mr Dunbar had relayed to me himself,' Dr Stanton wrote in his police statement at the time.

Yet despite her concerns, Natasha then told Dr Stanton she was happy to take him home and care for him.

Dr Stanton agreed Mathew should be discharged, especially

because Mathew was adamant about not having any more suicidal thoughts and 'felt silly for what he had done'.

'Mr Dunbar didn't have a serious depressive illness. He was very much depressed in response to what was happening in his life at that time,' Dr Stanton says, keen to drive home the fact he did not believe Mathew was suicidal at the time of his death. 'I am the only psychiatrist that ever saw him. I can tell you now, he didn't have a significant mental illness.'

Once Mathew was home, it appears Natasha changed tack, momentarily abandoning suicide research to focus on another method of death, one she might have more control over.

She also left him – just two days after returning home from hospital – to fend for himself at Pandora, while she went on a road trip to Scone, in NSW's Upper Hunter region, for a horse event.

There, she investigated an animal sedative, most commonly used on rams, called acepromazine.

Natasha's iPhone 7 searches, 17–18 June
- ace horse sedative
- is aceptomaxine (sic) human
- ace dose
- how to give an intramuscular injection
- muscles inback (sic)

Upon returning to Walcha, she expanded on her research, using her own phone at 9.11 pm on 18 June to search 'muscle in back'. Mathew's phone was then used to find out more about the effects of acepromazine. Although these searches were on Mathew's phone, Hatfield argues, this was Natasha attempting to 'lay a false trail'.

Mathew's iPhone 6 searches, 18 June
- how long until ace works

- ace injection
- ace promazine under
- ace humans

Natasha's intrigue seemingly grew as she browsed the results of the searches. She didn't wait long for her thoughts to marinate, swinging into action in just 12 hours' time.

27

PRACTICE RUN

Nurse Sally Heazlett paces outside the Supreme Court, taking nervous drags of a cigarette on Darlinghurst Road as she waits for the sheriff to call her into the courtroom. She's travelled down from Walcha to give evidence. I'm surprised she's here rather than her parents-in-law Bill and Di Heazlett, who I know had a strong friendship with Mathew. They were family.

I wonder how she fits into the case and why the prosecution wants her here in person.

By the end of the day, her evidence will be some of the most crucial in the case. It provides a rare insight into how Mathew was feeling in the weeks before his death.

Sally knew Mathew for about 20 years. She was working at Walcha Hospital on the day he was admitted with a swollen leg and mysterious calf infection on 10 July, less than a month before his death.

In his final weeks, this leg injury caused Mathew much grief. Natasha has wielded this in her defence, repeatedly telling police how Mathew was severely depressed about his leg and how it might affect his ability to run Pandora.

Listening to what the prosecution argues happened to Mathew before his hospitalisation, I'm rocked to the core.

Hatfield lays bare a series of events in a painstaking analysis, meticulously unravelling Natasha's web of lies as he compares her phone and internet searches against what Mathew said to several other people, including Sally Heazlett.

Sally's mother-in-law Di Heazlett believed this all along. She told me her theory sitting at her kitchen table in Walcha, but I'd quickly dismissed it as something too fanciful, even for the likes of a murderous, pathological liar.

The Walcha Veterinary Clinic hadn't been open long when the phone rang at 9.05 am on Monday, 19 June 2017.

Vet nurse Meleika McKinnon answered the phone to hear Natasha's spritely voice. She was calling to book in one of Mathew's dogs to get desexed. So far, the conversation was pretty standard for Mel, but it was about to take a strange turn.

Towards the end of the call, Natasha casually threw in that she'd need to pick up some ram sedatives when she dropped off the dog. Mel was taken slightly aback – it's not something Natasha had ever asked for and not something she really had any use for.

Diligently, she told Natasha she'd need to speak to the person who'd be physically administering the sedative, i.e. Mathew, and that she also required the specific weights of the animals it would be used on.

'Oh, no worries,' Natasha responds coolly, abandoning the subject before hanging up.

The request didn't sit well with Mel – she knew Natasha had nothing to do with the sheep at Pandora and wondered why she'd ask for such a powerful sedative. She decided to tell vet Rachel Greig as soon as she could.

Undeterred by the setback, Natasha began to ask around other vets in the area. She was persistent, searching the internet before ringing another vet in Tamworth at 9.14 am. She called this vet again at 9.51 am.

When Natasha dropped off Mathew's dog for surgery at the Walcha Veterinary Clinic, she didn't mention her earlier request to Mel.

Vet Rachel Greig was keen to talk to Mathew about Natasha's request. However when he arrived to collect his dog, 'he didn't appear to have any idea what I was talking about,' Ms Greig explains, giving evidence via video link from Armidale courthouse.

'I was taken off guard when he was in the clinic and when he said, "No, he didn't need it," then I felt a responsibility to ring him and just follow up to make sure he was aware Natasha had ordered it and to clear up any confusion.'

Despite having just spoken to Mathew in person, Rachel rang him not long after he left the clinic. 'I'm confused,' she said to him on the phone. 'There is a note in the back that Natasha rang yesterday and asked for a ram sedative.'

'I don't need any ram sedative,' Mathew replied.

'That's really odd. I don't know what's going on?'

Mathew said he wasn't shearing at the moment and had no idea why Natasha would need it. He only had two rams on his property; he only needed sedatives when shearing annually in November. It was June, however, and he didn't use the sedatives for crutching – the process of shearing wool from around the tail and between the back legs of sheep.

Sensing there was something more sinister at play, Rachel phoned the police and told them she was worried about Natasha's request for sedatives; she later made a formal statement. 'I was very concerned. I couldn't think of any reason that she would have asked for it that was a legal reason.'

Completely oblivious to the growing suspicions of Walcha locals, about a week after her failed attempt to source sedatives from the Walcha Veterinary Clinic, Natasha tried her luck at North Hill Vet Clinic in Armidale.

During a phone call, she told employee Lucy Miller she wanted to purchase acepromazine for her horse to get it into a float and travel to Queensland. Elaborating on the lie, she explained she couldn't purchase any from her usual vet in Uralla because they don't do a lot of horse work. When owner and vet Sarah Butler heard about the request, it immediately raised a red flag. She knew for a fact that the vet at Uralla does a lot of work with horses. She rang Natasha back and left a message, saying she wouldn't supply her the drug, because it wasn't a sedative commonly used for floating horses and because Natasha was not a known client.

Completely undeterred by three knockbacks so far, Natasha continued to try her luck with more vets. On 27 June, she used her mobile to call Creeklands Vet Clinic in Armidale. The call lasted for 162 seconds.

Later that afternoon, while inside the farmhouse at Pandora, Natasha again consulted the family Apple computer, researching how a human could be injected with acepromazine. Aside from momentarily shifting focus to google 'hyaluronic mask' – a beauty product for ageing skin – her searches about acepromazine continue into the early hours of the morning.

Apple computer searches, 27 June
- acepromazine human
- acepromezene (sic) suicide
- ace injectable dose
- acepromazine dose humans
- acepromazine human overdose
- acepromazine recreational
- acepromazine
- acepromazine inject

'This is a search consistent with those [detailed] previously, consistent with looking to kill someone, for using it to murder someone with the acepromazine and giving it to a human,' Hatfield tells the jury, as he dissects Natasha's actions with microscopic attention.

The following morning, Natasha hopped into her car and drove to Creeklands Vet Surgery in Armidale, about a 45-minute drive from Walcha.

This time, her persistence paid off.

Alarmingly, she managed to get her hands on 100 millilitres of acepromazine after claiming she wanted it to float her horse 'Bugs'. She'd been given enough to sedate 25–40 horses. When asked for her details, she told a young woman at the front desk that her name was Natasha Pascoe and she lived 4 Daily Street, Walcha – a non-existent address.

Now she had the drugs she so desperately wanted, Natasha doubled down, consulting Google again to investigate their potential effects on humans.

Apple computer searches, 1 July, 11.38 pm, to 2 July, 12.51 am
- what would acepromazine do to a human
- acepromazine injection suicide
- acepromazine murder
- acepromazine humans
- acepromazine suicide dose
- acepromazine overdose in humans

On 3 and 4 July, just five days before Mathew is hospitalised with a calf muscle infection, her iPhone is used to search:

- leg muscle injection sites
- leg muscles
- Suicide porm [poem]

She also reads a search result titled '10 ways to make IM testosterone injections less painful'.

As these searches occurred, Mathew was telling people how his mood was improving. He was feeling much better in the weeks since his admission to the Banksia Mental Health Unit.

During a telephone check-up, he reported having no concerns or suicidal ideation to the community mental health team at Tamworth Hospital. The following day, on 7 July, he told his GP Dr Allen he had 'no thoughts of self-harm' and had talked at length with Lance about some of the issues that had caused him to feel depressed.

His improved mood was at odds with searches carried out on his phone later that night; Hatfield argues these searches were made by Natasha to lay a false trail.

Mathew's iPhone searches, 7 July, 6.25 pm to 8.12 pm
- can you inject Valium
- suicide poem
- muscles for injection
- calf muscle

These searches were made on a Friday evening; at this time, Mathew reported completely blacking out. While he could remember some point during the afternoon of Friday, 7 July, he did not regain his memory until waking in a haze with an alarmingly swollen leg on the Sunday morning. He'd lost at least a full day and now had a severe leg infection with no explanation as to how it occurred.

Following the mysterious blackout, Mathew texted his friend Michelle Bray: 'According to Tash I went for a walk Friday night, and have no recollection of doing it, and Saturday I don't remember but Tash tested me and said I had a temp of 39.'

Mathew told the same story to a leg surgeon, who assessed his injury at Tamworth Hospital.

'Poor recollection of Friday night and all of Sunday . . . according to wife,' said Dr Leibenson's handwritten notes from their consultation (perhaps meaning to say the Saturday).

'Went on one hour walk . . . Friday night and was in bed all day with fever at 39 degrees on Saturday. When patient woke on Sunday . . . pain and swelling from knee to ankle with pain weight bearing.'

During the period of Mathew's blackout, Natasha busied herself with yet another series of disturbing Google searches.

Natasha's iPhone 8 searches, 8 July
- no urine 24 hours
- what happens if you don't urinate coma
- don't urinate unconscious
- fainting and urinating on yourself
- acepromazine humans
- acepromazine mellow yellow
- acepromazine overdose

'So the deceased clearly reports he lost the whole day. He can't remember. This is on the accused's phone, she's searching those things. He's out of it, unconscious, in a coma. Does she call an ambulance? Does she call anyone? No. She's googling these terms. And you might think, she knows precisely what has been given or administered to him at that time,' Hatfield says, as he summarises Mathew's weekend of lost memory.

There's enough evidence, he argues, for the jury to find that Natasha carried out a 'dry run' before the murder. Natasha had sedated Mathew in some way before injecting his calf with acepromazine in the hope it would kill him – she'd even googled suicide poems in the event that her plan went all the way.

'That accounts for the fog he was in, his loss of over a day,' Hatfield says.

Adding weight to Hatfield's argument was the evidence of Mathew's treating GP and leg surgeon, who both tell the court his leg infection had possibly been caused by a needle stick.

*

Natasha marched purposefully towards the front desk of the emergency department at Walcha Hospital, leaving Mathew several metres behind, hobbling down the hallway with child-sized crutches.

Sally Heazlett could see that Mathew was in pain; his leg had ballooned out and it seemed agonising for him to walk. He was pale and slurred his speech.

'I went for a walk on Friday night, and I don't remember anything about Saturday,' Mathew told Sally.

Natasha chimed in. 'He doesn't remember anything because he had a really high temperature.'

'Yeah, I had a really high temperature,' Mathew agreed.

Sally asked, 'How do you know you had a high temperature?'

Because Natasha had told him, he said.

After Mathew was admitted to the ward, and Natasha left to collect some more clothes, Sally began to ask her old friend a series of questions as she filled out his paperwork.

They'd been close family friends for a long time, often catching up at Bill and Di Heazlett's place, just down the road from Pandora. Mathew adored her sons and spoiled them, even buying them an ice-cream and slushie machine for one Christmas.

Sally asked Mathew a series of standard questions, including if he'd had any mental health issues, but was taken aback when Mathew explained he'd thought about taking his life a few weeks previously.

She gently asked him some more questions, keen to know what he'd been thinking, but could sense his hesitation.

'If I tell you, do you have to write it down?' Mathew asked.

'Yes,' Sally replied.

'I won't tell you if you have to write it down,' he said stubbornly.

'Why is that a problem if I write it down?'

'I don't want Col to see it . . . I will only tell you as my friend, not as my nurse,' he said, referring to Colin, who worked at the ambulance station attached to the hospital.

Believing it was important to hear what Mathew wanted to say, she agreed not to record their conversation. Sally asked him why he would even begin to contemplate suicide, when he now had everything he'd ever wanted: a partner and children living with him.

'She won't stop spending my money. I could lose the property. I've told her she needs to stop but she won't stop, she keeps spending,' he says, the words cascading from his mouth.

'Is it time to leave her?' Sally gently asked.

'I don't want to lose the kids,' he replied.

Sally asked him if he was still thinking about hurting himself.

'No, I know I was stupid and it won't fix anything,' he told her.

Worried, Sally told him that, if he ever got to that point again, he needed to ring her, her husband Mike, or friends Bill or Lance.

'I don't care if it's 3 am in the morning, you come and see me.'

Mathew promised he would, before telling Sally to relay everything he'd told her to the close friends she had just mentioned. Ordinarily, he was fiercely private, but perhaps he had reached breaking point.

Shortly after dropping off Mathew at the hospital and telling Sally he'd a high temperature, Natasha went home and googled 'high temperature' as if to double check the story she'd told. Later that night, she looked up 'vagina picture', 'porn vagina' and 'porn hairy vagina', then browsed various results.

It's confronting to think Natasha looked up sexual material while Mathew was in hospital, suffering from a severe injury that she'd likely caused by poisoning him. The searches are similar to the highly sexual texts she'd sent several Walcha locals in the lead-up to attacking Colin and burning their home down.

Mathew was later transferred to Tamworth Hospital, where he spent the next three nights.

While there, he texted friend Michelle Bray, saying, 'Swelling is going down. Not sure what caused it.'

While Mathew was recovering in hospital, Natasha used her phone to take pictures of her face and breasts, then searched the terms 'porn rape', 'she has no other options but to be good' and 'this rape scene is a bloody mess'. Porn is also a subject Natasha, bizarrely, later raised in police interviews as part of her defence.

Back at the trial, Sally tells the court she went to see Mathew after his transfer to Tamworth Hospital. As gently as she could, Sally explained to him she was worried about his relationship with Natasha and asked if he thought it might be time to leave her.

'Yeah, I think you might be right,' Mathew said, offering a rare insight into how he was feeling not long before his death.

I wonder if he'd ever told Natasha this, or if she'd caught wind he was having second thoughts about the relationship. Would things have been any different? Did it speed up her plans?

Sally also asked him why Colin was always hanging around at the farmhouse.

'Col is always there. Natasha says she wants him to be involved in the boys' lives,' Mathew told her, adding that Natasha and Colin often went away for weekends, with him footing the bill.

Mathew had confided similar concerns about Natasha and Colin's relationship to Lance.

Again, I wonder if he ever raised this with Natasha and, if he did, whether it played a role in his death.

28
PLANNING

Laura Kate's lily-white skin makes the red tear-stained blotches across her face all the more noticeable. Although Justice Lonergan has given her a certificate to ensure she won't be criminally charged for any of her answers, she's clearly nervous.

Sitting in the public gallery, Elaine, John and I find ourselves turning to one another with wide eyes, as we listen to another chapter of Natasha's unimaginable furphies.

What the jury doesn't hear – so Natasha can get a fair trial – is that the pair met during a three-month program they'd completed after getting out of jail. The jury are simply told that they knew each other, mostly communicated on Facebook and Laura once drove out to Pandora to look at some puppies.

In an incredible tale, Natasha told Laura that Mathew was 'her gay business partner', but she and her three children shared a home with him. She also said Mathew only had six months to live because of an inoperable brain tumour. This tumour made it impossible for him to sleep. If that lie wasn't twisted enough, Natasha elaborated, telling Laura that Mathew didn't have strong-enough medication for his pain because doctors believed anything stronger than what they'd prescribed could cause his tumour to grow.

THE WIDOW OF WALCHA

These lies laid the foundations for Natasha to avoid suspicion when, eventually, she asked her friend to illegally source some hardcore prescription drugs as part of her latest murderous plan.

About a week before Mathew's death, Natasha googled 'painless methods of suicide' and 'where to buy drugs' late in the evening of 23 July 2017.

The following afternoon, she upped the ante, searching 'getting a vein', and 'how to make veins pop out to shoot up'. Off the back of these searches, she contacted Laura, knowing she had connections who could help her source what she wanted.

The following set of messages are copied and given to each of the jurors to read; they detail Natasha's request for drugs to help Mathew sleep.

Natasha and Laura Kate Facebook messages, 25 July, 11.47 am to 1.13 pm
Natasha: Ask about the sedatives too
Laura: My besties got some Seroquel. Did you want to try them? Theyre antipsychotics technically but I used them to get to sleep in jail
Natasha: Hell yeh! Last time I gave Him them he slept well.
Laura: Ok cool. Shouldve let me know caus ehe just chucked out a full box of them cause hes doesnt take them anymore lol. Dunno if he still haa a prescription
Natasha: Pleeeeeade try and see if he does
Laura: He has 4 Seroquel. Theyre pretty strong though. 300mg. and fast release so thats cool.
Natasha: Serequel will be great
Laura: Ok cool. Can get paliperidone too. Its a different antipsych and ive never tried it so cant really tell you what theyre like. But my mate says they make him sleepy.
Natasha: Anything that will make him sleep is great. I'll take it all

Natasha: What do I owe for the pills? Just so I can have the cash on me.
Laura: Theres a full box of paliperidone. so 28. And 4 of the 300mg ceroquel
Natasha: Is he happy with $100
I need to go by 2 so I can get home for the kids.

Not long after their Facebook exchange, Natasha met Laura in the car park of Aldi at Armidale, where she handed over $100 in cash. In return, she was given the paliperidone and Seroquel. That afternoon, she popped into Creeklands Vet Clinic (where she got the ram sedative from a month prior) and bought an additional needle and syringe for $2.80.

With her purchases secured, Natasha drove back to Walcha. That evening, she searched more about the paliperidone and Seroquel she now had in her possession.

Natasha's iPhone 7 searches, 25 July, 5.52 pm to 7.32 pm
- paliperidone suicide
- overdose paliperidone
- can you inject paliperidone
- can you inject paliperidone tablets
- Seroquel
- Seroquel overdose
- how many Seroquel to overdose and die

Hatfield tells the jury, during his summary of all the evidence, it's clear Natasha bought the drugs to use on Mathew. 'So that is just after she has got them from [Laura Kate] who she told she was getting them to help the deceased sleep, but she has purchased them and googling on her phone "how many Seroquel to overdose and die". We say the inference is clear as to the purpose she got them, the purpose for which she got them and what she intended to do with them.'

On the final weekend of Mathew's life, Natasha decided to take her daughter on a camping trip to Dorrigo.

Although Mathew's leg was improving, he was still struggling. He was left behind at Pandora with Colin and the two boys.

Once away from the property, Natasha was glued to her phone, googling dozens of methods of death and suicides. It was Sunday afternoon when she finally found what she was looking for. After searching 'what to inject to kill yourself', she discovered a website where various people posted about methods of suicide. Scrolling down the posts, her eyes hovered over one written by someone based in Los Angeles, who posted a link to a blog recommending helium as the best method. From this point onwards, all her searches focused on helium.

Not long after reading this page, she googled 'suicide helium', 'spotlight helium' and 'gas bottle'. She then researched how to delete her web history and googled 'after suicide is there a crime scene'.

After returning to Pandora, she spent the next 24 hours researching her plan – where she could buy helium and equipment.

On 30 July, two days before Mathew's death, Natasha used her phone to search 'suicide bag' and 'helium hire Tamworth' at 1.20 pm, then switched to the Apple computer to look up 'helium gas Tamworth' and 'helium uses' at 2.12 pm. In between the searches, she texted her daughter about moving her horse to another paddock.

While Natasha was busy reading about helium, Mathew rang her mobile at 2.13 pm and 2.14 pm, but Natasha ignored his calls. Undeterred by her phone ringing, Natasha used the landline at Pandora to call Supagas at Tamworth.

Administration clerk Emma Worrell remembers the phone call well; she'd only worked at Supagas for one month when Natasha rang. She's pretty sure the woman on the other end of the phone had said she was from the *Northern Daily Leader*, the local paper.

'She told me she wanted a 3.5 cubic metre cylinder for an event she was holding . . . she needed it to be high purity,' Ms Worrell tells the court during her evidence. 'Usually, someone would tell me they would need a certain number of balloons and I would tell them what size they would need,' but she remembers Natasha mentioning needing 'high purity' several times during their brief conversation.

Despite learning they only stocked balloon-grade helium, Natasha ordered it, telling Ms Worrell that a man by the name of Mathew Dunbar would come in tomorrow and pay for it.

Increasingly paranoid about her plan for the following day, Natasha again used her phone to research whether she could cover her tracks. She deleted her latest round of searches, thinking there was no way anyone could recover what she'd wiped.

Natasha's iPhone 7 searches, 31 July, 7.42 pm to 8.07 pm
- can police see past web history
- can your internet history be tracked by internet provider
- how long do internet providers keep history

She then switched to the Apple computer to search 'helium tamworth' and 'suicide bag' – possibly to lay a false trail and claim that Mathew was researching his death the night before his apparent suicide.

29

THE FINAL DAY

Detective Senior Constable Graham Goodwin sits in the witness box, almost two months after the trial first started. He's been involved in more than a dozen murder investigations during his 35-year career. Up until now, Goodwin has spent most of the trial sitting outside the courtroom. He sat in court for the opening addresses, but has not been allowed to sit in court until his evidence is completed at the end of the trial.

Outside of court, he has helped to coordinate witnesses, especially from Walcha, making sure they were at court on the days they needed to be there. It's a long time to sit by yourself, wondering what's going on with the case you've worked on for four years.

In a fairly standard practice, Hatfield calls Goodwin into the witness box to formally tender a series of exhibits in court: crime-scene photos, statements, search-warrant videos, triple-0 calls and electronically recorded police interviews with Natasha.

Today, Goodwin sits in the witness box as Hatfield plays a compilation of security footage, which shows Natasha and Mathew at various locations across Tamworth on the final day of Mathew's life. While I've studied many pictures of Mathew, I've never seen any videos of him. I'm anxious to see what the footage shows. His aunt

Elaine sits behind me, close enough for me to hear her whisper, 'Oh my goodness, Mathew,' as we watch him walk onto the screen.

In the footage, Natasha strides down the corridor of Tamworth Hospital, a bright pink handbag slung over shoulder. Mathew is hobbling on crutches 10 metres behind her. He looks smart, wearing a grey-and-rainbow striped sweat with dark navy jeans, as he struggles to catch up with Natasha. Despite being left behind, he's smiling as he heads down the hallway, his transition lenses darkening from the glare of the bright white hospital lights.

It's about 9.50 am on 1 August 2017; Natasha leaves Mathew alone to wait in the corridor for his scheduled consultation with orthopaedic surgeon Dr Max Leibenson. He'd made the appointment to check on the progress of the mysterious leg infection which had landed him in hospital a couple of weeks back.

The footage shows Natasha power-walking into the cafeteria and ordering coffees for herself and Mathew. A few minutes later, she walks over to a newspaper stand and digs out her white iPhone from her handbag. She looks up a gas supply company and 'helium hire Tamworth' and finds the Supagas website, which advertises 'High Purity Helium 3.5m^3 Cylinder'. The prosecution argues that Natasha takes a screenshot of the advertised gas cylinder and sends it to Mathew.

Presumably, she's spoken to him about hiring helium – for one reason or another – and sends him the screenshot to indicate she's found somewhere they can hire it from. While she wants the helium, she also wants Mathew to be seen picking it up. Natasha then returns to Mathew before they both attend the appointment with Dr Leibenson at 10.30 am.

When Dr Leibenson first assessed Mathew's leg in July, he was unsure whether he'd ever regain proper movement. Amputation was a worst-case scenario but still a possibility. Mathew responded well to intravenous antibiotics, however, and by the end of his hospital stay, it looked likely that his leg would improve with physio.

'I advised him that I was extremely happy with his progress, and although his ankle was stiff, he was still only in the initial stages of recovery and it was likely to improve further with physiotherapy,' Dr Leibenson said in his police statement. At no point during the appointment did Mathew appear distressed.

Relieved to hear his leg was on the mend, Mathew agreed to return in six months' time for a follow-up appointment.

Natasha is smiling and appears to be chatting to Mathew as they walk out of the hospital and towards the car park. After dropping off a quad bike for repair, Natasha drives to Supagas and sits in the car while Mathew goes into the store. He pays $140 for a cylinder on his credit card and leaves a $100 cash deposit.

Manager Craig Smith helps to load the cylinder onto the ute while Mathew gets onto the tray to tie it down, explaining it's for 'a party'.

Now lunchtime, the pair drive to Gusto café in Tamworth. Security footage captures Natasha reverse-parking the ute on Peel Street with the gas bottle strapped to the tray.

While Natasha takes an outside seat at the café, Mathew goes inside and orders their lunch, leaving Natasha to peruse her phone. She brazenly uses this alone time to again look up ways to carry out her deadly plan.

For the six minutes she's alone, she searches 'suicide bag' and 'DIY Exit Bag Instructions', before browsing YouTube videos titled 'party store suicide bag', 'Helium Filled Exit Bag' and 'Man commits suicide by inhaling helium gas'.

While Natasha is deep in her research, security footage captures the moment Mathew returns to their outside table, using Facebook to check in to Tamworth Base Hospital ER.

'Going to be a long recovery, may need surgery in six months' time to walk properly but may have a limp for life. Infection has destroyed a fair bit of the calf muscle,' he posts.

Meanwhile, sitting right beside him, Natasha googles 'suicide bag connect helium' then watches an instructional video twice. This is the method she later uses to kill Mathew.

There's no sign that Mathew is aware of Natasha's plan. After lunch, he hops back into the car and makes a phone call to order fuel for the property on the drive home. He also calls a Tamworth nursery about buying some pear trees, while Natasha drives back towards Pandora. They arrive home at about 3.30 pm. It's an ordinary afternoon to everyone but Natasha.

After Mathew dutifully picks up Natasha's three children from the bus stop after school, he heads into town by himself to pick up groceries from the Walcha IGA. At the check-out, he tells Kim McKinnon about his doctor's appointment: his leg is improving and he's hopeful physiotherapy will help to restore the muscle in his leg.

Neighbour Ross King is the last person to hear Mathew's voice outside of Pandora, with the pair sharing a friendly call at 6.46 pm. In his evidence, Ross tells the jury the same thing he told me nearly four years ago: Mathew was making plans, they shared a few laughs and there was nothing to suggest anything was wrong.

The last sign of Mathew being conscious is just before 7 pm. He's a regular Facebook user, who routinely likes and replies to every comment made on his profile. In what are to be some of his final words, he replies to a comment made about his earlier Facebook check-in to Tamworth Hospital.

'Went very close to having leg cut off just above knee. Most of the calf now dead. Have to wait for it to scar,' he writes at 6.56 pm. Then nothing.

Three people respond to his post, at 8.08 pm, 9.46 pm and 11.23 pm. Mathew doesn't like or reply to any of these comments, or respond to a private message sent to him at 9 pm.

Sometime before or after dinner, Natasha prepares Mathew's final drink, pulverising a mixture of sedatives and prescription drugs in a Nutribullet. She pours the thick, pink smoothie into a tumbler. The sedative cocktail contains the Seroquel she bought from Laura Kate; clonidine, a drug prescribed to one of her sons; the sedative temazepam; and a quantity of acepromazine, the animal sedative she'd struggled to obtain.

At some point, Mathew downs the concoction, leaving a chunky residue at the bottom of the glass, which is later found in the dishwasher.

After stripping down to his boxer shorts – on an icy winter's night in Walcha – he falls asleep, heavily sedated.

Mathew is most likely out cold when Natasha contemplates whether she should use the paliperidone she'd purchased from Laura Kate at the same time she got the Seroquel.

'Can you inject paliperidone,' she types into Google at 10.27 pm.

As she moves about the house, carrying out the final steps of her plan, she sets up a false alibi, messaging Belinder Wauch on Facebook between 11.25 pm and 12.31 am, pretending she's still awake after being relegated to the couch.

Either questioning herself about what she's just done, or what she is about to do, she consults Google one last time at 12.36 am, using Mathew's phone to search 'is helium traceable autopsy'.

Her iPhone records the steps she takes around the house, moving a total of 21 metres between 1.10 am and 1.17 am, at a time Natasha later tells police she is asleep.

Once Mathew is sedated, Natasha attaches a piece of shower hose to the helium tank, which is positioned next to the bed where Mathew is sleeping. She then inserts the end of the hose into a plastic bag, which has been secured over Mathew's head with a white strip of elastic. The gas bottle is turned on; helium fills the bag. The helium displaces the oxygen in Mathew's lungs. He dies by asphyxiation.

Using Mathew's phone, she calls triple-0 at 2 am; lies fall off her tongue as she sobs and gasps for air on the phone to the operator. She claims Mathew is warm and acts out resuscitation over the phone for 15 minutes, cutting off the operator twice.

'He's warm . . . he's still warm. My ex-husband is a paramedic, he knows where to go . . . he's not breathing, no . . . he's cold, I can't get a pulse.'

Mathew is unresponsive when Colin and colleague Marion Schaap arrive first on the scene at 2.17 am to find Natasha doing CPR.

30

NATASHA'S FIRST INTERVIEW

It's strange to hear Natasha's sickly sweet voice, nearly four years since we spoke over the farmgate at Pandora. In the dark courtroom, her voice blares out of the speakers as the jury listens to her first interview, recorded just hours after Mathew's death. Elaine, John and I are all wearing headphones that the court officer has provided to help us catch every word. We all turn to look at each other when Natasha brings up John's name, especially because they've never met.

Combined with her chipper tone and sporadic chuckling, the lies make for excruciating listening. After the hour-long recording is finished, we all sit stunned in our chairs. I wonder if I misheard much of what Natasha said, because I can't believe some of the words coming out of her mouth.

For Goodwin, sitting opposite Natasha in the loungeroom of Colin Crossman's home in Walcha, less than 12 hours after Mathew's death, it's a stranger-than-fiction scenario. He last set eyes on her back in 2009, when he assisted in charging her at Nowra Police Station with Colin's attempted murder.

He does well to maintain his composure, telling Natasha that he and his colleague, Detective Senior Constable Rebecca McKenzie from

Tamworth detectives, are investigating Mathew's death on behalf of the coroner. He asks for her permission to record their interview on a handheld recorder.

Goodwin starts by asking her to explain the circumstances of Mathew's death – if she can. Not even a second passes before she launches into a well-rehearsed monologue about Mathew's depression.

'Mathew suffers from depression,' she says, with next to no emotion. 'He tried to kill himself a number of weeks ago. Um, the police took his guns off him. He then tried to overdose on pills that the doctor gave him.

'In regards to his leg. Um, yesterday we went to see the orthopaedic surgeon at Tamworth . . . and the news wasn't great. They said the majority of his muscle was dead, the calf muscle . . . he'd never get, he wouldn't get much movement than what he had, which was a huge limp. Um and he'd never be able to do any exercise or anything like that again. So, of course, that sent the depression like, right down.'

She scrunches her forehead and looks up to the ceiling. It's as though she's mentally ticking off a checklist.

'I spoke to him. I was up last night for a number of hours, just talking to him [saying] "It's not that bad. We can sell the farm,"' she says.

Goodwin doesn't ask any questions.

She keeps talking. 'Last night, he just asked to be alone . . . and he had said . . . we'd be better off without him.'

Natasha briefly outlines what happened on the night, and how she found Mathew, which she will elaborate on in great detail during a formal interview in two days' time.

Throughout the informal chat with Goodwin and McKenzie – and despite the death of her partner less than 12 hours ago – she persistently giggles and makes trivial small talk.

'You've probably seen my coffee machine,' she blurts out, knowing her home is a crime scene, crawling with police.

'Youse can give it a whirl, if you like. Just press a button and a cappuccino comes out!' she says with a nervous laugh.

At another point in the interview, she appears far more concerned about her pets than Mathew's recent death.

'This sounds a bit odd, but were you just at the house?' she asks Goodwin.

'Yeah,' he says.

'The . . . the ginger cat, he's okay?'

'He's still, yeah, he's still walking around.'

'The kids are devastated. They're so worried about the dogs and cats.'

Goodwin explains it will take some time before police have finished searching the house and surrounding property.

This causes the first note of distress in Natasha's voice. 'But again, all that's normal, isn't it? In an investigation like this?'

'Yeah, yeah, yeah. Yep,' he says. Then he asks her a series of questions about what happened on the night.

Natasha isn't interested in answering his questions, however, veering away from the events of the night as quickly as she can.

'I was telling you before about, um, Mat's uncle, that he hasn't had anything to do with . . . that [he] used to be a policeman,' she says, referring to John, who's seated behind me in the public gallery.

'Okay,' says Goodwin, bracing himself.

'And he's, um . . . been ringing everybody, telling them that I gave Mat an overdose . . . John . . . his mother's brother. It's . . . upsetting . . . someone who doesn't know me goes around and says something like that.'

Goodwin makes no promises to help her; he fobs her off by saying whatever happens will depend on where the investigation heads. He's keen to ask her something he already knows, but asks her straight out anyway: is she the main beneficiary of Mathew's estate?

She stumbles a little at first.

'No. Well, we've been together for three years, but I'm not sure who the beneficiary is. I know Lance is the executor,' she says coyly.

She continues to talk unprompted, quickly spinning a web around herself.

'I was also supposed to be an executor, and he had the will signed up and everything and I had to sign it . . . we just never got around to doing it . . . so I wouldn't think that would be . . . valid. Um, as far as I know. Lance thinks differently, but I don't think that's the case.'

Again, with no questions asked, she continues.

'TAS . . . The Armidale School is his main beneficiary. And I think Bill Heazlett, who lives down across the road and down a bit, he was supposed to get land in the will.'

'Do you know how much it's worth?' Goodwin asks.

'No idea . . . that's the boys' stuff!' she says with a giggle. 'We've got three thousand sheep, I know that.'

As Goodwin reaches what he thinks is the home stretch of this informal chat, things take an unexpected turn. Having spoken at some length about how depressed and suicidal she believed Mathew was, Natasha drops a peculiar bombshell.

'Mathew's gay – just to add another angle,' she scoffs.

Goodwin is keen to veer away from the subject, asking instead about Mathew's last movements, but Natasha is eager to bring up her claims of Mathew's homosexuality, planting the seeds to later use as her defence.

'I think he had a lot of issues due to that. Like, that was a lot of his depression . . . you know, being gay. One of his friends committed suicide recently, Craig Hoy . . . he was a really good friend of his and he was gay. And that really . . . um . . . Mat didn't get out of bed for about a week,' she says with some hesitation.

After a series of questions about her and Mathew's movements on the last day of his life, she mentions they'd stopped in at Woolworths.

'Mat loves grocery shopping. That's one of the things I love about [him], he's a great shopper,' she says. She pauses for dramatic effect before saying, 'Loved.'

'Oh, he's just so good, and he can always find bargains and every-thing and, yeah, it must be the gay in him!'

Lost for words, Goodwin looks to McKenzie. 'Um, do you have anything?'

'I don't think so,' McKenzie replies, but a few seconds later probes Natasha about the gas bottle purchase.

Towards the end of the interview, Goodwin explains they will need to conduct a more formal interview with her at Walcha Police Station, once she's spoken to her lawyer. He also would like her permission to examine her phone, at some point, to get a sense of the sort of things Mathew was saying and doing in the lead-up to his death.

'Oh, gee, I'm not good at keeping texts,' she says, scrolling through her phone before confirming she's got no messages from Mathew. She's deleted them all.

'As I said, sometimes, they can pull them up,' Goodwin explains, referring to forensic specialists.

'You mean the ones I've deleted? she asks.

'Past ones, yeah,' Goodwin says as he ends the interview at 1.38 pm, leaving Natasha on unsure footing.

After Goodwin and McKenzie left, Natasha was on her own; Colin had taken the kids out to get some food.

The following day, 3 August, McKenzie dropped in at Colin's house to ask Natasha whether she would be willing to provide her mobile phone to be downloaded. She said her lawyer advised her to let police see her text messages and call logs, but not her internet history.

'I've got nothing to hide, but I've been burned before by my browser history being misconstrued and used against me,' she said, possibly referring to the time her work computer was used to search 'poisons to kill' and 'how mortgage insurance works' before the 2009 house fire.

'That's up to you at the moment, but we would definitely be interested in looking at your browser history,' McKenzie said.

'I guess if I googled "how to kill your boyfriend" or something, like, that it would be of interest,' she said, in a bizarre attempt to make a joke.

Natasha told McKenzie she would talk to her lawyer about handing over her phone.

As soon as McKenzie was out the door, Natasha turned to her phone.

Natasha's iPhone 7 searches, 3 August
- what can the police get iphone
- can police access deleted web hidtory

About an hour later, at 3 pm, two more detectives called in at Colin's house to return his mobile phone, which he'd willingly given them earlier. Natasha was home, too, and the officers talked to her about whether she'd thought some more about handing over her phone for examination.

'I'm happy for you to have a look at my phone logs and text messages, but that's all. I don't want you looking at my browser history . . . It's just I have been set up in the past by police misinterpreting my browser history,' she said.

As soon as they leave, she again turns to Google.

Natasha's iPhone 7 searches, 3 August, 3.06 pm to 4.17 pm
- can police access deleted browser
- police want to copy iphone content
- cell phone data extraction
- how long does forensics take
- how long does it take to examine a crime scene

She gave police her phone at about 5 pm, giving them permission to download her text messages, photographs and contacts, but not her internet history. It was returned to her within a couple of hours.

Knowing she would soon be interviewed by police, as soon as she got her phone back she began to prepare answers. In one of the most telling searches, she looked up 'Craig Hoy Walcha' at 6.57 pm and again at 7.03 pm.

She'd already planted the seed in her first chat with police, linking Craig Hoy's death to Mathew's depression.

Defence barrister Janet Manuell raises Craig Hoy's death repeatedly throughout the trial, suggesting that Craig and Mathew had been in a close, sexual relationship. That it's possible Mathew had suicided, unable to escape the grief caused by Craig's death. Manuell probes nearly every witness from Walcha – ad nauseam – about their relationship, insinuating they shared a level of intimacy, but she never adduces any evidence to suggest the pair had an intimate relationship.

It's possible Natasha thought about using Craig's death as a defence, months before Mathew's death, revealing to anyone she could about how depressed Mathew was, even people she wasn't especially close to. During the trial, Hatfield reads the following message aloud to the jury:

'Mats been really depressed lately and not caring so much about the sheep. [My daughter] and I have been going around looking after them. With Craig's death he's even worse,' she wrote to Belinder Wauch, in a message on 15 April 2017.

'This tone of communication, we say, that she was happy to tell even casual acquaintances such as a friend she had in relation to horses – Ms Wauch – about his mood and the like, and we say, indicating or laying a trail for being prepared for Mr Dunbar's death, and she was prepared to breach his confidences and tell people about his [mental] state, and say things about his state and to exaggerate the condition he was in,' Hatfield argues.

Natasha was meticulous in setting up her defence, researching suicide methods on Mathew's phone whenever she could get her hands on it. If she was concerned about Mathew's mental health, Hatfield argues, she certainly didn't show it when she abandoned Mathew in the days just after Craig Hoy's death, going on a road trip without him.

Upon her return, she doggedly pursued her research about suicide, using the family computer so she could later argue it was Mathew.

Apple computer searches, 18 April

- how to commit suicide
- how many tablets suicide
- sedative suicide
- cyanide pill
- overdose pain killers
- lethal dose of clonidine
- Valium suicide

Hatfield goes to painstaking measures to point out, however, that Natasha first researched the subject of suicide the day *before* Craig Hoy took his life, searching 'suicide' and 'drugs used in suicide' on 10 April. These searches came following two months of Google searches researching ways to kill.

'So, any suggestion that the searches in suicide were those of the deceased, after the death of Craig Hoy, or somehow that instigated or triggered him making those searches, would appear not to be borne out by this analysis, because the first search in relation to suicide happens to be the day before,' Hatfield says, picking apart Natasha's defence in his closing arguments.

'There was a reference to them being "gentle souls" that had found each other in Walcha. You might think, overall, that the relationship was certainly close, but not some specially close relationship that deeply affected Mr Dunbar in the way that was contended, or which drove him to a particular result or conduct,' Hatfield tells the jury, adding that it is a matter for them to decide the extent of their relationship.

'You heard a lot of questions and examination in this trial directed at the deceased's sexuality. You might think [this was] an attempt to connect that with some type of depression. Our submission is that you will find that is not borne out by the evidence at all in this trial. That's the accused bringing up that angle as another reason, in addition to the leg being so bad, in addition to supposed problems with his mother, now, his sexuality apparently is another thing that troubles him so much that he would have reason to kill himself. We say [this is] all untrue, all completely untrue.'

Having done all the groundwork in the months before Mathew's murder, Hatfield argues, her searches about 'Craig Hoy' indicate she was researching and preparing for her interview with police the following day.

31

NATASHA'S SECOND INTERVIEW

Natasha looks down solemnly at her hands resting in her lap; her bright red nails are curled tightly around a crumpled tissue as she waits for her interview to begin at Walcha Police Station. It's 4 August, two days after Mathew's death, and she's squeezed between Goodwin on her right and Detective Sergeant Peter Rudens on her left, a homicide detective who's driven up from Sydney.

The three of them sit at a desk in a cramped office; a video recorder is set up at one end to capture the ultimately three-hour-long interview. Goodwin opens a plastic folder and states for the record that he and Rudens are interviewing Natasha as part of their ongoing investigations into Mathew's suspicious death.

Natasha has morphed into a grieving widow. She can barely manage to talk; a far cry from the giggles and small talk during her first interview at Colin's house, 48 hours ago.

She's about to say some horrible things, using Craig Hoy's suicide for her own gain, talking about his death flippantly and without any regard for his life. She's just as callous in her attitude towards Mathew, mocking him just days after his death.

Wrapping a grey knitted cardigan around herself, she begins to speak in a barely audible voice. She claims, on the morning of his death, Mathew received bad news from his orthopaedic surgeon. She claims it was possible he could still lose his leg because of the mysterious infection that had taken hold in mid-July: 'Mat sort of came out of there feeling pretty bad.' She then lists all the apparent problems with his leg, including that he would never walk properly again.

Following the consultation, she and Mathew dropped off a quad bike for repair in Tamworth. 'Um, then I'm pretty sure the next stop was, he wanted to go and get a gas bottle. I was assuming it was for the welding.'

Mathew mentioned needing to pick up a gas bottle when they were at the hospital, she tells the officers.

As though a lightbulb flicks on, Natasha's voice rises a few octaves as she excitedly asks Goodwin and Rudens if she can show them something. She reaches for her bright pink handbag and rustles through it before retrieving her phone. She flicks through her camera roll.

'I was looking for some photos of Mathew to put on the internet and I found, here, these two photos here.' She holds out her phone, pointing to screenshots of gas bottles from the Supagas website.

She claims Mathew's phone often had internet problems, and he was using her phone when she went to buy them coffees from the hospital's cafeteria, just before his leg consultation.

'Um, I think I left my whole handbag with him actually,' she says, unaware that she, her handbag and her phone were captured together on security footage just before the screenshots were taken.

Natasha tells Goodwin and Rudens that she's showing them the screenshots of the gas bottles because she has nothing to hide. She's sure they would have already seen them when they downloaded the contents of her phone the night before.

After running some errands in Tamworth, she outlines her version of events leading up to Mathew's death.

In the evening, the whole family feasted on sausage sandwiches – Mathew had four because 'he's a big guy'– washed down with a bottle of red they shared, a blend maybe.

Natasha appears confused about what happened next. It's as if she's trying to decide which path to take in a choose-your-own-adventure book. Eventually, she settles on a story in which she did some housework while Mathew watched a cooking show in bed.

At about 8.30 pm, she watched a recorded episode of *Top of the Lake* and then, at some point, Mathew got out of bed, had a shower and walked into the kitchen to talk to her.

'He was concerned because he said, "I'll have to sell the property." I've been running the property the last couple of months, as in the sheep. I bought (sic) them in for crutching and all that sort of thing, and I said to him, "Look, Mat, I can continue doing that with you telling me what to do. We don't have to make any decisions now . . . let's just see what happens," and I thought he was quite happy with that. I honestly thought that he'd agreed . . .' She trails off.

Towards the end of their heart-to-heart in the kitchen, Natasha says Mathew asked her to sleep in another room, because she'd accidentally kicked him in his sore leg a couple of nights prior.

'So he'd said to me . . . "I don't want you kicking me again,"' she tells Rudens and Goodwin with an animated laugh.

'Oh no, he said, "Well, can you just sleep on the lounge 'cause I really just need some alone time," which happens every now and again. He used to say that to me every now and again, and that was fine. He was a really private person.'

After being relegated to the couch, she claims she watched another episode of *Top of the Lake* while messaging her friend Belinder Wauch until late in the night.

'I remember we were laughing, because she was actually on the lounge as well,' she says, then eagerly reads aloud their message exchange.

In her version of events, she'd fallen asleep right after sending her last message to Belinder at 12.31 am but, at some point, woke up and decided to throw some more wood on the fire.

'The smoke alarm started going off, so I've turned . . . I found Mathew's crutch . . . I used his crutch to turn both alarms off.'

Feeling the need to tell Mathew what had happened, she recalls opening the door of their bedroom and, guided by the moonlight, walking around to his side of the bed and shaking him.

'I shook him. I said, "Mat" and he didn't answer me, and I thought, "Oh," so that's when I turned his lamp on.'

Later on in the interview, she remembers things a little differently.

'As soon as I walked in, I could hear [the sound of gas dispersing] and that's why I turned the light on. I wouldn't have worried about waking him up . . . I would've left but then I heard the noise.'

'Obviously, he had a bag over his head . . . I just sort of grabbed the bag and then something was sort of there around his throat, so I picked that up, too,' she says, her tempo increasing as she alternates between glancing at Goodwin and Rudens.

'So the first thing I did was rip the bag up . . . I pulled his arm out straight [and] I went to start compressions. I suppose I realised that he's put a tube up and he tried to kill himself. I didn't think he was dead, especially when I started the compressions. I actually started getting a bit of hope because he felt warm, so I thought that "Hey, we can do this."'

When paramedics Colin Crossman and Marion Schaap arrived, they took over doing CPR but, after about 20 minutes it was clear there was nothing they could do.

'Col turned around and said, "He's dead, Tash." And I got upset, I screamed at them to keep going and he said, "No, we're not keeping going," so I pushed them out of the way and I was gunna keep going, but two of the SES guys pulled me back,' she says, referring to the State Emergency Service volunteers who had also arrived on the scene.

It's about halfway through the three-hour interview. Goodwin is keen to move away from the night in question and probe Natasha more about her relationship with Mathew.

'I would say that Mat and I had a relationship. A normal marriage-type relationship without the sex,' she says in a matter-of-fact tone.

'Okay, yeah. And the reason for that was, why is that?' Goodwin asks, clearly uncomfortable with the subject.

'Mat preferred ... sexually preferred men to women,' she says, without offering any explanation why she was in a long-term relationship with him.

'Mat had even seen a sex counsellor in Sydney, um, to change the brain and the way he's thinking but ... it doesn't matter how hard you try to be straight, it just was never gunna happen,' Natasha says, laughing as she looks at Goodwin, hoping for a glimpse of encouragement.

He's doesn't give her any; instead, he is keen to ask her what Mathew was like when they first met and if she'd known about any problems he'd had. Appearing to wince with embarrassment, Natasha talks about Mathew being emotionally sensitive. Her high-pitched tone and excited pace are not dissimilar to those of a schoolgirl, venting about an annoying boyfriend in the canteen line.

'Mat ... he's a really sweet guy, but he's always had ... he just hurts more than normal. I could make him cry before I can make the kids cry. Not that I try hard but ... he was very sensitive. Things hurt him double what they'd hurt a normal person.'

'Yeah ... yeah,' says Goodwin, noncommittally.

Keen to fill the silence, Natasha laughs, talking more about Mathew's sensitive nature. 'Sometimes, I actually thought he had the mentality of an eight-year-old when it came to the emotional side of things. He just used to have his little two-year-old tantrums.' Again, she says this with a laugh, like she finds Mathew's sensitive nature funny.

Perhaps realising she isn't winning any fans, Natasha sits upright, pressing the reset button on her tone and tact. As Goodwin and Rudens listen patiently, Natasha describes how Mathew would lovingly get her car out of the garage each morning and park it alongside the house, ready for her to drive the kids to school.

'He was just the sweetest, most loving man you'll ever meet.'

Knowing Natasha had said some strange things about her relationship in her first interview, two days prior, Rudens steps in to ask her more questions. 'Just on that front, I know we've gone through your relationship before, but how would you describe it? Were you in a de facto relationship?'

'Yeah, yep,' she says, nodding.

'But no sex?'

'No sex.'

'Were you in love?'

'I loved him yeah, but more of a best-friend sort of love, um, yeah.'

'Were you planning to get married?'

'Um, yeah, yeah, he talked about that. We weren't engaged or anything like that. He was looking at rings, but I sort of avoided . . . I've been married enough, thanks!' she says in an attempt at humour.

Rudens and Goodwin remain stony-faced.

'He loved the kids?' Rudens asks.

'Oh yeah . . . you would never ask for a better stepfather for your kids. He was good with them and he was good with Colin, too.'

In a welcome line of questioning for Natasha, Goodwin asks her if, early on in the relationship, she'd had any concerns about his mental health.

Not even a tenth of a second passes before Natasha answers, nodding enthusiastically.

'Yes, he did tell me he had seriously thought about suicide a number of times and I thought, "Well, that's okay. I'm here now, he'll be happy."'

When they'd first met, she believed his suicidal ideations and depression were the result of his loneliness and strained relationship with his adopted mother, who he refused to speak to right up until his death. But she thought his mood had improved since she'd entered his life.

In an effort to move the interview along, Goodwin asks Natasha if there were any other red flags or incidents prior to Mathew threatening suicide in June.

It's the moment she's been waiting for.

'Mat, ah … Mat's … a good friend of his, Craig Hoy, passed away a few weeks prior to all of that … that hit him really hard. Craig was gay. Um, so I think it hit him hard.'

Craig had taken his own life two months prior to Mathew's suicide threat in June.

She says Mathew had 'always been a drama queen' but the death of his friend had sent his depression spiralling. 'It wasn't until Craig's death that he really, um … started mentioning dying.'

Mathew had been in bed for a week after Craig's death, she says, even though she hadn't witnessed anything of the sort, because she'd been away on a road trip. 'That was a couple of weeks prior to him going to shoot himself. I think that was the main thing, he was really down about.'

Speaking uninterrupted for several minutes, Natasha is keen to hammer home the possible link between Mathew's and Craig's death, even telling Goodwin and Rudens that Mathew had told her 'how he would do it'.

'Um, the day that all that happened – where he was gunna kill himself – he'd been talking about it a little bit. He said that he and Craig used to talk about it a lot, and he said [when Craig] actually went ahead and did it, it was almost like he was proud of him, like, "Hey, he actually did it, he's not in pain anymore."'

During the trial, her defence team doesn't produce any evidence to suggest Mathew ever felt this way, or said anything of the sort to anyone.

Goodwin moves on to the subject of Mathew's will. Even though he asked Natasha about it in their first interview, he's keen to hear her answers in a more formal setting.

Both he and Rudens have hard evidence proving she stood to inherit everything. And that she knew it.

'When I spoke to you on Tuesday, in respect of Mathew's will, do you agree, on that occasion, you told me that you were unaware who the main beneficiary was, of the will?'

'Yeah, yep,' she says, adding she'd spoken to Lance about it since, and seen a copy of Mathew's will, but still didn't believe she was the beneficiary. 'I don't think [the will] is active because I never signed it in front of solicitors.'

Goodwin asks her point-blank: what is her understanding of who benefits under the will?

Flailing around the subject, she claims Mathew wanted her to be an executor but, as far as she knows, the rest of the will was unchanged, meaning she would not inherit anything.

She folds her arms in front of her chest. 'I'm not really a wills person. I don't have a will myself and I don't like talking about death.'

After speaking to Lance Partridge, Goodwin knows that Mathew informed Natasha she was the sole beneficiary of his estate, during a phone conversation while she was in jail.

So he asks Natasha if she and Mathew ever spoke about his will over the phone.

'Mmmm,' she thinks about it for a second. 'No.'

Goodwin persists. 'Did you have any knowledge as to whether or not you're a beneficiary?'

'I didn't, but Lance told me the other day that I was a beneficiary, and I told him, "I don't want it if people start saying things" . . . they've been saying things lately, yeah,' she says, knowing several people were already pointing the finger at her.

'I said [to Lance], "I don't think that's correct, and even if it is correct, I haven't signed to agree to that like I was supposed to."'

Goodwin nods. 'Okay . . . alright.' As he contemplates his next question, Natasha begins to babble in a desperate attempt to conceal she knows anything about the will.

'Mat and I never really talked about it. I mean, I don't even like discussing my mum and dad's will, and I wouldn't know what was in that. I don't have a will myself, but I suppose death frightens me a little bit.'

Little does Natasha know that, before the interview, Goodwin found Mathew's will in an office filing cabinet at Pandora, which declared Natasha as the sole beneficiary. After placing it in a brown paper evidence bag, it was sent off for forensic testing, which later revealed Natasha's fingerprints on it.

'I haven't seen the will, so I can't . . . I've only seen what Mat . . . oh . . . what Lance has told me,' Natasha tells Goodwin.

After a stream of waffling, Goodwin again seeks to clarify her knowledge about the will. 'So, the first thing you knew about the possibly being a beneficiary, as far as you're aware, is when Lance told you a couple of days ago?'

'I knew Lance was the executor, and I said to him, "Can I go back to the house? I mean, are we allowed to, or do we have to move out now?" and Lance said, "No, the house is yours," and I said, "Well, no, it's not."'

Having questioned Natasha for more than two and half hours about her version of events, in the final 15 minutes, Goodwin and Rudens decide to change tack. They've played nice to elicit as much as they can from her, but they're keen to gauge her reaction under harder questioning.

Preparing to knuckle down, Goodwin leans in. As part of their investigation, police have interviewed several people since first talking to Natasha, including the surgeon who assessed Mathew's leg on the last day of his life.

'We've spoken to the doctor, and he was under the impression that Mat was quite . . . his leg injury wasn't as bad as what you're saying it was, and that Mat seemed to be in good spirits,' Goodwin says, looking straight at her.

Despite being taken off guard, Natasha is quick as a flash.

'Well, you've seen Mat's Facebook. That's not the impression we got.'

But then it falls apart. Her head shakes furiously and she struggles to string a sentence together. She backtracks slightly, explaining the doctor did mention there were some improvements to Mathew's leg.

'So, um, yeah, no, I . . . I was there, it was definitely, um, look, he . . . he didn't say he was gunna, um, he did say that it was definitely improving.'

Before she can recover, Goodwin goes in again. 'We've also made some inquires at Supagas at Tamworth,' he says, referring to the store Natasha had ordered the gas from but asked Mathew to pick up.

'Who's that?' she asks, feigning confusion before suddenly pretending to remember it was the 'gas place' Mathew had bought the helium from.

Goodwin explains a Supagas employee is adamant that a female rang up and ordered the gas.

Natasha doesn't bat an eyelid, possibly confident in the knowledge the helium was ordered from the landline at Pandora, and not her mobile phone.

'Oh, well, you're welcome to look on my phone and see. I never ordered any gas or anything. That wasn't me. I did not ring up and order gas.'

Goodwin isn't letting it go so easily. 'They also said that the woman who ordered the gas specifically asked for the 3.5 cubic metre bottle of pure helium. What can you tell me about that?'

'I have no idea. I did not ring up and order the gas. You can, well, you've got my phone records. Mat was the one that went in there, arranged it and picked it up and put it in the car.'

'The female also said the lady that did the order [the gas] said that Mat Dunbar, male by the name of Mat Dunbar, would be picking up the gas the next day.'

She casually shrugs her shoulders.

'Um, that wasn't me. I have never ... I have never rang up and ordered any gas.' Natasha denies having anything to do with ordering the gas another half a dozen times.

Goodwin ups the ante. He says the Supagas employee was adamant that a woman ordered the helium.

'Obviously, that sort of thing raises our suspicions a bit and that's why I stated it's obviously a suspicious death,' he says.

This, combined with the fact that, at 12.48 am on the morning of Mathew's death, his phone was used to google whether helium would show up in an autopsy.

Looking back and forth between Goodwin and Rudens, Natasha keeps her calm.

'Yeah, okay, well, he was obviously trying to work out if it was gunna be detected. He didn't want me to get in trouble for anything. I don't know, that's all I can think of,' she says.

Goodwin isn't letting go so easily. 'And so, the question we ask is . . . if someone's gunna commit suicide with helium, why do they care?' he asks.

'I suppose he was checking that they would know what killed him. I don't know.'

'Did you use his phone to make those inquires?'

Making direct eye contact with Goodwin, she calmly replies, 'I most certainly did not.'

'If he didn't want you to get in trouble, or anything like that, is there a reason why he wouldn't write a note or something to explain what happened?'

Looking down at her lap, Natasha's voice softens as she closes her eyes, summoning tears.

'I keep asking myself that same thing. Why didn't he write a note or anything . . . I have no idea.'

Goodwin throws the baton to Rudens. Glancing between his notes and Natasha, Rudens gesticulates in her direction with a blue pen in hand. He asks whether she's ever carried out any Google searches regarding suicide. She looks in his direction, raising her eyebrows to indicate confusion, before looking down as she thinks.

'What I'm asking you [is], could this have been an assisted suicide?' Rudens clarifies.

Arms folded and right hand clutching her left wrist, Natasha shakes her head.

'No, I would not assist him, no.' She thinks about it more, her head shaking back and forth.

'No, definitely not an assisted suicide . . . no.'

Natasha's lips quiver for several seconds then she lets out loud sobs, gasping for air in between. Despite the tears, Rudens doesn't mince his words.

'The way we see it is, it could be natural causes, it could be suicide, it could be murder. Okay, that's how we are treating it. Now, did you have anything to do with Mathew dying?'

Taking her hand away from her mouth, Natasha turns to Rudens and lowers her voice. 'Most certainly not,' she says defiantly, followed by loud sobs.

'Okay. Did you put the bag on his head?' he asks.

'No, I did not.'

'Did you carry that cylinder of helium into the bedroom?'

'No, I certainly did not.'

'Did you give Mathew anything that night . . . a sedative?'

'No, I didn't even give him his Endone.'

'Or something that may have put him to sleep?'

'No, no, most certainly not,' she screams, her hysteria reaching a crescendo.

This is just the beginning of her rapid unravelling.

32

NATASHA'S ARREST INTERVIEW

The fluorescent white light hanging overhead reflects off the shiny black polka dots stitched onto Natasha's grey knitted jumper as she sits in a room devoid of colour. The interview room at Tamworth Police Station is an all-too-familiar place to her. She rests her tightly interlaced fingers on the edge of a grey Laminex table. Goodwin learns forward to press record on the video. The time is 3.42 pm on 18 November 2017, just a few hours after Natasha's arrest at Pandora.

Just like her police interview at Walcha Police Station, three months earlier, Goodwin sits on her left and Rudens on her right. This interview will play out very differently, however. For starters, police are now armed with Mathew's toxicology reports and a dossier of Natasha's phone records – including all her deleted web searches.

During the first 10 minutes, Goodwin and Rudens tag team, trying every tactic possible to get her to admit she ordered the helium. They try to catch her off guard – presenting a still image of security footage, which captures her in the Tamworth Hospital cafeteria on the last day of Mathew's life. This photo proves she had her phone and handbag with her, just before she looked up the Supagas website and took screenshots of helium cylinders.

Previously, Natasha had told police she'd left her handbag and phone with Mathew – who was waiting to see his orthopaedic surgeon – when she went to get coffees. Even though she's caught in a lie, and can see that security footage has captured her holding her phone, she remains chillingly calm.

'Would you agree that that's you in the photo?' Goodwin asks.

'Yes.'

'In that photo . . . is that your mobile phone?

'No, it would be Mathew's,' she says, explaining they often swapped phones because Mathew's phone had poor internet service. The police show her a zoomed-in photo of the phone, showing a white-coloured cover. Mathew's phone was black.

'Maybe I swapped phones with him when I went to the toilet,' she says, with a nonchalant shrug. She gets confused, first saying, 'that's definitely my phone' and later, 'I still think that it was his phone. I don't know. I know you're trying to trick me into something, but I seriously don't remember.'

At one stage during the interview, Goodwin presents Natasha with evidence proving that a woman ordered the gas from the landline at Pandora the day before Mathew's death. The Supagas employee distinctly remembered speaking to a woman.

'Well, it wasn't me, so I don't know who it would have been. Mathew had a very feminine-sounding voice'.

Goodwin repeatedly asks her if she ordered the helium.

She repeatedly denies it. 'I can't say anything about that. Look, I did not ring and order gas, and I think I was home.'

There's an answer for everything. Lies cascade off her tongue like water over a cliff. The passion behind her responses is so strong it's like she truly believes what she is saying and can't believe the injustice of the situation in which she finds herself.

Goodwin puts on a pair of rectangular-framed glasses and reads out a Google search she'd made – and later deleted – at 5.42 am on 1 August, the last day of Mathew's life.

'Can police see web history,' Goodwin reads.

He's quickly interrupted. 'Oh, that's definitely – I'm not a morning person.' She laughs. 'I would not have been on my phone in the morning.'

Goodwin persists. '"Can police see internet history" – did you make those searches?'

'No, definitely not, not at that time of morning. That would have been Mathew.'

'Why would he be concerned as to whether or not police could see his internet searches?' he asks.

'I can't answer that for you, I'm sorry. You're asking me what Mathew was thinking. I can't answer that.'

Natasha gets wildly more creative in her responses to the next series of questions. Her answers aren't logical, however; she's making things up on the run, having only just learned the police have recovered data from her phone. Data she thought would never be found.

Goodwin asks her if she's ever, at any time, made any searches about deleting internet history or what police can find.

She admits she did, after Mathew passed away. 'I was trying to protect Mathew.'

'Why?' Goodwin asks.

'Because, um, he looked up gay porn and stuff on the computer, and I didn't want any trouble.'

Goodwin looks lost. 'Why would he get in trouble for that?' he asks, exasperated.

'Well, I don't know. I don't know if anything was legal that he looked up.'

Goodwin nods slowly, twirling a pen in his right hand as he takes a few second to think.

'Okay. Do you ever look up that sort of porn, or anything like that?' he asks, knowing she does from her phone records.

'I must say "yes", but definitely not gay and not the naughty stuff he looks up.'

Goodwin pauses, allowing Rudens to jump in.

'What naughty stuff?' Rudens asks, shaking his head incredulously.

Natasha feigns confusion. 'Sorry?'

His face reddens. 'What "naughty stuff", that he looks up?'

'Oh well, the bad stuff, like, um, I don't know. His just seemed worse than mine.'

Frustrated, Ruden's face contorts. He's about to lose it. 'And what you're saying is that you were concerned that police would find that?'

'Uh-huh. Yes, I was. I didn't think it was legal.'

'Pornography?' he asks with increasing exasperation.

Natasha plays stupid. 'Don't you get in trouble for that? If they find images on your phone and that? I don't know, that's what I thought.'

Police have never found any evidence of pornography on Mathew's phone.

Later, Goodwin confronts her by reading out a series of searches she'd conducted, all with the aim of covering her tracks.

He starts by reading the search: 'Can police read text messages that have been deleted.' Then he accuses her, 'You're worried we are going to find all the searches you have done.'

Natasha's head shakes furiously. 'I was concerned about the porn . . . [that's] what I was concerned about, the porn that had been searched.'

Rudens can't take much more. He jumps in, raising his voice. 'What sort of porn was Mathew looking up?'

'Websites, they were gay websites, and just things like that.'

'You thought he'd get in trouble because of that?' Rudens asks, arms crossed, looking straight at her.

'I thought he'd get into trouble, or I'd get in trouble.'

This has gone on long enough for Rudens. He's busting to state the bleeding obvious. 'But he's dead!' he exclaims.

Natasha doesn't miss a beat. She has an answer for everything. 'I didn't want his name tarnished. I didn't want me to get into trouble either.'

Police find pornographic material and searches on Natasha's phone, but never on Mathew's. While she'd made up a cover story about Mathew searching porn, in fact it was her. It doesn't make sense at all.

Goodwin moves on to another series of searches, which Natasha made at Gusto café in Tamworth, shortly after getting Mathew to pick up the helium tank.

In another attempt to trap her, Goodwin explains police have security footage that depicts her using her phone outside the café.

'From 12.24 to 12.33, your phone is searching "suicide bag connect helium", "exit bag" and then "inert gas".'

Natasha thinks carefully, adding 'uh-huh' after every few searches are read aloud. She's rattled.

Goodwin continues to read: '"Suicide kits", "party store suicide bag", "man commits suicide by inhaling gas" and "do-it-yourself exit bag instructions".'

'Oh, I didn't . . . I remember . . . I don't remember any of that, I'm sorry. I don't remember any of the times or anything. Sorry, I can't answer any of that.'

'But you had your phone with you?'

'I don't remember . . . I'm sorry, I don't remember, I don't know,' Natasha says, lost for words. She embarks on a tear-riddled soliloquy.

'Not that this is relevant – or that you care – but I'm dealing with post-traumatic stress syndrome. I'm seeing a counsellor next door here at Centacare.' She animatedly points over her shoulder to prove such a place exists. 'I've been trying to change the story, that's how we are dealing with it, okay?' she says, pausing to channel more tears.

'Because every time I walk into the house, I see Mat with the bag over his head, and it scares me. It's flashbacks, and the therapist is trying to get me to change the story so that it's a happy ending. And so I've been trying not to remember this story and change the story, so it's really, really hard, because I've been trying to forget all of this. And you're asking me these things and I'm thinking, "I've been trying my hardest to forget these things and I don't remember a lot."'

Goodwin isn't having a bar of it, refusing to acknowledge a word she's said. He tries to move on to the subject of the will.

Rudens doesn't want to let her off the hook, however. He doesn't believe a word she's said about 'changing the story' for her mental health. 'That psychologist told you to change the story . . . for what reason?'

This gives her an opportunity to bring the focus back to her supposed grieving. She's more than happy to answer. 'I can't sleep, I can't focus, I can't do anything. And what the psychologist said – when they're working with people from Afghanistan [who] fought in the war – they teach them to, in their head, change, like, make it a happy ending. So, now I'm trying to change myself to, now, when I see Mat with the bag over his head, I'm trying to think of Mat at peace now. This is what he wanted. I thought, "He went peacefully," and that's the story I'm trying to tell myself.'

With a clear hint of sarcasm present, Rudens asks if she's been told to 'change the story' about anything else in the lead-up to or after Mathew's death.

Natasha turns up the volume, fiercely gripping onto this new defence. 'You ask my psychologist and he will tell you, that's what he calls it!'

Before letting the subject go, Rudens has one more crack. 'What we're finding is that you have changed your story a number of times.'

'Changing the story is what the psychologist calls it when you're trying to change the memory,' Natasha spits back.

Although Natasha had thoroughly researched all the drugs Mathew ingested – before and after his death – Goodwin informs her about the toxicology results for the first time.

'There's also an animal sedative located in his vomit. What can you tell me about that?'

Natasha hesitates. 'Um, that was, he'd asked me about, um, acepromazine. That's why I was considering . . . I thought maybe he'd taken some of that, too.'

He confronts her with the fact she'd unsuccessfully tried to purchase the sedatives from the Walcha Veterinary Clinic.

'Oh no, that was a total misunderstanding . . . even the vets knew that,' she says.

When Goodwin asks where Mathew would have bought the animal sedative from, she explains she has it for her horses and Mathew had an old bottle of it, which he kept for sedating the rams for shearing.

'Every horse owner has a bottle of ace and a bottle of penicillin. They're two fundamentals.'

She feigns confusion about when and where she got it from but, later, admits to buying it from the vet in Armidale for Bugs, her horse. 'And we used it the next day because I needed to fix the horse's tooth and the horse trod on it and smashed it, and my daughter can verify that. She was there.'

Rudens jumps in and doesn't hide his scepticism. 'Smashed the bottle of ace?'

'Yeah. He's trod on the bottle of ace.'

Goodwin says police never found any acepromazine or empty vials of it on Pandora, despite a thorough search of the property when Mathew died almost three months ago. 'Can you explain that?'

Not even a second passes before she's conjured up a new story. 'Oh, last weekend, my dad and I were cleaning out the back shed . . . and there was a little bottle of acepromazine,' she claims.

Goodwin later holds a receipt in his hands, proving Natasha bought acepromazine from a clinic in Armidale, using a false name and address.

When confronted with it, she maintains she's done nothing wrong. 'Yes, that was my purchase, that was my date. That information seems wrong. There is no reason why I would give wrong information, because I wasn't doing anything illegal or inappropriate, or anything like that. That's all I can tell you.'

Natasha blames the girl who put the transaction through. 'The girl took forever to do that. She was struggling, she was finding it really,

really hard. She had to call somebody in a couple of times. I mean, that's the only explanation I have.'

Goodwin shakes his head. 'Well, I find it hard to understand how someone can get a surname wrong, an address wrong, a phone number wrong when they're getting the information from you.'

'Well, I'm sorry. I gave her the correct information. Like I said, I wasn't doing anything wrong.'

It's time for Goodwin to go in for the kill. 'We believe that, obviously, you've given false particulars to them to cover up the fact that you were purchasing acepromazine in Armidale.'

Incredulous, Natasha replies, 'Well, I've never covered up that I purchased acepromazine. As soon as you asked me about it, I said I did.'

Goodwin asks if she can explain why there is acepromazine in Mathew's vomit, indicating he must have ingested it orally on the night he died.

This time she brings on the waterworks. 'No. I can't imagine it would taste very nice. It'd be horrible. Since Maty died, the one comfort I've had is – and a doctor told me – that dying by helium gas would be peaceful. Now, you're telling me that he died of an overdose and it's . . .' She breaks down, unable to finish her sentence.

'I'm not telling you he died of an overdose. I'm saying he's got acepromazine, along with a lot of other drugs, which are unprescribed to him, in his system. And you told us in an initial interview that you looked after his medication.'

Goodwin is reaching the end of his tether, twirling a pen in his hand as he considers his next move. 'You gave him the drugs and the acepromazine, didn't you?'

'No, I didn't.'

'In his drink.'

'No, I love Maty. Maty was the most brilliant man in the world.' Natasha sobs loudly.

'And once he was basically sedated in bed, you put the bag over his head and put the helium into the bag to kill him, didn't you?'

'No, I did not,' Natasha says, hysteria rising.

'And the reason that you did that was because you well and truly knew that you were in line for the will, and that you were gunna inherit the property.'

'That's not true.'

He prods her again. 'Didn't you?'

'No, it's not true!'

'You're just making things up to fit a story . . .' Goodwin says, causing a volcanic eruption from Natasha.

She leans in towards him and screams, 'I think you're the one that's making things up to fit the way you want it to be, because that's not how it happened at all!'

Goodwin arms himself with a pile of paperwork – enough to make a loud thud if it were dropped on a table – and leans back confidently.

'So, [we're] just gunna go through a few of the searches that are found on your phone in the days leading up to Mathew's death. Okay? These are from 29 July. "What to inject to kill yourself" . . . on the same day, "murder by injection". Do you want to say anything about that?'

'No. I didn't . . . they weren't my searches.'

Rudens jumps in. 'How do you explain it? How do you explain that on your phone?'

'Mathew looked it up on my phone.'

Goodwin goes on to read dozens and dozens of searches, from '99 undetectable poisons' and 'the science of getting away with murder' to 'hydrogen peroxide murder' – all searches deleted from her phone.

After a pause, he reads more. 'Again, "murder by inducing heart attack", "murder by stroke", "stroke murder", "what causes heart valve disease", "where to buy drugs". All on your phone, all prior to Mathew Dunbar's death.' He continues through a lengthy list of Google searches.

'"What are mass murder pills", "suicide pills", "Oxycontin murder", "What does Valium taste like", "Are some benzodiazepines bitter while others are tasteless". The reason you're researching this is so you can put it in his drink that he takes his medication in to poison him.'

She maintains Mathew carried out the searches and the reason they were deleted is because she deletes her browser history by habit every week.

'I would never have poisoned Mathew or hurt him in anyway. He wanted to go, and he wanted to go quietly,' Natasha says.

'We're just wondering, why is it . . . where you're saying Mathew is contemplating suicide . . . why is he researching murders and how to get away with murder?' Goodwin asks.

Natasha is quick with her answer. 'When they took his guns away from him, he said to me, "They're not going to stop me from killing myself, just because they've taken my guns away." I think Mathew was desperate.'

'People don't – if they want to kill themselves – don't research that,' Goodwin argues.

It doesn't matter what evidence he's got or what he says, however, there's no way she's backing down. 'Mathew researches everything! You can ask anybody. He sits for hours and researches everything.'

Her denials leave Goodwin in disbelief. 'You've never done these searches? Correct?'

'I never did these searches, no.'

Why then, he asks, was she searching acepromazine on her phone after Mathew died, if she wasn't aware he'd taken it?

''Cause he asked me about it, um, a few weeks prior. He said to me, "Do you know what would happen if a human took acepromazine?"'

Goodwin scoffs. 'So all of a sudden – after he's dead for twelve days, you decided to check out what would happen to a human?'

Natasha decides she needs to change tack; she pulls out the victim card. 'There was a rumour around town that I'd poisoned him with sheep drench and stuff like that. And I'm thinking that they must have found something in his system, so then I started thinking . . . I remember him asking me about the acepromazine.'

If she won't admit to her post-murder searches, Goodwin asks, then how does she explain the searches about whether police can retrieve deleted text messages and internet history?

'You're worried that we're gunna find all the searches that you've done on your phone.'

Again, Natasha blames the searches on the fear of Mathew being caught with viewing porn.

Goodwin asks how she can explain searching for 'plead not guilty to murder', 'wife poisons husband', then reading an article titled, '*Woman on run for two years after poisoning husband's cereal to avoid having sex with him*'.

Natasha stutters, struggling to explain the last round of searches. Eventually, she accepts that she read the articles.

'I did, yes. Since Maty died, I don't sleep a lot and I sit there, and I search everything. I've been watching a show called *The Killing*. Um and yes, I have been searching a lot of things. I want to know what he was thinking.'

Not acknowledging what she's just said, Goodwin continues to read out her web browser history: 'temazepam', 'The victim poisoned by her husband', 'Geneva woman pleads guilty to killing husband with poisoned smoothie'.

Natasha admits to reading these articles. 'I want to know what he was thinking. I've rung the coroner; I've been trying to get information.'

'About poisons?' Rudens asks.

'Yeah. I want to know what he did.'

Goodwin points out that she's consistently maintained Mathew killed himself by using helium. There was never any mention of poisons in her previous interviews.

Her face turns crimson. 'I'm the one that's been hearing about poisoning! Every time I go down the street, people say to me, "Oh, there's that killer and she poisoned her husband." And my kids come home: "I heard today, Mum, that somebody said you were a killer."

I'm trying to find out everything I can. Nobody tells me anything. The police don't tell me anything, the coroner won't tell me anything.'

Rudens jumps in, shaking his head in disbelief. 'So, you're just searching websites out of pure curiosity, because people are accusing you of poisoning your partner? Is that what you're trying to tell us?'

'Well, yeah, basically. Yes, I'm looking up different things. I'm trying to make sense of everything.'

Rudens asks her straight out. 'Did you poison him?'

'No, I didn't. Mat was the best thing to ever happen to me. I definitely did not poison him. I didn't hurt him.'

33

BOMBSHELL EVIDENCE

About a week into Natasha's trial, whispers about new 'bombshell' evidence begin swirling. Several sources tell me it's 'jaw-dropping', something I can't miss. Although no one will outline the specifics, I know a woman has recently come forward with new evidence. Apparently, it's pretty damning; a mid-trial gift that has landed squarely in the laps of the prosecution.

On Day 13 of the trial, Hatfield informs the judge that a new witness 'came to light' and that their evidence would go towards 'consciousness of guilt'. This means Hatfield will rely upon something Natasha has said or done after Mathew's death as evidence of her consciousness of guilt. The court hears the mystery witness lives in South Australia and has expressed her willingness to give evidence via video from her home state, or travel to Sydney to give evidence in person.

After following the case for the past four years, I didn't think I could learn anything more shocking than what I already knew. I am very much mistaken. What Natasha did is equal parts stupid and outrageously disturbing. What I hear today, however, is only a small fraction of what this integral witness will tell me after the trial.

*

After the jurors take their seats in the courtroom, Hatfield rises to his feet. He explains that what they are about to hear relates to the time Natasha was in jail, waiting to face this murder trial.

A woman wearing a long-sleeved navy shirt, who looks to be in her mid-40s, appears on the screens hung on the right- and left-hand sides of the courtroom. While her blonde hair appears to be freshly blow-dried, and her face is elegantly made up in nude tones, she can't hide how uncomfortable she looks. I wonder if she's going to be physically sick.

Natasha, dressed in black today, can't seem to raise her head to look in her direction.

The jury hears the woman, Mandy, is a disability support worker. She's known Natasha since they were teenagers, after both going to Colo High School in North Richmond, a semi-rural suburb in the Hawkesbury region on the outskirts of Sydney.

The court hears she and Natasha were part of the same close-knit group of friends – six girls – who used to pen letters to one another.

After finishing high school, Mandy and Natasha lost touch but, years later, bumped into each other at the Richmond shops during the Black Christmas bushfires in 2001. Following that, it was another nine years before they reconnected on Facebook, where they would sporadically comment on each other's photos and posts.

When Mandy found out about Mathew's death, she was under the impression, from reading Natasha's Facebook posts, that he had suicided. She reached out to Natasha a few days afterwards, sharing her own deeply personal experiences regarding suicide to comfort her old friend. They reconnected quickly, speaking on the phone and messaging each other, confiding in all aspects of their private lives.

Much of their conversations centred on Mathew's death, with Natasha leading Mandy to believe he had taken his own life. In a Facebook post, Natasha complained about the police searching her property. Mandy concurred their actions were outrageous, in the context of believing Natasha was grieving the loss of her partner.

'Based upon what she said, you thought she was being treated unfairly by the police?' Hatfield asks her in front of the jury.

'Yes,' Mandy says.

'There was no indication by her to you that she was being investigated?'

Mandy agrees; Natasha never mentioned anything about police suspecting her involvement.

Following Natasha's arrest in November 2017, Mandy contacted Natasha's mother, Maureen, to let her know she wanted to help and support her friend in any way she could. She believed Natasha and had no reason to think she'd lied about Mathew taking his own life.

In 2019, when in Sydney to see family, Mandy visited Natasha twice at Mary Wade Correctional Centre. During these visits, Natasha talked about her case at length and denied any wrongdoing. Afterwards, the pair began writing to each other, just as they'd done in high school. In total, Mandy ended up receiving seven long letters from Natasha. Each letter reveals so much, but it was the fifth letter that would harm Natasha the most.

Mandy remains on the screen in the courtroom, as Hatfield picks up the letter and reads it to the jury in its entirety.

Natasha's letter to Mandy, December 2019

Dear Beautiful Mandy,

I hope [your daughter] likes her letter i sent her. I received your letter, obviously and her drawings are so cute. ♥ You can tell [your partner] that i would have done the same with the Huntsman. I have a pathological fear of spiders! I was driving once and a large spider crawled across my dashboard. I leapt out of my car and the man working in the pizza shop had to jump behind the wheel and park my car. Once i called Colin (who is a paramedic) and was screaming so much that two Ambulances and two police cars turned up sirens blasting. Colin had been having coffee with the copper after a big job so they had all responded to the hysterical emergency spider situation.

It sounds really horrible what your poor [son] is going through, but with a wonderful mother like you, i'm sure he will be fine.

It was so wonderful to see you, twice. I feel like the luckiest girl in the world to have you as a friend. I'm going to train a special pony for [your daughter] so she can ride when she comes to visit Aunty Tasha. Hey, wouldn't it be great if your son and my daughter get married? We could be nanna's together!! :) OK so I'm getting ahead of myself.

Ive been going through the brief of evidence and it's amazing how people lie and seem to have been manipulated by the police. Some lies i can prove are so but others are there word against mine. I have very little faith in man kind. It awful how money makes people so greedy. The people who were taken out of Mat's original will say the worst things, and they have never even met me. I have played by the rules the whole time and look where it's got me.

Mat was so much more than just his money. He was kind, generous and wore his heart on his sleeve. He was tall, handsome and smart. Every night he would exfoliate and rub cream into my feet. He would actually remind me of this after i had a shower, i wouldn't ever ask him.

Every morning he would get my car out of the garage and have the heater on, warming so the kids and i had a warm car waiting for us. He always made a fuss out of every meal i cooked saying things like 'you should write a cook book together' or 'you could go on Masterchef'. And can i just tell you my cooking is very basic.

He was such a great guy and instead of being remembered for being a wonderful man, who was troubled, and yes his death was a sad tragedy, but not a crime. But he is being remembered as a wealthy man who everyone thinks they deserve a piece of his property, who was allegedly murdered.

It makes me so sad Mandy, if you ask any of those so called witnesses:-

- What was his favourite colour?
- What was he allergic too?
- His favourite TV channel?
- What he had for lunch every day?
- His name on his original birth cert?

Anyway i just get so upset because i am the only person who would be able to answer these, and many more questions regarding my Maty.

By the way the answers are:-

Sky blue

Tomatoes – Get nose bleeds

CI on Fox

Ham sandwich – Every bloody day

[Mathew's name on birth certificate]

I was watching an episode of *Frasier* when Niles needed him to lie in court and say he didn't know that Niles was in love with Daphne, so that Niles could get a 'clean divorce'. Frasier knew that the oposition was using dirty tactics and the correct thing would be for Niles to win, however he struggled with the moral dilema. It got me thinking that if only i could ask somebody to say that Mathew told them he was planning his suicide, maybe a few or several days before he passed. My mum talked to Mat the night he died and she has already provided a statement to police so i can't ask her to do it.

So Mandy i'm going to make you a proposition and see if you can be the one to help me. Please don't judge me, there is no pressure here. Your friendship is the most important thing!!!

Once i am found 'not guilty' which would be pretty much assured if you help me, than i automatically get the inheritance Mat wanted the children and i to have. I would be willing to give you $20,000 which I'm sure would help you buy out [your partner's] family.

If you agree to do this I was thinking the following details would be sufficient.

1. I knew you had once attempted suicide and we talked over Facebook imessages about my fears for Mathew and his talking about suicide.
2. You offered to talk to him for me as you could tell him you understood his anguish.
3. You phoned the house home phone when i knew Mat would be there alone so the house was quiet. I had told him you wanted to talk to him so he was prepared for the call.
4. You talked to him for around 40 minutes and he told you:
   - he had been planning his suicide
   - he wanted to die at home
   - he had already had 2 attempts and he didn't want to fail again.
   - he had been looking up different suicide methods.
   - He loved the kids and i but he was convinced we would be better off without him.

All true comments by the way, just not said to you from him.

You suggested to Mathew:-
- He get a good councilor (psychologist)
- That you knew exactly how he felt and told him it would get better
- You suggested he call lifeline or go back to Banksia House before he took any action towards suicide.
- To give the anti-depressants a chance.

If the lawyers ask for your phone records, just say it was over 2½ years ago and you don't keep them. It would mean that you have to talk to lawyers about your suicide attempt and i'm sorry about that, it must be hard for you to talk about.

My solicitor is Randall Legal at Lismore and Tracey Randall is my solicitor. You could contact her if you wanted to be pro active. Tell her you wanted to talk to my <u>first lawyer</u> when you heard i was arrested and you knew it was wrong. Tell her that he took your <u>details</u>, but didn't pass them on to me or take a <u>statement</u> from you. I couldn't even remember his name so the fact that you have these facts are great.

You could send Randall legal an ~~call~~ email and tell them that you came and saw me last week and i told you i never received the message from [my] first lawyer. You could tell them that i told you who my new lawyer was.

That all sounds really good. It could even get dropped before it goes to trial. Is all they have on me is those web searches and once they know Mat confirmed to you that he had been searching suicide, they have nothing.

Anyway, just disregard those last few pages if you like. As i said, your friendship and support is the most important thing.

I forgot to tell you to say hi to your mum for me, hey i sound like Rove. Tell [your son] that if he marries [my daughter] she is use to having to remove spiders for me.

I will finish now and will write again when i get your other letter you said you sent.

Give my love to all the family

Love and hugs your grateful friend

Tash xxx

After reaching the end of the letter, Hatfield pauses for a short time. I look at the jury: most of them are wide-eyed; some shake their heads in disbelief.

'Is it the case that, when you received the letter, you did not do any of the things she asked you to do?' Hatfield asks Mandy, looking at her on the screen in front of him.

Tucking a few blonde strands behind her ears, Mandy replies loudly and clearly. 'That's true, I did not.'

'You didn't put the proposed plan into action?'

'No, not at all.'

Mandy tells the court, she didn't write back to Natasha but, soon enough, another letter landed in her mailbox.

Again, Hatfield reads the entirety of the sixth letter to the jury.

Natasha's letter to Mandy, 2 January 2020

Dearest Mandy,

Happy New Year my darling friend. I hope you and your family have a great, safe year. This year is going to be great, i can just feel it!

I was just reading your letter again and noticed you said that you have written a novel. Really, that's amazing. Tell me more:-

- Title?
- What's it about?
- Are you getting it published? Maybe i could help you with that.

In my last letter i offered you some money to help me and i just wanted to say im sorry if the amount i offered you offends you. I'm very generous with my friends, Mathew taught me that and i can give you as much as you need.

This reminds me of a funny saying which i can't remember word for word but it was something like . . . if your ever in trouble, i won't be there to support you cause i'll be next to you helping you hide the body. LOL.

Thanks Mandy, you are the best friend anyone could ever have.

Love

Tasha xxx

As Hatfield reads the letter, Mandy's head is lowered, but she slowly looks up after he's finished. Again, he asks if she did anything to put Natasha's proposed plan into action.

She did not. Mandy never wrote back, but Natasha later called her from jail, asking her if she was okay. Mandy didn't want Natasha to know she had received the letter, so pretended all was well, getting off the phone as quickly as she could.

I will soon learn more about why Mandy did this.

Despite not hearing from her friend after offering cash for a false statement, Natasha wrote back to Mandy on 14 January 2020. She never got a reply.

Mandy tried to ignore what Natasha had asked her to do for more than a year but, as time went on, her gut told her that she must come forward. After hearing through the media that Natasha's murder trial had started, Mandy decided to contact the prosecution.

The jury hears she called the office of the Director of Public Prosecutions and explained what Natasha had asked her to do. The following day, she met with detectives in Adelaide, who took a statement from her. She also provided the incriminating letters.

When she gave her statement, Mandy had no idea that the prosecution had already included a Facebook chat between herself and Natasha as part of their case. Just days after Mathew's death, Natasha sent Mandy a Facebook message, proving she knew she stood to inherit Mathew's estate: 'I am the only beneficiary of the will though so that part should be easy.'

This message is completely at odds with what she told police following Mathew's death.

The defence, who accept the jail letter was written by Natasha, decline to ask Mandy any questions.

When she learns there is nothing more she needs to say, Mandy breaks down and sobs.

34

PROSECUTION CLOSING ADDRESS

Back in November 2017, I'd met Natasha's mother briefly when I knocked on the front door of the farmhouse at Pandora. It was a very busy time for them with shearing, she told me, and Natasha wouldn't be back at the house until dusk. Nathan and I returned at dusk, and spoke to Natasha at the farmgate, just a few days before her arrest.

Because her mother Maureen was listed as a potential witness to be called during the trial, she was prevented from coming to court until all the evidence had been heard. As soon as she was allowed, Maureen power-walked into the Darlinghurst court complex, keen to show her daughter support. From my seat in the public gallery, I watch as Maureen opens the heavy timber doors. Once inside, she peers to the right, where her other daughter and her husband are seated, before turning left and taking a seat as far away from them as possible. Natasha's sister, who often sits with Elaine and John, is clearly not there in support.

As she's led into the courtroom in handcuffs, Natasha beams at the sight of her first supporter in court. Maureen blows her multiple kisses from her brightly painted red lips. A Cheshire cat grin spreads across Natasha's face; she flaps her arms, waving with over-the-top animation.

I'm sitting in front of Elaine and John, who haven't missed a single day of the trial, and they certainly weren't going to miss today. They miss Mathew terribly and want to witness justice for him.

Today, Hatfield will begin his closing address, summarising all the evidence heard in the past eight weeks. He will analyse the evidence and emphasise certain parts, arguing that this was a case of murder beyond reasonable doubt.

Up until this point, he's presented evidence to the jury through questioning witnesses and tendering exhibits, such as Natasha's phone records and videoed police interviews. Now, he will explain the relevance of this evidence and argue what the jury should infer from it. In his final arguments, he will be as persuasive as he can, explaining his case and how each piece of the evidence fits into the larger puzzle.

Once the jurors are seated, Hatfield rises to his feet, a thick wad of notes resting on a lectern in front of him. He starts by explaining murder has a physical and mental element to it. 'You have to do a thing which causes the death of another person and, at the time you do it, you have to have a certain state of mind. Now, in this case, the physical element, the thing which Natasha Beth Darcy did to cause the death of Mathew Dunbar, was the application of the exit bag apparatus to him while he was sedated and turning on the helium gas. In relation to her state of mind, the Crown case is that – at the time the accused applied the exit bag apparatus to the deceased, and turned on the gas – that she did so with the intention of causing his death,' Hatfield says.

He highlights the hundreds of death-related internet searches, where Natasha had been at the time and in what context she'd carried them out. He pinpoints when and how she'd obtained the various drugs, the other events occurring at the time and how they all fitted into her murderous plan.

Using a pen to mark off each event as he deals with it, he guides the jury through a meticulous timeline until the end of his address, which lasts several days.

'Our submission to you is you would be well satisfied this was a case of murder rather than suicide,' he says, before hammering the point home. 'There is no evidence, we say, that is consistent with any knowledge or involvement of the deceased in this being a suicide that he had been pursuing. It all points in the other direction.'

The only rational conclusion they could draw, he tells the jury, is that it was Natasha who gave Mathew the cocktail of sedatives.

'It is consistent with the searches on her phone, searches relating to taste, overdose, murder. None of the deceased's regular prescribed drugs were consumed in the cocktail or left on the bench there – the Endone, the sertraline and the like.'

There is no evidence that Mathew had any knowledge about Natasha's plan; she alone watched the instructional videos on how to kill him – at the café in Tamworth, following his hospital appointment.

'We submit [that] only the accused was capable of putting the apparatus together on the night. She was awake and moving around. She knew how. She was up at the time, messaging Ms Wauch. We submit to you the deceased was not, he was, you will find, in bed sedated and that is consistent with the timeline.'

Although he spent weeks preparing for it, Hatfield never gets the opportunity to question Natasha, because she opted not to give evidence. Without the opportunity to confront her in person, Hatfield therefore spends a large portion of his address highlighting the hundreds of lies she told in her various police interviews.

'Lies told by the accused that, we say, are important lies, lies not just going to her credibility but lies, we say, she told because she knew what she had done. Lies showing a consciousness of guilt. She only, we say, told those particular lies because she was guilty of murdering the deceased,' Hatfield says.

Lies about the months and months of murderous searches she undertook, even when she was away from Walcha with her phone. In particular, she lied that she only researched how to delete phone data so the police wouldn't find Mathew's pornographic searches.

'There was no porn searches on the deceased's phone, and you have the truncated description of various porn searches on the iPhone 7,' Hatfield tells the jury, who have folders filled with Natasha's phone data. 'So the person looking at porn was her, not him. You might think that explanation there is completely false, a completely false explanation for why she looked up those things. And the reason that she looked them up was because she was concerned about how her history might implicate her, that's the reason for those searches.'

He reminds the jury Natasha searched for each of the four drugs found in Mathew's system after she killed him: clonidine, temazepam, Seroquel and acepromazine. 'Each of which were searched postoffence and before she was informed about the toxicology results.'

He also spends considerable time sifting through the lies she told about acepromazine, her attempts to purchase it and, when she did, what she did with it. 'We say these lies about obtaining the acepromazine are consciousness of guilt lies. She denies and she lies about her efforts to get acepromazine, because it would implicate her in the murder of the deceased.'

He points out parts of Natasha's final police interview, after her arrest, where she claims the bottle of acepromazine she'd bought was smashed while her horse Bugs was having his teeth done.

'So, on the accused's version, she gets the one hundred mils from Mr May, and it is smashed the next day because the horse steps on it,' he says, with a note of sarcasm.

'So that would been, what the twenty-ninth of June? The whole bottle of acepromazine is smashed by the horse. You might think that is quite implausible . . . the acepromazine in the deceased's body was, in fact, that bottle the accused bought from Creeklands Vet Clinic and, we say, also used on the seventh of July to inject in his calf.'

Hatfield highlights her lie about finding a bottle of acepromazine while she was cleaning out a shed with her dad, just a week before her arrest. This was never found during the extensive police search. He also notes the implausibility of Mathew adding acepromazine to the sedative smoothie blended in the Nutribullet, then returning the bottle to the shed.

Hatfield's incredulous tone reaches a peak.

'What is this suggestion anyway? What, the deceased poured the milkshake himself and then, what? Went and took that bottle of acepromazine and put it back in the middle shed, late at night, on the first of August, just before killing himself?' he asks.

'You might think it is completely implausible, she is just giving that, or manufacturing that detail to try and identify a source of acepromazine other than the one that she bought from Creeklands Vet.'

Methodically, Hatfield runs through everything Natasha did. She convinced Mathew to change his will. She carried out months of murderous searches. She bought acepromazine under a false name. She sourced Seroquel and paliperidone from her jail friend. She ordered the helium. She watched instructional videos. She gaslighted him and goaded him to kill himself. She tried to kill him by injecting his leg with acepromazine. She searched each and every one of the drugs mixed in the Nutribullet, then fed a sedative cocktail to Mathew. She searched about what police could find and how to delete all her phone data. On top of that, she tried to bribe a friend to get off a murder charge and had violently attacked her estranged husband, Colin, twice in the past.

'She has a tendency to sedate her partner with prescription or other drugs or poisons. And that she has a tendency to do so with the intention of obtaining a financial or other advantage for herself.'

Towards the end of his address, Hatfield slows down. 'The accused had a strong motive. She had nothing. She had no income. She pursued the deceased online. She insisted she be made the beneficiary. She stood to gain substantially by his death.'

Hatfield pauses, making eye contact with as many jurors as he can. I can tell he's about to finish and I take a deep breath, preparing to get every word down.

'In this courtroom over the last two months, it might seem that we have opened Pandora's box, looking as we did at the issues in

Mathew Dunbar's life from every angle, and forensically examining the circumstances of his premature death at only forty-two years of age,' he says, his hand resting on the lectern as he takes another breath.

'In modern times, that idiom, "opening Pandora's box" has come to mean any source of great or unexpected troubles. You might think it a sad, but apt, description of the role played by the accused in the end of Mr Dunbar's life. He may have desperately wanted love and a family, but what did he get? A cold and calculating person, who was determined to kill him and inherit his wealth.'

He delivers his final plea. 'As my role in this part of the process of justice draws to a close, the time is approaching when the outcome will be in your hands. When that time comes, I ask you this: deliver a just verdict, a verdict of guilty to the charge of murder that Natasha Darcy murdered Mathew Dunbar.'

35

DEFENCE CLOSING ADDRESS

I've been waiting the whole trial (as no doubt have the jury) to hear what evidence there is that proves this is a case of assisted suicide. At the start of her trial, Natasha stood up and told the jury she was not guilty of murder but 'guilty to aiding and abetting suicide'.

In her opening address, her barrister Janet Manuell spoke about the defence of 'assisted suicide' at length, but hasn't raised the subject again in the past two months.

In his closing address, Hatfield reminded the jury that there was no evidence presented during the trial to suggest Mathew's death was an assisted suicide.

It's not long before we all find out why.

Manuell rises to her feet to begin her closing address. She speaks clearly and with confidence. 'The Crown told you he needs to exclude as a reasonable possibility that Mr Dunbar died by his own hand. If you think there is reasonable possibility that he died by his own hand, then the Crown cannot satisfy you of the elements of murder,' she says.

Just as she did in her opening address, she asks the jury to think about who Mathew was. 'Who is Mathew Dunbar? What do we know of him? What did any one person know about him?'

Throughout the trial, Manuell cross-examined most of the prosecution's witnesses with persistent questions about his spending habits, poor relationship with his mother, sexuality and history of depression.

'We know Mathew Dunbar had difficulty establishing and maintaining relationships,' she says, then asks the jury to think about the stress this would have caused a fourth-generation farmer, unable to have a family of his own.

There was evidence during the trial that Natasha's overspending had been the main source of stress for Mathew before his death. Manuell acknowledges this, but argues that whatever money Natasha spent was merely that associated with the cost of raising a family.

'She gave Mathew a family life he never had before. Anyone with children knows they constantly cost money. Mr Dunbar had gone from just himself to having to look after a family of five, a responsibility he accepted. The expenditure of a family of five was always going to be a shock to him.'

Manuell turns to the 'issue' of Colin Crossman and the time he spent at Pandora. 'Colin Crossman is still around in 2017, even after that incident in 2009. [Natasha's third son] wasn't born until 18 months after the incident, which you might think in itself is a curious feature.'

Even though Natasha and Colin were separated, Manuell explains, he was the father figure in the children's lives and, naturally, wanted to remain so.

'Issues around families can be tricky. Adults move on but, where kids are involved, it's not so easy. Mr Dunbar had a bit of trouble with the idea of Mr Crossman being around . . . of course, he was going to see the children when he wasn't working.'

I wonder why she's raised the subject of Colin. Perhaps it's an attempt to water down the damning tendency evidence by showing Colin and Natasha still have an amicable relationship, despite the 2009 hammer attack and house fire. Or perhaps it's to explain why Natasha allowed her ex to spend time at Pandora, despite the obvious distress it caused Mathew.

Manuell then confronts the issue of the Google searches, and the prosecution's case that Natasha searched for ways to poison Mathew as early as February 2017.

'But is that the only reasonable inference you can draw from those searches?' she asks, suggesting that those searches on the Apple computer could have been made by Natasha, Mathew or one of the three children.

It's also possible, she argues, that Natasha or the kids carried out the searches about killer spiders and poisonous plants and mushrooms out of curiosity, having just moved to a rural property for the first time.

'Were there lots of redback spiders around the property? Were there spiders in the house, the usual creepy-crawlies? Ms Darcy had only been on Pandora for three or four months. It was all new to them. Why wouldn't Ms Darcy and the children want to know more about what they were seeing?'

The questions continue, thick and fast.

'What's to say she wasn't out in the property one day with the kids, using it to search for mushrooms or fungi they couldn't eat, and that the searches were made for that reason?'

Pausing, it's like a thought-bubble pops from her head when she adds, 'When's mushroom season around Walcha?'

Manuell concentrates heavily on searches made on the family computer in April 2017, which included 'How to stop suicidal thoughts'. 'Who makes a search for something like that? Who do you think would make a search for "how to stop suicidal thoughts"? You'd think it would be someone who was having suicidal thoughts.'

Manuell goes on to present alternative explanations for many searches, but by no means all of them.

'Things might look suspicious when you first see it, but are there any other reasonable explanations for the evidence that you've heard?' she asks.

Unable to explain away all the lies Natasha told, Manuell concedes her client wasn't being honest. 'Think about it; one of the problems with lying is that, once you've told one lie, you've got to keep telling a whole lot more lies if you're going to keep up with the original lie.' She gives no explanation about what the 'original lie' is.

'Some people fess up to the original lie, some people don't – and they just make things worse and worse and worse. That's what's happened here – Ms Darcy has made things worse and worse for herself by the repeated lies she's told.'

She asks the jury to ponder why people might lie. 'They might think they've been unjustly accused . . . they might think nobody is going to believe them.'

As Manuell nears the end of her closing address, she asks the jury to turn their minds to the sedative cocktail blended in the Nutribullet. If Natasha had spent five months carefully and deliberately planning Mathew's murder, as the prosecution argued, why didn't she wash the glass tumbler containing the cocktail's residue?

'If she had had a guilty mind, don't you think she would have turned on the dishwasher, an easy way of getting rid of any evidence, or getting rid of the evidence as to what had been in the Nutribullet container and the glass? All she had to do was press the button to turn on the dishwasher. And it wasn't done.'

Manuell tells the jury there are 12 reasons why the prosecution could not exclude the possibility Mathew had taken his own life. These were:

1. Mathew had a history of depression.
2. Mathew reported suicidal ideation in 2009 and June 2017.
3. The family computer was used for various methods of suicide, including 'how to stop suicidal thoughts'.
4. There is evidence proving Mathew bought the helium from Supagas (the Crown had not excluded him from being 'an active and knowing participant' in obtaining the cylinder), and it was unlikely he'd been 'duped' into believing it was for a party.
5. It was unlikely that Natasha watched an instructional video about

how to suicide using helium for a second time, when Mathew returned to their outdoor table at the Tamworth café.

6. Natasha's phone was used to watch an instructional suicide video for 1 minute, 48 seconds at the Tamworth café, when the defence argues Mathew wasn't using his phone, inferring he watched it with her.

7. It was implausible that Natasha watched an instructional video on how to use helium after the helium tank was purchased.

8. Mathew had time and opportunity to prepare for his death, when Natasha and the children took their cat to the vet on the afternoon of 1 August 2017.

9. It would have been difficult for Natasha to remove a small part of the helium cylinder, which allows gas to be dispensed.

10. Mathew's DNA was present on the shower hose, which had been connected to the helium cylinder.

11. Mathew's DNA was present on the elastic band that had secured the bag.

12. It was implausible that Mathew drank the cocktail of drugs blended in the Nutribullet: 'Drinking a drink which must have been thick with pulverised tablets . . . we know it had all those crunchy bits in it'.

During her closing arguments, Manuell summarises the evidence of expert psychiatrist and internationally recognised suicide researcher, Matthew Large. He was the only witness called for the defence, aside from Natasha's solicitor Tracey Randall.

It's not unusual for the defence to call far fewer witnesses than the prosecution. Sometimes, defence barristers don't call any witnesses at all, and wait until their closing address to pick apart the prosecution's case and sow seeds of doubt.

The opinion of Dr Large is at direct odds with that of Dr Clive Stanton, who had assessed Mathew during his brief visit to the Mental Health Unit at Tamworth Hospital, following his suicide threat.

Based on his reading of medical notes, Large tells the court he would have diagnosed Mathew with having a major depressive order of mild severity.

He believes Mathew 'had a whole range' of objective suicide risk factors, including his history of depression, a previous suicide attempt and the fact he was a farmer.

Large disagrees with Stanton's assessment of Mathew having an objectively 'tiny risk' of dying by suicide: 'I think it's kind of glib to say patients who are discharged from a psychiatric hospital have a tiny risk of suicide.'

He's also sceptical of Stanton's assessment that Natasha 'emotionally manipulated' Mathew and that their argument was the cause of his suicide threat. 'All relationships have difficulties and suicide is rare-ish,' he concludes.

Under cross-examination, Hatfield suggests Dr Stanton was in a better position to assess Mathew, having met him in person.

'I don't think so ... your gut feelings about things doesn't work particularly well,' Large replies.

A fiery argument erupts in the middle of Manuell's closing address, which the jury does not hear. Hatfield raises the issue after the jury files out of the courtroom for their lunch break. He's clearly been stewing on it.

During her arguments just prior to the break, Manuell invited the jury to speculate that, on the final day of his life, Natasha and Mathew watched an instructional video about helium together at Gusto café in Tamworth. She did this by highlighting timestamps, which showed the video was played for a second time when Mathew's phone was not in use, after he had ordered lunch and returned to their table outside.

Hatfield tells the judge this is unfair, given that Manuell has abandoned the defence of assisted suicide.

'It is a problem because of the way this case was inappropriately opened by my learned friend, raising matters about assisted suicide and the like, and fleshing them out to some extent in the opening, about which there is no evidence ... it is unfair to the Crown. Completely unfair to the Crown.'

He asks for Manuell to withdraw it in front of the jury.

This is the first time Justice Lonergan hears that the defence of assisted suicide has been abandoned. It's not exactly clear when Natasha's legal team decided to abandon this defence, but they'd informed the prosecution about it via an email just before Hatfield delivered his closing address. Justice Lonergan was not privy to this development.

Despite the shock revelation, Justice Lonergan keeps her cool.

She asks Manuell a series of questions. 'How can you fairly invite the jury to reason that way, when your own client said she never looked up those things? How can you ask the jury to speculate that she was actually sitting there with the accused, showing him these videos?' Justice Lonergan asks.

Manuell fights back with a question. 'Did I say to the jury that they were sitting there together, looking at the videos?'

Exasperated, Justice Lonergan doesn't hold back.

'Oh, that's the inference. That's exactly what you are inviting them to do, Ms Manuell. Let's not play games about what's being inferred here, or what really you are inviting the jury to infer. Without stating it, that is absolutely clear, that's what you are inviting the jury to infer. Absolutely clear.'

There's a bit of back and forth then Justice Lonergan decides she can't wait any longer to find out what she's been wondering for the whole trial.

'Let me raise this now because I don't think this issue can wait any longer,' she says, her clasped hands resting on the bench.

'What is the evidence you say supports an assisted suicide case, or are you going to disavow that case? What's happening with that? I have been quite patient with waiting for that position to be revealed. I've been careful not to press you on a final position in respect of that, but with this current objection taken by Mr Crown, I need to know what's going to be said about that. What is going to be said about that?'

After the lunch break, Manuell clarifies the defence position, telling the court: 'I will not be asking the jury to consider an offence of aid or abet suicide. That issue is now off the table.'

Justice Lonergan asks why the defence was raised in the first place.

Manuell explains there was discussion about it between the parties during the course of negotiations in the lead-up to the trial. 'It had been floated as an idea and the Crown had the opportunity to accept that offer before the commencement of the trial.'

Hatfield looks as though he's about to lose it. He tells the court that Natasha's legal team only informed him of the decision to adopt the assisted suicide defence on the day the jury was selected. He was hardly given any time.

'I was ambushed by a text message 20 minutes beforehand and left in the position that we completely delay the empanelment [of the jury], or proceeding in some other way,' he says in a raised voice, referring to a text message Manuell sent him. He's fired up.

In light of how the defence opened their case, and the decision for Natasha not to give evidence, he argues, it's unfair how the defence is 'filling the gaps' and inviting the jury to speculate whether Natasha and Mathew planned his suicide together.

'It's been happening throughout the closing address ... she's attempting to plant seeds or give explanations on behalf of her client at this time. And it's quite inappropriate. It's very unfair to the Crown.'

Justice Lonergan agrees. 'There is a pervasive sense of unfairness in having opened on a case of assisted suicide that has not been specif-ically withdrawn by you, Ms Manuell ... here's the jury, still in the dark, thinking they might be looking at things that might feed into assisted suicide and, therefore, their mind gets that idea locked into it, even though, in reality, it is not going to be left to them because there is no evidence of it.' She also points out that she's been in the dark the whole time, too.

'One wonders why it was opened on, if there wasn't any evidence to be led to support it.'

After another 15 minutes of debate, Justice Lonergan puts her foot down. 'I take the view that the area to which the Crown has taken objection is speculation,' she says. But Justice Lonergan won't ask Manuell to withdraw what she's said in front of the jury at this critical point in her closing address.

'I will deal with it in summing-up, in the way I consider appropriate and fair, and we press on,' she says. 'Summing-up' is when a judge summarises all the evidence for the jurors, including the prosecution and defence cases, and gives them directions about the law.

In her summing-up, Justice Lonergan tells the jury: 'There is no evidence at all in the trial that Ms Darcy helped the deceased . . . or spoke to him about any intention he had to commit suicide. There is evidence she went to collect the helium with him . . . [but] there is no evidence of a shared discussion with him and the accused about what he might do with that helium. There is no evidence that Ms Darcy knew of the deceased's intention to kill himself but refrained from telling anyone. You must not speculate that the accused would have said those things if she had elected to give evidence.'

Following a little more than two days of her closing address, Manuell finishes much in the same way she began at the start of the trial.

'If you think there is a reasonable possibility that Mr Dunbar died by his own hand, you must acquit the accused. It's a fundamental right that Ms Darcy doesn't have to prove anything. It is for the Crown to establish the charge beyond reasonable doubt.'

36

VERDICT

A cold front brings strong winds and icy temperatures to Sydney, cloaking the city in grey on the morning the jury is sent out to reach their verdict. The courtroom feels a little emptier without John and Elaine, who reluctantly flew to Broome to visit family; they'd rescheduled this trip multiple times as the trial dragged on. The trial started in March; it's now mid-June.

Just before Justice Lonergan finishes summing-up all the evidence, Mathew's childhood friend Belinder Wauch slips into the courtroom. She flashes me a reassuring wink as she closes the door quietly. Detective Senior Constable Graham Goodwin is here, too, sitting to my left in the front row of the public gallery.

Natasha trudges up the stairs from the cells below and into the dock, wearing a blush-coloured knit and sporting a new look. Her mane is ironed straight today, leaving me to wonder whether she's allowed a hair straightener in her cell.

Her efforts to present herself on the trial's final day fail to hide her swollen face and puffy eyes. It's as though, after swallowing all the evidence she's heard in the past 10 weeks, her body has bloated. While I've been taking note of the jurors throughout the trial, I feel the urge to take a good, long look at the people who will shortly be asked to make the ultimate decision. The overall casualness of their collective appearance doesn't seem to align with the grave and serious job they are about to undertake. One of them obviously plans to watch the State of Origin tonight, proudly donning his NSW Blues jersey. Another looks like he's snuggled into his faded grey hooded jumper, about to watch a movie, while the juror next to him has adopted a couch-couture look, too, dressed in an oversized, stretched grey T-shirt.

The women seem to take more pride in their appearance, as does the foreman; a man who looks to be in his mid-50s or 60s, who is often dressed in collared shirts. He's taken meticulous notes through-out the trial and remained alert for every second.

Justice Lonergan tells them their decision must be unanimous; they must all agree about the verdict they reach. If they have any questions, or want to check certain parts of evidence, transcripts will be made available to them. Before she finally sends them out to deliberate, she reminds them that, at any stage, if they have a question or want her to repeat a direction of law, they can send a note through the sheriff, and she will open the court and formally respond to them.

'Now, I will send you out to deliberate,' she says at 10.47 am on 9 June.

The court officer leads them out of the courtroom.

I make eye contact with Goodwin, who raises his shoulders and eyebrows in a who-know-what-will-happen kind of look. Natasha looks over to the public gallery and flashes a smile in Belinder Wauch's direction. Belinder doesn't return the smile. Corrective service officers take Natasha back down to the cells beneath the court.

Now, we wait.

While the judge leaves the courtroom, prosecution solicitors Andrew Baker and Hugh Buddin, and the defence team remain on the floor. All with takeaway coffees in hand, they go through the list of exhibits tendered during the trial. Belinder and I stay, too, chatting in the public gallery.

A jury can take anywhere from a few minutes to several weeks to make their decision. The wait is often a draining and exhausting experience – long stretches of boredom interspersed with pockets of wild stress – as you wonder what the jury are thinking and how long they will take to come back.

My nerves are in overdrive, being so connected to the case and knowing so many of Mathew's friends and family, who are all praying for a guilty verdict. So many people want justice for him.

Rightly or wrongly, I also hope she will be found guilty. I've never invested so much time in a case, both professionally and personally. I truly believe Natasha murdered Mathew and the thought of her getting off makes me feel sick. But you can never predict what verdict a jury will deliver.

At 11.45 am, I notice Justice Lonergan's associate open the court's side door and descend into the room. I overhear her explaining there is a jury note. An electric current surges from my feet to my head. Is it a question or the verdict? Does anyone know? In a lot of trials I've covered, the judge's associate can inform the legal teams about whether the note contains a question or the verdict.

Depending on whether the judge is mindful of the media, the associate will also alert the NSW Supreme Court media liaison officer, who will then give reporters a heads-up about whether a verdict has been reached. I check my inbox – there are no emails to say either way.

Usually, there's only about 20 minutes between the time the jury sends a note to when the court reopens. Or however long it takes for all the lawyers to get back to court.

At 12.01 pm, there are two loud knocks on the courtroom door, indicating the imminent arrival of the judge. She walks in. Taking her seat at the bench, she unfolds a piece of paper. Justice Lonergan reads the note aloud: 'Your Honour, could we please have a copy of the full transcript?'

The request invokes a collective slump from almost everyone present in the courtroom.

The jury might take some time to reach a verdict if they are intent on going over the entire trial transcript. It's possible they only want to look at certain parts, or perhaps they feel a responsibility to ask for it after the judge told them it was something they could request. Either way, they won't be reaching a verdict in the next five minutes.

Justice Lonergan summons the jury back into the courtroom, informing them a copy of the transcript will be delivered to them during the course of the afternoon.

Confident it will take a few hours for them to receive the full transcript, Belinder Wauch and I walk down Darlinghurst Road, in search of sustenance. Not far from St Vincent's Hospital, we find a little hole-in-wall Japanese restaurant. Feeling guilty I'm not waiting outside the courtroom door, I boot up my laptop and log in to the NSW Supreme Court portal, knowing that a video of the courtroom will begin streaming if the jury has a question or reaches a verdict.

After devouring bento boxes, washed down with miso soup, we walk back to court. We are greeted with news at 2.15 pm. There's another jury note but again no indication as to what it's about.

After the prosecution and defence have all returned to the courtroom, Justice Lonergan enters to read aloud the most mundane of notes: 'Can we please be excused from jury duty at 3.30 pm today?'

I begin to worry, as do those closest to Mathew. What's taking them so long?

The jury doesn't make a peep the following day. I try to calm my nerves and focus on writing a feature story about the trial, which will run in *The Sydney Morning Herald* and Nine's online website after a verdict is reached. At 4 pm, the judge calls the jury into the courtroom to formally release them for the day. She also has a note to read. In it, the jury asks for another early mark, requesting to leave by 1 pm the following day, the Friday of the June long weekend.

By this stage, the jury have been deliberating for nearly two days. If they're asking for tomorrow afternoon off in advance, it doesn't sound like they're close to reaching a verdict anytime soon.

I've always desperately wanted to be a fly on the wall in a jury room, keen to see what their thought process is and how they go about dissecting a case. In this case, I particularly want to know the thought process behind the requests for early marks. Are they dragging out their decision to score an extra-long weekend? Or are they deadlocked and unable to stand sitting in a room together for six hours a day?

Friday afternoon rolls around and the jury file into court. My suspicions about the delay being deliberate is heightened by the smiles on many of their faces. This doesn't look like a group who are gridlocked or fatigued by endless debate. Or people agonising over a life-altering decision. On the flip side, they do have a duty to be thorough; it's possible they are simply taking their role seriously, going through all the evidence before making their decision.

They are sent home for their extra-long weekend at 1 pm.

The following Tuesday at 11 am, having only deliberated for an hour after the long weekend, the jury send another note to the judge. Neither the defence nor prosecution know whether it's a question or the verdict. One by one, Hatfield, Manuell and the other lawyers file into the courtroom and take their seats.

The hairs on my arm stand upright as corrective service officers bring up Natasha from the cells to hear the contents of the note. She appears chipper, smiling at her legal team and sipping from a plastic water bottle as she makes small talk. I wonder whether she'll look so cheery in a few minutes.

Justice Lonergan enters the courtroom and sits down at the bench.

'They have reached their verdict,' she tells the court, then calmly asks the court officer to bring in the jury.

There is complete silence as we wait. Every second is agonising. I wonder if John and Elaine are watching online from their daughter's home in Broome. I take several deep breaths. The jurors file into the courtroom and take their seats.

Justice Lonergan's associate asks the foreman what verdict they have reached.

The foreman stands at 11.42 am.

'Guilty,' he says loudly and clearly. His fellow jurors nod in unison, suggesting the resoluteness of their decision.

Natasha stares straight ahead in the seconds after the verdict is read out. Not a muscle in her face moves, her eyes vacant. Her deadpan expression comes as a surprise. I half-expected her to scream out, 'I'm innocent!'

My phone begins to vibrate on the chair next to me.

'Hooray!' Elaine texts, followed by several clapping emojis. Ever dedicated, she and John were watching online when the jury handed down the guilty verdict.

Three years and 10 months after he was murdered, there is finally justice for Mathew.

After all this time, his family and friends can start to heal. And everyone living in Walcha can now breathe easy, knowing Natasha will never walk among them again.

Goodwin is smiling widely, waiting in the public gallery for the opportunity to celebrate with the prosecution. Tears roll down Hatfield's cheeks.

Once word begins to filter through Walcha, many more tears will flow.

PART FOUR

A HISTORY OF DECEIT AND DECEPTION

37

WHAT THE JURY DIDN'T HEAR

There is so much the jury didn't hear during the trial, including one of the most staggering revelations of the case. Not even Natasha may have realised this was playing out as she took the final steps towards ending Mathew's life.

About a week into the trial, a legal argument played out in the NSW Supreme Court, revealing the actions of local police in the lead-up to the murder. But the jury were kept in the dark, waiting in a room nearby.

While the jury heard evidence from the Walcha vet, who contacted police after Natasha inquired about ram sedatives, they did not hear from many other Walcha locals, who had come forward to police with grave concerns about Mathew's relationship with Natasha.

Their concern was real; local detectives were in the initial stages of forming an investigation – even setting up a strike force – to look at Natasha's motives for being involved with Mathew and why she was trying to source ram sedatives. It's almost inconceivable: police were investigating whether Natasha might be planning to harm or kill Mathew before she actually did. After the trial, I learned one particular officer did all he could to prevent Mathew from coming to harm, but Natasha acted far more swiftly than anyone anticipated.

*

As he sat in a monthly meeting at Tamworth Police Station on 27 July 2017, local Walcha police Sergeant Anthony Smith felt the collective weight of the town's concerns on his shoulders. Almost two weeks prior, he'd filed an intelligence report in the NSW Police database, outlining his concerns for a local Walcha farmer, who recently became involved with a woman known to target her partners for money. Smith was yet to receive any response.

Smith worked at Walcha Police Station within the Oxley Police District, an area covering 45,000 square kilometres in country NSW, including the regional towns of Tamworth, Gunnedah and Narrabri. There are 22 police stations in the district and, once a month, police from across the region travel to Tamworth to discuss local issues, investigations and updates.

During this meeting, Smith waited patiently for someone to raise the intelligence report he'd filed on Natasha Darcy. But as the meeting drew to a close, he realised it was up to him. It was now or never. He flung his hand high in the air.

'I think a bloke in Walcha is going to get murdered. Who do I talk to?' Smith asked the room.

A mix of bewildered and blank faces stared back at him.

Immediately sensing everyone's disbelief, Smith added, 'I'm fair dinkum!'

He was advised to contact the Tamworth detectives' office. He wasted no time in heading straight there, seeking out Detective Senior Constable Craig Dunn, who knew Natasha all too well, after interviewing and later charging her with the two attacks on Colin Crossman in 2009. Unable to find him straight away, he relayed his concerns to Senior Constable Graham Goodwin, who had assisted Dunn in charging Natasha all those years ago.

Goodwin listened intently as Smith explained the latest on Natasha, and how she'd latched on to a local farmer who was desperately looking for love. A few months into their relationship, the new boyfriend was already well and truly besotted, and willing to turn a blind eye to her prior crimes. He stood by her while she served 18 months in custody and, after getting out of jail in October 2016, she moved straight into farmer Mathew Dunbar's property with her three children. From that point onwards, all who knew Mathew reported witnessing his rapid decline.

'The town was talking about her well before that, but certainly, once she got out of jail and moved to Pandora, once that happened, the talk was very strong. People were asking me, "Isn't there anything you can do?" They were basically saying, "We know what she's capable of and she just wants his money,"' Smith says.

Smith informed Goodwin there was also information to suggest Natasha was trying to source ram sedatives, running him through the intelligence report he'd compiled in mid-July 2017, less than two weeks before Mathew's death. The report said:

> Due to this relationship Dunbar has ceased all communication with previous friends who have voiced their disapproval to his relationship with the POI [person of interest]. Prior to this relationship Dunbar was considered to be living a comfortable lifestyle with considerable wealth.
>
> Police have real concerns for the welfare of Dunbar. As the POI's history highlights, her partner at the time becomes the victim of her criminal enterprise. Dunbar is not accepting of the POI's previous criminal behaviour blaming all the listed matters on police victimisation of the POI.

Upon hearing Smith's concerns, and knowing her background, Goodwin decided to start an investigation into whether Natasha was trying to source ram sedatives and looked into how they could potentially catch her in the act.

'I basically said, we will try and do some covert surveillance on her to see if she was trying to buy these drugs and to see if we could do anything about it,' Goodwin says.

'Mathew wouldn't believe anyone that told him he shouldn't be with her and then we learned about the sedatives. That's why we decided to do the job. We certainly didn't think it was going to happen there and then.'

When Smith was first posted at Walcha Police Station back in 2013, it didn't take long before Natasha landed firmly on his radar. He arrived when she'd falsely accused a Walcha man of indecently assaulting her daughter. All the charges were later withdrawn and dismissed. Natasha had met the man through the local pony club and there was no evidence to prove any of the allegations.

'At one stage, she alleged this fellow was driving constantly past her house. I hid out there one day and he never showed up. This fellow had an awful time tied up with it, I don't think anyone believed he was capable,' Smith recalls.

Only a few months after arriving in town, Smith came face-to-face with Natasha. He interviewed her after she was accused of stealing cash from Walcha Royal Café, where she worked part-time. Charges were never laid. He later spearheaded an investigation after she falsely accused her ex-partner of assaulting her and was involved in taking out an apprehended violence order (AVO) against her.

Being the local sergeant, Smith was well trained in ignoring town gossip, but the talk about Natasha and Mathew snowballed into much more. In the months before Mathew's death, more than half a dozen people had come to Smith, genuinely concerned for Mathew's welfare. This fear about the relationship was a topic he could not escape at work or off duty. He distinctly recalls being bombarded by concerned locals at the Walcha Show in March 2017, to the point where his wife commented about how impossible it was for him to get away from work when working in a small town.

After learning Mathew had changed his will to make Natasha the sole beneficiary of his entire estate, Smith grew even more worried, but the alarm bells really started ringing when the local vet called him to report Natasha's suspicious attempts to buy ram sedatives.

'I'd been receiving information for a long time with people very concerned about the relationship. Initially, I thought, I'm not a relationship doctor, but once we learned about the sedatives and when Lance informed me about the will – that she'd been made the sole beneficiary – those two factors, you're thinking, "We've got something here."'

'That, combined with all of her criminal history, where her partners seem to be the victim of her criminal enterprises.'

Smith spoke to several of Mathew's friends, his mother Janet and even rang his uncle John Schell, knowing he was a former officer himself, to see if he could talk any sense into Mathew.

This is the same John who watched all of Natasha's trial a couple of seats behind me in the courtroom's public gallery with his wife Elaine. Both spoke fondly of Smith and all he tried to do.

'Anthony Smith called John and told him to warn Mathew about Natasha. When John contacted Mathew, he wouldn't hear anything bad about Natasha,' Elaine tells me one day after court during the trial.

'Even when John told him that Natasha was known to the police, he wouldn't listen and ended up hanging up on John. Sadly, that was the last time we spoke to Mathew, as he wouldn't take our calls after that.'

Smith even drove out to Pandora to speak to Mathew himself, but he was not receptive.

Smith and Goodwin discussed a game plan, even looking at potentially tapping Natasha's phone to try and catch her out.

'I was getting information. All the information was giving me a strong belief but that's all I had, a belief. It got stronger and stronger, which led to the intel report.'

On the same day Smith raised his concerns at the Tamworth police meeting, Mathew's friend Stuart Wellings walked into Walcha Police Station to speak to someone about his growing fears. Stuart, who knew Mathew through the poultry club, spoke to Senior Constable

Tony Souzu. This was the same officer who had been called out to Pandora following Mathew's suicide threat.

Stuart Wellings informed Souzu that he was worried about Mathew. He looked unwell, he was displaying memory loss and was suffering after a mysterious leg infection that, at one stage, looked like it could require amputation. He couldn't quite put his finger on it, but he was very concerned about Natasha's background and how she was affecting all aspects of Mathew's life.

An impending sense of doom lingered over Walcha. Five days later, everyone's worst fears were realised.

Smith woke to the sound of his phone ringing in the early hours of 2 August 2017.

'Souzu rang and said, "We've got a deceased out at Pandora." He said, "I'm fair dinkum."'

Shortly after waking up to a nightmare, Smith got dressed and ran down to Walcha Police Station before driving out to Pandora with Souzu.

'I think we were in a fair bit of disbelief and thinking, "Has this really happened?" I can't put words to it, it didn't seem real. You couldn't think someone would ever do that,' he says, recalling the 15-minute drive on Thunderbolts Way out to the property.

'I had this belief it was going to happen, and it happened. I was speechless and I felt a bit of guilt. What did I miss? Did I not react soon enough? Was there anything more I could have done?'

Smith's prior knowledge, however, was critical in treating Mathew's death as a murder from the start.

'When I got to the house and realised what had happened, I rang Goodie [Goodwin] and said, "It's happened, mate."'

Smith declared Pandora a crime scene before Goodwin arrived and took over, swiftly and decisively, organising a crime-scene warrant, arranging for forensics and getting extra officers out to the property.

296

Goodwin recalls Smith filling him in over the phone as he drove from Tamworth to Walcha, and explaining Natasha's version of events. 'I was certainly going to use every resource possible to see whether it was a suicide or not.'

'I was aware, after speaking to Smithy, the problems with Mathew having his guns taken off him, but we would treat it at the highest level [a homicide] until we could prove otherwise.'

Goodwin acted with lightning speed, sending out detectives to interview employees at Supagas, where the helium was bought, and to the hospital to find the surgeon who had assessed Mathew's leg the previous day. Within hours of Mathew's death, Goodwin got confirmation that it was a woman who ordered the helium, and that the surgeon's prognosis of Mathew's leg injury was directly at odds with Natasha's claims.

'That showed she was lying from the outset, very early on in the piece,' he says.

Although he kept an open mind, Goodwin knew this was a homicide after he organised for the digital forensic unit to download Natasha's phone.

'They downloaded and showed me some of the searches like "how to get away with murder" and "acepromazine murder". As soon as I got those, I thought, "Well, no one googles that." I was pretty sure it was a murder.'

Many police believe if Natasha had killed someone in a different region or state, and staged it as a suicide, she might have got away with it.

Because he knew her background, however, Goodwin ensured a lot of evidence was gathered that may have been overlooked.

'I think if she'd done it a fair distance away, there is a high likelihood that a lot of evidence that we were able to gather may have been lost, or may have not been sent for testing, like the Nutribullet.'

The forensic teams also collected samples of Mathew's vomit and the bedroom carpet for testing, which ended up revealing traces of acepromazine, something which police may not have done if they were not aware of her background.

'The ace would probably not have been detected. If she'd gone interstate, we wouldn't have become aware of that, unless we saw something in the papers. It would have made it a lot more difficult to prove, if at all,' Goodwin says.

His colleague Craig Dunn agrees. 'If she'd moved interstate, she would have spun her lies and the cops would have cleaned up the crime scene. She possibly could have got away with it. But because she did it in the same area, and a few of the cops knew her, our interests were already raised that, if something happens, it is to be treated suspiciously right away.'

Goodwin, Dunn and Smith have all talked about how easily she could have got away with murder – anywhere but Walcha.

'It could have easily been treated as a suicide. He'd tried to kill himself a couple of weeks before, and it could have been seen as he's been successful this time,' Smith says.

Even though the knowledge of local police helped to bring her down, they were still powerless to stop her.

'It gives me no joy that she's been convicted, because it doesn't give him back and I feel like I let him down. I was getting stuff that, in hindsight, turned out to be true but I wasn't able to stop it.'

Smith continues to replay the events leading up to Mathew's death in his mind. 'That's the disappointing thing, I couldn't save him and that haunts me . . . because I know he was a genuine bloke – he wouldn't harm a fly. I knew something, but I couldn't stop it.'

38

JAIL LETTERS

Cradling a goblet-sized glass of shiraz – and slouched on a chair so close to the gas heater there's a real risk my stockings will melt – I notice my phone light up on the kitchen bench. It's been two days since Natasha was found guilty. I feel so drained, the act of standing up and walking over to look at what's on my phone seems like it would take a Herculean effort.

Despite Natasha being found guilty in mid-June, she will not face a sentence hearing until October. This is where the prosecution and defence put forward arguments about the length of the sentence she should receive. Mathew's family will have the opportunity to read out or write a victim impact statement, outlining how his murder has affected them.

About half an hour later, and coinciding with the need to pour more wine, I drag myself away from the heater to see what's on my phone. There's a Twitter notification, indicating I've been sent a direct message from Mandy, Natasha's high school friend, who she'd written to from jail, offering her $20,000 in return for a false statement.

I am overwhelmed she's contacted me. After watching her give evidence, I sensed there was much more to her story. I wanted to get in touch but wasn't sure how it would be received.

Mandy's message

Hi Emma. I'm just reaching out in the hopes that I can remain anonymous for now, although you have my name, I'd prefer no one to know I'm talking to you yet. You may or may not know that I am the high school friend who Natasha Darcy wrote to from jail. I see you are writing a book and am wondering if you would like to chat with me at some point. If you're writing it, you may as well have the facts.

Kind regards,

Mandy

A few days after her message, Mandy and I arrange to talk on the phone.

She tells me, as she read Natasha's jail letter, the sickness in her stomach rose with every word.

'I knew where it was going and, as I'm reading it, I was thinking "No, no, no, no, no . . . don't do it!"' she says, talking candidly from her home in Adelaide.

She recalls pacing around her living room in a panic, putting the letter down and picking it back up again repeatedly. She winced as she read the letter, hoping Natasha was not about to ask her to lie for her. Her worst fears were soon confirmed. Natasha asked her to make a false statement to help get her off a murder charge.

'I was thinking, "Oh my God, she did it, she actually asked."'

Anger came first. 'I thought, "How dare she! How could she ask me to do that? Who does she think I am?" Then I thought, "Maybe she's panicking, and she doesn't really mean it." I was hoping a letter would arrive the next week, and she'd apologise and tell me to ignore it.'

A letter did arrive but, to Mandy's horror, Natasha did the opposite of retracting her request. She offered more money.

'I don't know how many times I said, "No, no, no, no, no!"'

She even read the letter aloud to her husband at the time, who'd said, 'She's sooooo guilty.'

'I said, "Don't say that. She's my friend, she's just messed up," and he just kept saying, "Guilty!" But I told him, "I just don't want to believe it."'

Mandy was trying to forget about the letters when Natasha rang from jail, obviously keen to have some sign her friend would agree to her farfetched plan.

'She said, "Are we okay?" and I said, "Yeah, yeah," but was really thinking "No, we are not."'

'I didn't want her to know I had received the letters, and I didn't want to talk about them as I still hadn't fully processed them. She never rang me back. Maybe she picked up on my nerves, but that was the last communication we had.'

Mandy says she knew what Natasha had asked her was wrong but tried to brush it to one side. Getting involved in Natasha's mess was the last thing she needed, when she was going through a separation, dealing with her own mental health issues and looking after three children.

For the next year, Natasha's proposition niggled at her and, as the trial approached in March 2021, she felt an impending sense of dread. After googling Natasha's name, she realised the trial had started; she couldn't shake the feeling she needed to do something.

'I still didn't want to believe she'd done anything wrong, and I felt like I was betraying her. I felt like the worst friend in the universe, but I knew I had to do this because I knew what I had was evidence. I thought, "If she's innocent, then she'll get found not guilty regardless of what I do or show." At the end of the day, I had what is considered evidence and I knew that withholding it was not a good thing.'

On the Tuesday morning after the Easter long weekend, Mandy rang the office of the Director of Public Prosecutions repeatedly from 8 am. Eventually, someone picked up. She told the woman who'd taken the call that she thought she might have some evidence in relation to the Natasha Darcy trial and asked to speak to the Crown prosecutor, Brett Hatfield.

'She told me to hold, and I was patched straight through.'

She and Hatfield spoke at length.

The next day, Mandy spent five hours at a police station in Adelaide as one of the state's most seasoned homicide detectives took her statement.

She went right back to the beginning, to when she had met Natasha at Colo High School.

They'd played netball and socialised in a tight-knit group with four other girls. She remembers Natasha's family living on a large acreage in Freemans Reach, a town on the Hawkesbury River about 65 kilometres north-west of Sydney's CBD.

'She was a really big personality: a big character, always laughing, silly and loud. She was always a lot of fun, and we were always laughing at something she was doing,' Mandy says.

After graduating in 1992, the pair lost touch but bumped into each other at the Richmond shops, just after fires had ripped through the Hawkesbury region during the 2001 Black Christmas bushfires. More than 100 fires burned through parts of New South Wales and the Australian Capital Territory for 23 days, fuelled by westerly winds. More than 100 homes were destroyed. Miraculously, no one died.

Mandy remembers their meeting well. She'd just found out she was pregnant with her second child; Natasha was the first person she'd told after seeing her GP. At the time, Natasha was pregnant with her daughter and still living in the Hawkesbury area with her then-husband – a man I would learn much more about in coming weeks.

Another decade passed before they connected again – this time through Facebook in June 2013. They would sporadically like each other's photos and posts on Facebook, but had minimal contact.

It wasn't until 5 August 2017 – three days after Mathew's death – that they would properly enter each other's lives once more.

Mandy felt sick to her core when reading a Facebook post of Natasha's, which explained how Mathew had suicided by 'gassing himself'.

'I reached out because I had not long gone through my own mental health stuff and attempted suicide a few times, and I told her I understood what Mathew must have felt and told her that, if anyone said anything negative or mean about what had happened, to let me know,' Mandy says.

'I didn't want her to be angry at him and I wanted her to understand it would be hard for her to understand what it's like to be suicidal.'

Mandy sent Natasha her mobile number and told her to call anytime she needed. Within minutes, Natasha wrote back to her kind offer.

Natasha and Mandy Facebook messages, 5 August 2017, 9.28 pm
Natasha: Thank you so much. It's so confusing right now, there are so many 'if only's' I'm sure people blame me. Why didn't I make him happy? Why didn't he want to stay with us if he loves us?' I keep going from sadness to anger then blame all over again.
Mandy: You did make him happy . . . and you're probably the reason he held on so long. Oh sweet. You're grieving . . . just let yourself go through the whole range of emotions
Natasha: But when it comes down to it, he was sick and if I had of saved him in time, he would just try again.
Mandy: Yes. He would have.
Natasha: Thank you for understanding. It hurts so much. You're a great friend.

Open and raw, Mandy writes from the heart, explaining what being suicidal felt like, in the hope it would help Natasha.

Natasha and Mandy Facebook messages (continued)
Natasha: I'm in tears now. Good tears.
Mandy: Oh I'm glad. And I'm glad I can explain how he felt. I saw the things he wrote about you and your babies. You gave him the only happiness he ever really had.

Natasha: You explained his pain to me better than anyone. Are you all ok now?

Mandy: Yes I am. And I'm glad I went through it . . . especially right now . . . I knew there was a reason & one day I would know why.

Natasha: I'm so glad you came out the other end of it. Thanks for taking the time and explaining it to me. Goodnight my dear old friend xxxx

It's hard for Mandy to read back over their old messages.

'I feel sick that I was so open and vulnerable about my own suicide attempts. I told her all this stuff and I now wonder, did she use any of that when she was talking to the police, or did she use that as part of, or to shape, her defence?'

Believing that Mathew had taken his own life, she'd felt sorry for Natasha when she'd read a Facebook post in which she'd written about Pandora being left 'trashed' by police, who'd left black fingerprint dust all over the walls after searching the property.

'When I spoke to her on the phone, she said people were being really mean to her and that everyone was blaming her for Mat killing himself. She said, "I feel like everyone is blaming me because I didn't stop him."'

When a mutual school friend sent her a link to a news article, Mandy was 'devastated'.

Natasha had been arrested and charged with Mathew's murder.

'I didn't think there was any way she could have done it, because we had shared so much, and I believed her. I believed my friend and I had no reason to doubt her. I didn't know anything about her past and it's not like I googled her. We had reconnected on Facebook but it's not like she said, "Oh hey, I've been locked up before."'

I ask Mandy if Natasha had ever spoken to her about being charged with Colin's attempted murder. Natasha had briefly mentioned it in a letter, Mandy says, but denied any wrongdoing, claiming her dealings with the 'horse industry' had led to her family home being burned down in Walcha.

The letter, penned to Mandy at some point in 2018, is wild reading. It's an invaluable insight into how Natasha explains away her criminal past, particularly the house fire of 2009.

Natasha's jail letter, 2018
Dear Mandy,

It was so great to get your letter. I'm crying and have now read it about 10 times. I feel like the whole world is against me at the moment. Even the people who knew Mathew well and know the truth of what happened have abandoned me now. I'm so glad you and your beautiful children are doing so well and i'm sorry to hear you and [your husband] have separated, but glad he's supporting you and darling [your daughter].

I'm so proud of you almost finished your studies. Well done, that's a real accomplishment especially considering you also have three children and a difficult relationship situation.

You are a 'super star'!

Thank you for your offer of sending me things but that's not possible unfortunately, and there is nothing i need anyway. Your support means the world to me though. Today you have picked me up. I cry most days, for my children, for Mathew (still) and for everything that I've lost. Please pass on my address to [mutual friend] if she wants it. I can't express how much it means to me to have your support, i thought everyone hated me, except my kids, my parents and my ex-husband that is.

My ex-husband Colin is supportive as he can be. The media have been really bad to him and the kids, especially me. Very little of what the media have reported has been true. They said i purchased the helium bottle which he used to end his life with. I didn't! the police even have CCTV footage of him purchasing, collecting and the loading it on his ute. They said we don't have rams on our property and had no use for any sedative, which is also not true and they also said he had only months prior to his death, changed his will, however it was in 2014 when he did that. Very little about his mental health has been mentioned and nothing regarding his stay in a Mental Health Unit on suicide watch, just weeks before his death. It's all just bad about me. My poor children, my heart breaks for him every day and for my children especially. Colin loves them but he is very hard on them. I know my life is over, i'm now only living for my children.

We all make mistakes in life and bad choices, but i would never hurt anyone or anything. Unfortunately for me when we moved out to the country and i got involved with the horse racing industry and my love of the animals and the horses being hurt, drugged and stables burned down and as a result of me saying i was going to the police, suddenly my house was burnt down. The police didn't investigate the real culprits, however i do have some sense of justice hearing that one of the men is now serving a long jail sentence for another matter. But at the time Colin and my parents and i decided the best thing would be to plead guilty, as we had already paid over $200,000 in legal fees and needed it to stop. Pleading guilty was the worse thing i ever did as the police now believe i'm guilty to everything, even something as sad but obvious as a suicide.

I'm actually in a reasonable place here at Mary Wade Remand Centre. I have a nice new room to myself (there are only two single rooms here) and i am in a house full of Asians, who i love. The Aussies don't like working and this is a working house, so i hang with the Asian ladies and they are lovely. I'm the boss's secretary and i find job, work, position for the inmates. I'm treated well at work and it makes my days go faster.

Actually there is something you may be able to help me with if your able. I have recently seen on 60 Minutes on 25.11.18 7pm, a Dr or a Professor who is in charge of something called the 'Innocens

Project' in Perth, she has short brown hair and works with the university or something. She fights for people who are found guilty and who are actually innocent. That's not me, however i would like to make contact with her, She may be able to offer me advice. Would you be able to google her. Only if you have time that is.

I hate asking people to do things for me but i have very few tools at my disposal.

Anyway i'm probably boring you silly. Do something for me though. Kiss your kids and hold them every chance you get. Tell them you love them and how proud you are of them. And then every day tell yourself what a wonderful mother you are. I'm so grateful to have you as a friend.

Lots of love

Tasha xxx

Following this letter, Mandy spent hours researching the Innocence Project, making phone calls and printing off information for Natasha. At this point, she still believed Natasha had been wrongly accused.

'I was fully invested in helping her. I'm a disability support worker and I would stop and help anyone I could,' Mandy explains.

Knowing Natasha's mother, Maureen, was the only person who was visiting her, Mandy decided to visit Natasha in jail when she went to visit family in Sydney in December 2019. 'I knew she needed a friend and I wanted to let her know that I was there for her. I did this because I believed her.'

During her two visits, Mandy recalls they talked about the case at length. Natasha convincingly explained away any evidence against her, including that none of her DNA had been found on the helium tank.

During the trial, Hatfield always maintained the prosecution case did not rely on DNA to prove its case. The jury heard that several items – including the helium tank and plastic bag – were not ideal surfaces from which to extract DNA and fingerprints, so it wasn't surprising Natasha's DNA was not present.

'I was thinking, "You poor thing, oh no." I left thinking, "I think she's right and she'll get off."'

Mandy says the reality of the situation only fully dawned on her as she talked to the detective taking her statement. He spent a lot of time going through the letters, pointing out parts that showed Natasha had groomed her from the start.

'I think I knew, deep down, but I didn't want to believe it. I wasn't hearing from anyone in Walcha, or Mathew's friends or family, it was just what she was telling me.'

She'd come forward with the letters, still feeling like she was a terrible friend but, looking back, she is relieved she spoke up. And after realising Natasha had preyed on her vulnerabilities, her sympathy quickly turned into rage.

'I was horrified, I was shocked and I just couldn't believe it,' she says, taking a few seconds to think.

'I was angry at her because she'd taken advantage of me. Everything I said to her was for the right reasons and the fact that she took advantage of that, and tried to use it against me to make me help her, makes me so angry.'

In Natasha's last letter to Mandy, she'd even had the gall to tell her she was on 'suicide watch'.

'She was just taking advantage of someone's vulnerabilities, which is exactly what she did to Mat. I felt like I betrayed her right up until the end, but now that everything's come out – and there is no way she is innocent – I'm glad I came forward. Maybe I could have saved a life. What if she got away with it? Who was next?'

Mandy is still in disbelief that someone she considered a friend was, in reality, a murderer who had put her own life in jeopardy.

'She could have put me in jail and, if I wasn't as strong as I am now and didn't have my head together, I could have been in a really bad place. How dare she risk my life and play on the most vulnerable part of me? She could have caused me to take my own life.'

Looking back at all the letters, particularly the letter in which she'd been offered money to lie, Mandy now sees how dismissive Natasha had been of her feelings, asking her to talk about her suicide attempts in a sick attempt to help herself.

'She did not care about me one bit, and that becomes obvious in the letters. You don't bring something like that up. I'm glad I went through what I've been through so I can help others, but someone taking advantage of that for their own selfish gain ... fuck her. Fuck her.'

Mandy is clear that part of the reason she chose to reach out to me was because she wanted to impart a message to people suffering from suicidal ideation. She hopes that, out of everything Natasha did to her, she may be able to help someone else.

This is her message:

'I promise you: you can feel better and recover. Please use the big emotions to fight, to hang on and, when you feel better, share your story and you will probably save someone else's life. I know I have, and that is one amazing feeling. No one understands or is more trustworthy than someone who has been there before. Your story can save lives. The world needs people like you; you are so important. I promise you; you can feel better.'

39

RETURN TO WALCHA

Towards the end of the trial, I travel up to Walcha one weekend to catch up with Lance Partridge, his wife Trish and Mathew's mum. I also touch base with Mathew's neighbour, Ross King. We talk over tinnies at the rugby as we watch the Walcha Rams thrash the Gunnedah Devils 50–7.

About a week later, I return for a different reason.

I want to talk to the two men Natasha committed crimes against: Colin Crossman and her partner after him, Fred Nicholson. I don't think Colin will ever speak to me, but I don't feel comfortable writing a book that includes so much about him without at least approaching him and offering him the chance to talk. I'm also in town with Nine's *A Current Affair* cameraman 'Rattle' on the off-chance Colin does want to talk to me and is willing to go on camera for a TV story I'm working on.

I've taken a punt Colin will stop in at Café Graze for a coffee, a place he visits habitually.

We've been parked opposite the café for less than an hour when we see an ambulance pull up out front. I find myself holding my breath as Colin climbs out of the driver's seat and walks into the café. The last time I saw him was three years ago, when Nathan and I followed Natasha to his house and took photographs.

I debate on whether to jump out and approach him right now, but um and ah about it for too long. Colin walks out, gets into the ambulance and drives towards the hospital. We drive that way, too, and park a few hundred metres up the road from the main entrance, hopeful that Colin may come out at some point.

As we sit in the car, I decide to bite the bullet and try to contact another of Natasha's ex-boyfriends, Fred Nicholson. Natasha spent 18 months in jail after stealing his credit card and falsely accusing Fred of assaulting her. I know he's moved to a town nearby and I have a possible mobile number for him. I call it.

It's a bit of a shock when the phone rings, and even more of a surprise when the man who answers the phone is indeed Fred.

'I've been waiting a long time for someone to get in contact with me,' Fred says with a hint of playfulness.

I sigh with relief, thrilled he hasn't hung up on me.

Fred tells me he always thought someone would end up writing a book about Natasha. He's surprised no one got in touch with him sooner. He's also waiting for the movie.

I explain what I've learned about him from Natasha's court files, and ask if there is any chance he would mind talking to me about his experiences with her.

He's currently on his way to Tamworth to get a haircut and do his weekly grocery shop, so can't talk right now, but is happy to chat.

I ask if he minds me driving out to his property later this afternoon, explaining that I'm in Walcha. We arrange to meet at his property at about 2 pm and, after hanging up the phone, I cancel my flight back to Sydney and organise a hire car in Tamworth so that Rattle can drive home to the Central Coast. I have no idea how long I will be with Fred, and I don't want to be rushed.

At this point, we're still sitting outside the hospital in the hope of seeing Colin, but I'm feeling increasingly uncomfortable about the prospect of ambushing him outside his work.

The best course of action, I decide, is to drop a letter in his mailbox, giving him the opportunity to talk to me if he wants and eliminating any possible confrontation.

Parked at the entrance to his property, the same place I'd seen him and Natasha unloading the washing machine back in 2017, I've got one foot out the door when I see an ambulance rapidly approaching.

'Fuck, fuck, fuck,' I mutter to myself, making the split-second decision to follow through with the letter delivery. I'll try to hand it to Colin if he stops before driving through the gates to his property.

As I walk towards the gates, Colin pulls into the driveway and winds down his window.

I'm still about five metres from the car when I begin to explain who I am, but he interrupts.

'I know who you are,' he says calmly, catching me off guard.

Nodding, I launch into a bumbling spiel about why I would like to talk to him, but he stops me again.

'Listen darlin' – I'm not speaking to anyone and I never will,' he says clearly, hands still on the steering wheel.

I try to explain I've got a letter, outlining what I'm doing, but he doesn't want a bar of it.

'I'm not going to read your letter; I don't want to read your letter,' he says.

It's clear where he stands and, while I can't push it any further, there's still a burning question I've always wanted to ask.

'Look, um, just before I leave, ah, I've just always wanted to know: why have you maintained a relationship with her?'

'Why do you think?' he asks. 'I've got kids with her.' He winds up the window, cutting me off as I thank him for his time.

I nearly break into a jog as I power-walk back towards the car where Rattle is waiting.

I try to imagine where he's coming from as the primary carer of Natasha's three children. It wouldn't do any of them any good if Colin spoke to the media about their mum. It's impossible to know how awful and hard it's been for Natasha's kids but, at the very least, they've had someone who's kept them together.

40

FRED

After hiring a Mitsubishi Pajero near Tamworth Airport, I punch Fred's address into Google maps. It's a golden afternoon as I drive towards Nundle, a tiny town with a rich gold-rush history. Nundle is nestled between the slopes of the Great Dividing Range and the Peel River, where people still fossick for gold, sapphires and crystals. The countryside is breathtaking.

Driving into Nundle, a village of just 300 people, feels like entering a magical time capsule. Many of the buildings have their original facades intact, including the Peel Inn, the sprawling corner pub built in the 1860s, and the Nundle Woollen Mill, one of the last spinning mills operating in Australia.

Fred lives on a small acreage not far from the town's main drag, in a house perched halfway up a hill. As I make my way up the dirt driveway to his house, his prized horses are grazing in a paddock near the front gate. Standing on the porch with his hands tucked into his jeans, Fred pulls one hand out to wave as I get out of the car with a six-pack of Great Northern beer.

I needn't have brought beers. Fred's not a big drinker; he insists on me trying his liquorice tea. He pops the kettle on. While it boils, I study Fred's impeccably tidy and ordered home, the walls festooned with photographs of his horses. It's strange to be standing in his home, after I've spent days studying his police statements and all the court documents detailing what Natasha did to him. Fred looks into his tea, stirring it thoughtfully.

'I really think I dodged a bullet, I really do,' he says, referring to his brief relationship with Natasha.

'If I was a mullet, then Mathew Dunbar was a marlin.' He repeats this analogy a few times, explaining he believes he was small fry before Natasha turned her sights towards a bigger fish.

'I had a smaller property, and he had a lot more money. I could have been in the same position as Mathew Dunbar which, when you think about it, it's quite nerve-racking.'

We sit down on his grey leather couch, brimming with colourful cushions. I start by asking how he met Natasha.

In August 2013, Fred was in the process of converting an old shed into a house on a block of land he'd recently acquired, when he decided to put down his tools for the day. His brother and his wife, who lived nearby, were headed to Walcha to run some errands. Fred jumped in the car with them to give himself a break.

After paying his phone bill at the post office in town, Fred wanted to grab a coffee from Café Graze, but his sister-in-law wanted to try out the quirky Walcha Royal Café, a popular pitstop for bikers on Fitzroy Street. Fred remembers a bubbly waitress with bleached-blonde hair stopping at his table and saying flirtatiously to him, 'I know you,' to which Fred said, 'No, you don't.'

Natasha kept her eye on him until he and his brother went up to the counter to pay for their coffees and muffins.

Much to Fred's embarrassment, his brother chuckled and said to Natasha, 'He's single and looking for a good woman.'

Fred elbowed him in the ribs. He quickly forgot the awkward encounter but was remined of it a few days later, after taking a break from working on his block to visit his brother. Not long after walking through the doors, his sister-in-law passed him a piece of paper. It was the number of the waitress they'd met at the café. Natasha somehow tracked down his brother's number, rung his house and, once getting through, began asking a lot of questions about Fred.

Fred says he mulled over calling her for about a week before his brother jostled him, encouraging him to 'give it a shot' because she was obviously keen.

'I rang her and the rest is history, I guess,' says Fred.

Natasha was not backward in coming forward, telling Fred, when they had first arranged to meet, that she was attracted to him and very interested.

A little more than a year later, Fred and Natasha ended their romantic relationship. Then, in September 2014, Natasha called him out of the blue and asked if she could catch a lift to Armidale next time he was headed that way. Thinking it was an innocent request, Fred drove her there. He ran a few errands, finishing at Horseland to pick up a few things. Before heading back to Walcha, Fred pulled in at Hungry Jack's for a quick bathroom stop, leaving his wallet behind in the car's centre console. He only realised his credit card was missing when he got back to Walcha. Natasha feigned worry and offered to help him find it.

'She was quick as a flash, grabbed the phone, looked up Horseland, rang the number and spoke loudly, talking to an employee, explaining how I might have left my credit card there.'

After hanging up, Natasha told Fred the store had his credit card and would hold onto it until he came back.

'I said, "I'm going back to get it now," and she said, "No, no, no. I'm going into Armidale tomorrow, so I'll get it," while knowing the card was securely in her pocket.'

Fred reluctantly agreed but soon regretted his decision. The following day, he got a text from NAB. His credit card had exceeded its limit. Fred spoke to local Walcha Sergeant Anthony Smith, who quickly arranged for police to check security footage of the stores Fred's credit card was used in. In the footage, Natasha is captured carrying out an almighty shopping spree. She's at Dick Smith Electronics, where she casually buys three iPads and a laptop, giving a false name and address to staff when finalising the $3294 purchase. She also makes several $500 cash withdrawals at ATMs in Armidale, buys herself a new wardrobe at Noni B and stocks up on groceries at an IGA.

In total, police could prove she racked up at least $7476 on Fred's card.

Police were keen to lay charges straight away, but Fred wanted to give Natasha an opportunity to explain.

'I rang her and she told me all these lies about one of the children's fathers not paying child support, and how she was in the family law court and needed the money to pay for legal fees. She'd said the court case was coming up and that she'd pay me back.'

Too trusting, Fred agreed and asked police not to lay charges.

Local Walcha Sergeant Anthony Smith – who knew about her criminal past involving Colin and would later be the first officer on the scene to Mathew's death – said to Fred, 'You'll be back.'

When Fred heard nothing from Natasha after her alleged family law court date, he decided to confront her.

'There is no court case and I'm not getting my money back, am I?' he asked.

A wide smirk spread across her face. 'That money is gone.'

Fed up with the lies, Fred called the police, who later charged Natasha with 12 counts of dishonestly obtaining property by deception. Natasha told police a series of conflicting stories when she was called into Walcha Police Station. At first, she said she was trying to claw back some of the money Fred owed her. When it was clear this defence wasn't cutting it, she later claimed she had permission to use his card.

'What he's doing is vindictive. He found out on Facebook I was seeing somebody and then he's, um, started all this,' she told police at Walcha Police Station, during an interview on 15 January 2015.

Her new partner was Mathew; she started seeing him a couple of months earlier. After she was charged, she wasted no time in getting in touch with Fred.

She began with a softer approach, calling him to ask why he went to the police. Then she bunged on the tears, wailing as she told him he'd ruined their beautiful relationship. A relationship that, in Fred's mind, was already well and truly over.

Not long after hanging up, she pelted him with the first of many text messages. 'Your vindictive. This is not to do with money. You have ruined something wonderful, just because you didn't want me with Mathew. If only you knew the truth.'

Fred didn't respond, bracing himself before the next barrage of texts, including 'Now its definitely over' and 'I officially hate you'.

It was getting dark, but the messages continued to flash up on Fred's phone as he drove towards his property on the outskirts of Walcha. Each text sent his anxiety levels higher and higher. He prayed for her to stop. But what would he do if she didn't?

As he got closer to home, his phone rang again; a distraught Natasha was on the other end. She was waiting for him outside his front gate. His stomach dropped.

'I just wanted to say goodbye to you. I won't be around in a few days because I am going to kill myself,' she said through sobs.

As he pulled up to his property's front gate, he noticed Natasha parked to the left of his driveway in a silver Volkswagen. Cautiously, he walked to his gate to unlock the padlock but couldn't see any movement in her car.

'Oh my God, I hope she hasn't done it here,' he thought to himself, slowly opening the gate. He'd better go and check. Filled with dread, he walked towards her car and, as he edged closer, Natasha lowered the driver's side window. *She hasn't killed herself at least*, Fred thought.

'Tash, you're not to be here, you cannot be here,' Fred said.

'All I wanted to do was say goodbye, because I won't be here in two days. Can I talk to you?'

At this point, she was bawling, repeating threats of suicide. Not knowing what to do, Fred told her to hop into his car and drove up around his house, parking in his shed.

Blotchy-faced, with tears and snot flying everywhere, Natasha begged him to call the police and take back his statement.

'Tell the police you forgot you lent me the card and say that you didn't realise [I'd] spent so much money on it.'

Fred felt the need to placate her, fearful she was going to make good on her threats. He chose his words carefully: 'I will see what I can do.'

There was an immediate shift in Natasha's demeanour. Now, she was rambling about the wonderful life they could have together. Fred was keen to get Natasha off his property, but she asked to use his bathroom, promising to get out of his hair afterwards. Fred unlocked the front door of his home but, sensing she was up to something, decided to wait outside. From here, he had a clear view of his bedroom and watched in horror as Natasha walked up to his bed. She peeled back his doona and slowly took off all her clothes. She hopped into the bed and lay there naked, seductively waiting for him. Fred was paralysed. She'd totally lost it. He stood outside for 15 minutes; there was no way he was going in there.

Realising she couldn't lure him to bed, Natasha eventually got dressed and reluctantly walked out of the house without mentioning her attempt at seduction. Fred bid her farewell and quickly locked the front gate, watching her car drive off.

Rattled, Fred managed to fall asleep. But this was far from over. At 8.51 am the following day, his phone started beeping. It was Natasha.

'I just finished talking to the Legal Aid solicitor, and he said the police can run with it unless you change your statement. You need to go and ask to change your statement to "you forgot you loaned me the card but didn't realise I'd spent so much." That way, they can't go ahead with it. But you need to make sure you actually change the statement in print.'

Fred hardly had a second to take it all in when his phone beeped again.

'Please delete the last message before you go in! XXXX'

Getting no response, Natasha sent another message.

'Don't let them hurt your ego. Remember we will have all we dreamed about and more! I love you. Delete this as well.'

Her onslaught of texts and calls continued to weigh heavily on Fred's mind.

Trying to get her to back off, he told her he'd try to get in contact with police the following day, but had no intention of doing so. His stalling tactics had no effect.

Between 8.23 pm and 9.08 pm, Natasha called Fred six times. She was an unhinged rollercoaster about to hurtle off the edge. The suicide threats continued – screaming and yelling – repeatedly telling Fred he'd ruined their relationship.

Feeling stressed and helpless, Fred thought, *Make her stop*.

The threats of killing herself were too much and she knew it. Fred's father had suicided and the hurt still ran deep. After the barrage of calls, however, Natasha still wasn't finished; she was frantic, desperate.

'I loved you and held out for over 6 months because I loved you, and now I have no choice but to be with him,' she texted, referring to her new relationship with Mathew.

With her tactics not working, she tried something new. She told Fred she had some documents to show him. He mistakenly thought the documents might help him pursue her later in his planned civil action to claw his money back.

Finally winding up the night's communication, she told him once again she loved him, but then decided to send a final warning message.

'I will do anything to protect my kids and if this goes ahead I'll have to have the Nowendoc camp draft [a cattle-mustering event] audited for embezzlement.'

Fred knew he'd done nothing wrong, 'It is legal u will loose . . . go ahead.'

Fred didn't manage to get a full night's sleep; his phone started going off at 3.34 am. It was Natasha, asking what time he would be in Walcha so she could show him the documents.

Fred wasn't sure now whether it was worth trying to get hold of the documents. He needed more dirt on Natasha but was unsure whether any good would come from meeting her again.

After another full day of calls and messages, he declined to meet her, citing sickness.

Natasha didn't let up, however, telling him she was looking forward to seeing him, had gone to the trouble of taking her daughter to a friend's house, and had baked a slice for him. She also offered him a massage and a cuddle.

'I want to make love to you again, slowly,' she added.

Fred had absolutely no intention of engaging in any romantic rendezvous. But he wanted more proof of the money she'd taken. He agreed to meet her briefly to see the documents, but was afraid of going to her house. He arranged for them to meet at the gate outside her property. *Better to meet her in public*, he thought.

It was pitch dark when Fred pulled up on the road outside Natasha's house at about 9 pm. She walked to the gate, holding a bundle of papers in one hand and, oddly, a bottle of wine in the other.

Alarm bells immediately rang in Fred's ears. Something wasn't quite right. Natasha told him she'd accidentally brought out the wrong paperwork and tried to get Fred to hold the bottle of wine while she headed back to the house to fetch the right bundle. Holding the wine bottle at the base, she thrust the neck of it at Fred, who briefly touched it to prevent it from coming into contact with his chest. As soon as he touched the bottle, Natasha recoiled, telling Fred he better go.

'I thought, "What the hell is going on?" I thought I was being set up for something, but I didn't know what,' Fred says.

Natasha acted quickly, sprinting back to the house as Fred drove off. When she got inside, she told her daughter in a panicked tone to call Mathew and lock the doors. Without hesitation, she smashed the wine bottle and used the jagged edges to cut her arms and neck.

She was sitting on the front-door steps when Mathew arrived. He'd just sped from Pandora to her house in town. Mathew hopped out of his ute and shone his torch around the house to see if he could see anyone, then walked up to Natasha. She told him Fred had held a bottle to her neck and assaulted her, demanding to know who her new boyfriend was. Mathew caught a glimpse of her injuries and immediately called triple-0.

When police arrived, they immediately sensed something was amiss; they asked Natasha to come to the station right away to make a formal statement. Mathew came, too, genuinely concerned someone was out to harm his new partner, and volunteered to make a statement.

In his signed statement, he told police he and Natasha had been in a relationship since November 2014, but had no children together. That night, he'd driven straight from Pandora to Natasha's house after receiving a phone call from her daughter at 9.04 pm.

'She said Fred was there. She sounded distressed and upset. I immediately got out of bed, got dressed and went to Natasha's house. Tash told me Fred was asking who she was seeing. I then decided to ring triple-0 after seeing the marks left on her neck and arm. Tash appeared to be in shock from the incident,' Mathew told police in his statement.

While Natasha made her statement at the station, Mathew went back to the house and drove around the surrounding streets with a torch to make sure Fred wasn't there.

In her statement, Natasha told police Fred had unexpectedly turned up at her house, marched straight into her kitchen and, after sighting two wine glasses on the bench, demanded to know if her new partner was at home.

'I pushed him on the chest directing him out the back door. I saw that he had picked up the wine bottle and was holding it in his left hand . . . holding it by the neck of the bottle,' Natasha claimed.

She claimed Fred violently smashed the wine bottle, grabbed her shirt and held the jagged edges to her throat. But he'd backed off the minute she told him her daughter had phoned Mathew, who would arrive any minute. He placed the bottle down and scurried off to his car, leaving in a hurry.

Sergeant Anthony Smith knew from the get-go what they were likely dealing with. It was Ground Hog Day for him, but he was obliged to call poor Fred into the station and question him about the allegations. Fred was happy to give his version of events and volunteered his phone to police; the calls and texts instantly corroborated his story.

'I just . . . [was] very suspicious why she'd give me the bottle out there, wanted me to touch the bottle. It's just odd. And you don't offer anyone a bottle, a drink out of a bottle,' he told police.

Fred was released without charge, leaving police to weigh up their options as to what action they should take.

Fred says he will always be grateful for the care and concern shown him by Smith, who'd said it would be safest if he stayed with his brother for the time being.

'He said to me, "There's something I want to tell you and I really want you to take it on board. This woman has the potential to harm you," and I'll never forget the look on his face when he said that to me. He meant it.'

About a week after Natasha falsely accused Fred of attacking her, he received an Express Post envelope with his name clearly written across the front.

Tearing it open, he peered inside to find several pages torn from a notepad.

The first page reads: 'YOU MAKE YOURS GO AWAY & I'LL MAKE MINE GO AWAY.'

He knew it was Natasha, blackmailing him to drop the fraud charges and, in return, she'd retract her fake attack story.

Police were quick to act. The Express Post satchel was tracked mail, allowing police to review security footage of the West Tamworth Post

Office at the time and date it was purchased. In it, Natasha is clearly visible, buying the envelope. Once again, Natasha found herself in a small interview room at Walcha Police Station. But for once, she exercised her right to silence.

She was charged with perverting the course of justice and making a false representation resulting in a police investigation. Police also slapped her with a third charge, the details of which can't be published for legal reasons, but involved her coaching a witness to make a false statement. This time, she was not getting off so lightly.

In June 2015, she was sentenced to 12 months' jail with a non-parole period of six months. She appealed the decision, her lawyer telling the court she had no criminal history until reaching her 30s, and suffered from anxiety and depression. Lawyer Peter O'Connor told the court his client was in protective custody, having been stabbed in the head and hand by another inmate, and later threatened with a syringe.

When she faced a separate court hearing for perverting the course of justice, Mathew gave evidence on her behalf. He told the court he and Colin were facing considerable hardship, raising her three children while she was in jail.

'They are struggling without their mum,' Mathew told the court.

While Natasha was already in custody for stealing Fred's credit card, Judge Stephen Hanley later sentenced Natasha to a further two years behind bars. This was for attempting to get Fred to change his statement, her threatening letter and the assault allegation she'd fabricated, all while still on parole.

When Fred learned Natasha would spend a minimum of 18 months in jail, he felt a great sense of relief. This was double the time she'd served for torching her home and leaving Colin sedated in his bed.

Fred was never under any illusions with Natasha. She was never going to be the love of his life, but she was good fun and a distraction following a tough period in his life.

'Whenever I'd see her, she'd have a big smile on her face, always smiley and bubbly. She could really turn it on,' he tells me. 'She's very convincing. She puts on a personality where butter wouldn't melt in her mouth.'

He says he wasn't the only one fooled by her charm.

A couple of close mates had given her the tick of approval – as had his family when he'd introduced her to them following his sister's death in 2014.

'Looking back, she probably just came to sticky beak and see what my family was like, but everyone that met her thought she was quite nice.'

During their relationship, Fred had been completely oblivious to Natasha's past. She'd obviously never mentioned it, and no one in town had breathed a word about it to him. He first sensed something wasn't right when he was talking about Natasha with a mate in town one day and had mentioned 'she wasn't a bad person'.

'He never answered after I said that and I thought, "Hmmm, that was a bit odd, he didn't say anything at all."'

After their on-again, off-again relationship ended, a local farmer explained how Natasha had attacked Colin with a hammer and burned the family home down.

'I said, "Why didn't you tell me about this 12 months ago?" and he said, "We weren't game as we didn't want our houses burned down."'

During their time together, Fred found that, if he ever quizzed Natasha about something she'd said or questioned a story that didn't add up, she'd defend herself with lightning speed.

'If ever I tried to correct her and say, "You said this," she would come back at me as quick as a flash. She would come back with a totally different story and convince you it was true. I'm talking in seconds – bang – without even thinking about it, she could come up with a story.'

Another warning sign struck when Natasha had brought her three children to stay with him for a weekend at his newly built property.

'She said, "If I come and live here and work, I'd be entitled to half of this." A bit of a light bulb went off then and I thought, "That was a pretty strange thing to say."'

He tells me that, everything she did, she always did with purpose. 'She was always thinking about how to do things or manipulate situations – pre-plan things. Looking back now, I can see it.'

Fred doesn't know the ins and outs of Natasha's relationship with Mathew, but believes she had her sights set on him before they ended their relationship. He recalls she'd found two lambs on the side of the road – which he didn't think needed rescuing – and took them home to hand-raise. She claimed she couldn't bear the thought of the lambs being sold for slaughter, but Fred distinctly remembers her making a very odd comment.

'She said, "These lambs will do a lot for me",' a comment Fred now believes was in reference to her plan to lure Mathew in.

'She goes, "I'll contact Mathew Dunbar, because he's such a nice person and he won't harm them."'

Fred's theory makes me think back to those first Facebook interactions between Mathew and Natasha. In October 2014, Natasha had thanked Mathew for allowing her 'babies' – Sugarfoot and Lou Lou – to live on his property. Had the lambs been part of her plan?

Fred thinks so. 'The lambs were a lead-in to Mathew Dunbar. I think it was all premeditated to get those lambs. She was always scheming. Looking back, whatever she did it was planned out, step by step,' he said.

Looking back at what happened, Fred is glad he's still alive to tell the tale.

'I'm probably more embarrassed. I was a bit older than her, and she hoodwinked me. That's my nature, I'm probably too trusting but I just didn't think she could be capable of what she did. I've since learned people are capable of doing anything.'

After we've finished our teas, Fred takes me out to feed his horses, including two stunning chestnut foals he keeps on a hilly paddock behind his house.

The sun disappears, highlighter pinks and oranges staining the sky. We zoom up a hill in a battered, old Suzuki Vitara, the backseat brimming with hay.

'I feel so sad and sorry for poor Dunbar. He didn't need to die like that,' he says, stroking the face of one of the foals.

'All he wanted was a family and she preyed on that. She could have had a comfortable life, living with him on his property, but she was greedy. I've always said, he died too early for no great gain.'

Staying across the trial had brought a lot of memories back for Fred and he was worried she'd get off.

'I'm hoping she stays in jail for the rest of her life, she deserves it because it was just so premeditated. The main thing is there is justice for Mat Dunbar,' he says.

We hop back in the Suzuki Vitara and head down the hill.

41

PREVIOUS LIVES

People often ask me if something happened to Natasha as a child, or whether there was a traumatic event that could in some way explain what led her to becoming a murderous psychopath. By all accounts, she grew up in a loving, blended family and was lucky enough to grow up with horses on their small acreage. Friends say her parents were big believers in the value of hard work, with Natasha and her siblings all working part-time jobs during high school.

She had a close relationship with her mother and stepfather, who officiated at her and Colin's marriage, and still maintained contact with her biological father.

It's hard to work out when and where her obsession with money came from. Or when the lying started. In her 20s, she'd led a modest life, always maintaining a job, but somewhere along the line, money became her sole focus, something she was willing to kill for.

While I'd hoped to interview her family to learn more about Natasha's past for this book, I understand and respect their decision to keep to themselves.

Despite not digging as deep as I would have liked into her upbringing, many people have helped to fill in some gaps about her life prior to arriving in Walcha, including former work colleagues and two ex-partners.

When I get hold of Natasha's old boss Sarah on the phone, she's happy to chat about Natasha. As an employee, she had been a constant source of grief for Sarah. When Sarah joined Provet – a veterinary distribution company – in 2000 to become the general manager of the business's NSW operations, Natasha had already been working there for a couple of years. Natasha was a travelling merchandise salesperson, working out of her car to sell in-vogue collars, leads and pet products to vet clinics across NSW.

Learning this, I think back to her claims about being a vet when she moved to Walcha. Natasha seems to fit the definition of a pathological liar: a person who compulsively fabricates stories or embellishes facts to gain attention or achieve an advantage. There's often a tiny element of truth to her outlandish lies.

Sarah was never a fan, she tells me. 'She wasn't someone I wanted to associate with. I found her to be really ditzy and over the top.'

She also didn't enjoy Natasha's constant 'oversharing', particularly about her sex life. 'She used to share so much personal stuff but, in reality, it was all lies and she would take a lot of time off because of the lies.'

Quite early in their working relationship, Natasha explained she was undergoing IVF, because she was desperate to have a baby with Chris[8], her husband at the time.

'She used to tell me you can't lift your legs off the lounge for three days after doing IVF and came up with all these wild stories, which meant she couldn't come into work,' she says, almost as if she's still in disbelief at Natasha's ability to lie.

'One time, she said she was going off for an egg collection and had a week off work. She'd said, "I've had insemination and I can't stand up or sit in a chair, I need to be lying down for a long time." I knew it

---

8   Name has been changed

was all lies, but I was very new in that role, and she was friends with senior management, so it was hard for me to do anything.'

Although Sarah didn't want to know anything about her personal life, Natasha was keen to share. She openly told Sarah and other colleagues that her husband was secretly homosexual and their marriage was purely one of convenience.

'She kept saying how much she hated sex, so it worked for her,' Sarah says.

Despite claiming she wasn't a sexual person, Natasha later revealed she was living a thrilling double life and having an affair.

'She told me this guy was fantastic in bed and I was thinking, "I thought you didn't like sex."'

Never really paying too much attention to Natasha's stories, Sarah hadn't given much thought to Natasha's claims about her husband being gay until two decades later, when reports surfaced from her murder trial.

Sarah was shocked by media reports revealing Natasha's claims about Mathew being homosexual and that they didn't have a sexual relationship.

'I was horrified. I rang the police the next day and told them this was the same story she told me when I'd first started working with her. I called police at Tamworth and said, "I don't really believe Mathew would have been gay. This is the same story she'd spun back in 2000."'

The 18 months that Sarah managed Natasha as an employee were nervous ones. The lies she'd told were so elaborate, Sarah found them impossible to disprove. 'She was difficult to manage. She would say one thing and do another – you never really knew what she was up to, and you really never knew if she was working.'

Whenever she was confronted about where she'd been, what she'd been doing or why she didn't answer her phone, Natasha often turned on a 'bucket of tears very, very quickly'.

'Whenever I had worked up the courage to talk to her about things, she'd be in a flurry of tears and say, "Are you trying to accuse me of something?" She was always on the back foot, always on the defence, but nothing would stick to her. She was like Teflon.'

Sarah remembers hearing about Natasha being charged over the house fire, which Colin survived.

'At that point, she was living down in Nowra and there was very little information around about it, but I thought, "Wow, there you go."'

She always knew Natasha was a liar but, when the news of Mathew's murder first hit the news, she was shocked to hear the lengths she had gone to.

'I thought, "Holy Christ, this girl is really, really sick." I look at her as being a very dangerous woman.'

Sarah's husband, who also had the displeasure of managing Natasha when she later worked for an internet arm of Provet, believes she is 'very unwell'. He was eventually able to fire her after seeing her on the side of a road in Canberra when she'd claimed to be hundreds of kilometres away, working in another region.

Sarah hopes Natasha will remain in jail for the rest of her life. 'I hope they don't let her out. I think she's a dangerous psychopath and I don't think she is someone who can be rehabilitated.'

After the trial, I also call Amanda. She was another of Natasha's work colleagues but someone who considered her a close friend. Amanda was tasked to train Natasha when she started working at Provet in 1997. Although they lived in different cities, the pair quickly became close friends, talking on the phone and catching up whenever they could.

I sense it's difficult for Amanda to talk to me.

'I feel like I'm betraying her in some sense, but then I think, she's murdered a man and we haven't been in touch for a long time,' she tells me.

Back in the late 1990s, the pair were travelling merchandise managers. Amanda serviced the area from the NSW Central Coast to Queensland, leaving Natasha to cover the Greater Sydney area.

'She came up a lot and I would go down there. We had these big vans with a big display of products – leads and collars – and we would drive to all the vets, where people would climb in the back and take what they wanted.'

When they'd first met, Natasha told her she'd escaped from a violent and controlling relationship up north.

'She said she had married or moved to Queensland with a policeman, who hit her. Her father, who was a pastor, went to Queensland and brought her home, and that's when she got a job at Provet,' Amanda recalls, with a hint of hesitance, perhaps wondering whether anything she'd been told was true.

In reality, Natasha had married a dog handler, who worked for the Royal Australian Air Force (RAAF) base at Richmond, close to where she grew up. She met DJ in her early 20s while working as a vet nurse at a clinic in Windsor. After marrying in 1996, they moved to Queensland, but later separated. Her family helped her to move back to Sydney.

Not long after her return, Natasha told Amanda she'd met another man, but that had ended badly, too.

'She said to me, "That's it, I'll never be in another relationship for love."' This was something Natasha would often say.

Early on in their friendship, Natasha claimed she couldn't have children, following a terrible car accident that damaged her ovaries. Amanda never questioned her; she had no reason to.

'She was very happy, smiling. I always thought she was a little ditzy, but she was lovely.'

Just as she had told her boss, Sarah, Natasha confided in Amanda, telling her she was in a relationship with a man called Chris, but that he was secretly homosexual.

Natasha told Amanda they married to 'keep up appearances for his family, mainly because they didn't want him to know he was gay.'

Amanda recalls meeting Chris once at an industry ball, where all the Provet representatives invited their partners.

I already knew Natasha had been married to a man named Chris, having read about him in her old court files. I wondered if he had any idea Natasha was telling people he was homosexual, or that their marriage was one of convenience, just as she had said about her relationship with Mathew.

In about 2002, Amanda recalls, she and Natasha were attending a conference in Sydney together and staying in motels nearby. Amanda remembers asking Natasha if she wanted to grab a bite to eat one night, but Natasha already had plans. Excitedly, she divulged she was having an affair with an older man named Mark[9] and told her the sex was fantastic.

Not long after this, Natasha became pregnant, telling Amanda that Mark was the father. In reality, the baby's father was Chris. Elaborating on the lie, she claimed she became pregnant during her secret rendezvous with Mark at the conference in Sydney.

'She told me she really, really liked him. He was into cars and had grown-up children.'

Because Chris and she had been trying to conceive via IVF – so the story went – Natasha thought he would be thrilled to learn she was pregnant. Mark, on the other hand, was apparently 'angry' about the pregnancy, and wasn't interested in having any more children.

Natasha went on to give birth to a baby girl. After separating from Chris, she moved in with Mark and became pregnant again. She maintained that Mark was the father, but they had separated by the time Natasha gave birth to her second child, a baby boy.

Amanda recalls Natasha telling her she'd met a man named Colin online, when her son was just a newborn.

Amanda met Colin when he and Natasha dropped past her home in Maitland, during their move up to Walcha.

'He was really lovely and nice, doting on her and the children. He was treating the children as if they were his own,' she says, adding

---

9   Name has been changed.

that she and her husband both agreed he seemed like a 'lovely guy' when they'd left.

Once Natasha settled in Walcha, she sent Amanda a few letters and photos of her children, describing the beautiful life they'd built and how happy they were.

Later, Natasha invited Amanda to her and Colin's wedding on Great Keppel Island in Queensland but, because she had three children, it was impossible for her to go. Amanda was taken aback when she heard Natasha had been charged with Colin's attempted murder.

'I just didn't see her doing anything like that, but I try to see the good in everyone.'

Amanda was equally shocked when one of her colleagues at Provet called to tell her Natasha had been charged with the murder of a farmer, who she was living with at Walcha. After hanging up, she googled the case, needing to read it with her own eyes.

'I had always thought she was very harmless.'

Had she not known about what had happened to Colin, she says, she would never have believed it.

After our phone call, I'm more desperate than ever to track down Chris and Mark.

Before I contact them, however, I decide to get in touch with a woman called Belinda, who allowed Natasha to sell swimming accessory products from her and her husband's company. From reading court documents, I knew this woman was a friend of Mark's and thought she could give me a sense of whether she thought he'd be willing to talk to me.

Belinda was hosting an intimate party for a friend's 50th in her Melbourne home when Mark arrived with Natasha, his new flame, in 2003. They'd flown down from Sydney for the event. Belinda recalls Natasha being loud, vivacious and the centre of attention.

'She was lovely, very over the top, but lovely,' Belinda says, adding that Natasha was eager to reveal details about her and Mark's sex life, and how great he was in bed.

She recalls her whizzing around the party, laughing and working the room, leaving guests dizzy in her wake.

'I remember her outside on the deck and someone saying, "Who's that crazy blonde that Mark's brought?"'

Belinda tells me that, at the time, she had a toddler daughter about the same age as Natasha's daughter. She got talking to Natasha at the party and explained how she and her husband ran a swimming accessories company.

'She said, "I'm a mum looking for work ... oh, I'd love to do something like that."' This comment eventuated in her selling their products on a commission basis in Sydney.

'She went into the pools and people loved her.'

Apart from the odd email and phone contact regarding sales, Belinda wasn't especially close to Natasha, but always found her friendly and easy to deal with.

'I didn't know her intimately. I'd had a couple of dinners with her, and she was always lovely, pleasant and there was never a problem. I found her quite endearing.'

About the time Natasha separated from Mark, she rang Belinda to tell her she was pregnant with her second child. She was adamant Mark was the father, and said she was angered and upset by his reaction to the pregnancy. She told Belinda she thought he was an arsehole. Natasha also spoke about her 'heartbreak' in an email she'd sent in May 2005.

Email from Natasha to Belinda, Tuesday 17 May 2005, 12.35 pm
Hi Belinda, how are you?
I'm settling in nicely to my new house. It's a shoe box compared to the old one, but cosy. How is your family going? My baby is due in 7 weeks today so I'm getting very uncomfortable. It's hard work looking after a 3 year old, 33 weeks pregnant and a broken heart but as one of my friends said, I'll be a stronger person for it.

Belinda maintained contact with her because of the business, but 'the wheels started falling off' their working relationship after Natasha moved to Walcha.

Natasha was paid on a commission basis only, and was not supposed to receive funds directly. She sold the products on and off while living in Sydney and later in Walcha, using a shed at her and Colin's house to store the stock.

At some stage during their working relationship, Belinda remembers sending invoices to various businesses for the products Natasha had sold them, but was surprised to learn the money had already been paid to Natasha directly. This was not the deal.

In the end, Natasha owed the business up to $20,000; money that has never been recovered.

Belinda remembers calling and emailing about the missing money, and trying to organise for the remaining stock to be returned, when Natasha set fire to her home in January 2009.

Natasha had used the fire as an excuse, emailing Belinda to apologise for the delay in sending stock back.

Email from Natasha to Belinda, Monday 23 February, 9.45 am
Belinda, I understand that you need these things urgently, but unfortunately I have had a major catastrophe in my life.

The police still have my computer and I should get it back by the end of this week. It's not like CSI where they take forensics and test them on the spot. These things take ages to get tested. I have not been able to get access to my house until now because it has been too dangerous. We have now been told we can go in and get things after Friday 27th Feb. I need to go to filing buboard [cupboard] on Saturday when I drive down but I need my computer for all the dates I made payments ect.' I understand your fustration but if you had receipted the payments correctly we would not have a problem so it's not all my fault exactly.

Thanks
Tash

336

At one point during their email exchange, Belinda was caught off guard when she received an email from Colin, informing her Natasha had been arrested.

Email from Colin to Belinda, Thursday 11 June, 5.12 pm
Tash is in jail. I will advise her of your email but you will not get her via email or phone.

After receiving this, Belinda called Natasha's phone straight away. Colin picked up.

'He answered,' she says. 'He was really emotional and wanting help, wanting us to support her.' He then asked her to be a character reference for Natasha to help her case.

'It was just unbelievable. I was just flabbergasted. He didn't want her to be found guilty. [He was] saying he loved her and all this stuff. I thought, "This is insane."'

She recalls Colin being 'totally supportive' of Natasha, despite her being charged with his attempted murder. Belinda was asked to make a statement to the police, which she did, and never heard from Natasha again.

Despite knowing Natasha was found guilty of setting fire to her family home, Belinda was still shocked when she heard Natasha had been charged with the murder of Mathew Dunbar.

'I couldn't believe it. It's really sad, she's taken somebody's life and it got to that point. It's really sad for the kids ... immediately, you think of the kids.

'I always found her to be lovely, but I'm a trusting person, so I take people at face value. From Mark's perspective, he's very lucky.'

On the subject of Mark, she tells me he's a pretty approachable guy. She suggests I try to get in touch.

I hang up the phone, hoping he will help me to separate what little fact there is from fiction.

42

THE EXES

I'm desperate to get a firsthand insight from Natasha's ex-partners, whether they saw any signs of what Natasha would end up doing. But I'm a highly talented procrastinator. So I swivel endlessly in my office chair, tidy my desk drawers and dust photo frames in my study as I work up the nerve to send Mark a text.

Hi Mark, I was going to call but I thought text might be better so I didn't put you on the spot. My name is Emma Partridge and I am writing a book about the life and crimes of Natasha Darcy. I'm also the crime editor at Nine News Sydney and have been reporting on the murder of Mathew Dunbar since 2017. I am not looking to drag your name into anything I am doing but I am really hoping we could meet or have a chat on the phone about Natasha. As you would be well aware, her capacity to lie has made it difficult to separate fact from fiction and I am hoping you might be able to clarify a few things for me. I found your name in old court documents where Natasha had spoken about you and also heard about you from some of her former colleagues at Provet. At the very least I'd love to explain more about what I'm doing and see what you think. Call me anytime if you feel comfortable. Cheers, Emma

I leave my phone on my desk and walk out of the study. Staring at a phone, waiting for an answer, is up there with watching paint dry.

When I come back with a tea, I'm surprised to see a missed call. It's Mark. I call him back straight away. The warmth and humour in his voice puts me at ease. He's happy to chat on the condition I don't disclose his full identity. He has a wife and children, and doesn't want them dragged into Natasha's story in any way.

Mark has watched the trial at a distance but tried not to get too sucked into it.

'I was just fascinated with the stories I was hearing,' he says, 'and I was thinking, nothing has changed. Her story changes every day, and it's scary because that's what it was like with her.'

Mark describes his time with Natasha as a 'rebound relationship' after separating from his wife of 23 years. He reckons he's erased a lot of their relationship from his memory as a self-preservation mechanism. Although they lived together, renting a home in Kellyville in Sydney's north-west, Mark says this was more out of convenience after moving out of his family home.

'We started seeing each other, but she got incredibly intense. There were situations where she was quite volatile and did weird things.' Like the time, he says, she pulled a knife on him in the kitchen during an argument. His back was turned to Natasha at the time, but his Newfoundland – a giant and loyal breed of dog – suddenly grabbed her hands with its jaws, holding her until Mark turned around.

'I thought the dog overacted at the time but, in hindsight, clearly that wasn't the case,' he says. 'I remember turning around and she sort of joked and said, "You must have thought I was going to do something."' Perhaps she was.

He also distinctly remembers Natasha putting a pillow over his face and holding it down as he lay in bed one night.

'She tried to suffocate me. I don't get overly flustered and I pushed her off and said, "What are you doing, you idiot?" I'm an ex-swimmer and can hold my breath for one-and-a-half minutes . . . she probably thought she'd been successful,' he says with a chuckle.

Gobsmacked, I tell Mark about the time Colin had made a statement to police, unsure if he'd been the victim of a suffocation or just had a vivid nightmare. Just like Natasha had done to Colin, Mark tells me, Natasha had also hounded him about taking out life insurance.

'She made up stories continually. Everything was a story, nothing was real. I quickly came to the realisation and said, "I'm outta here."'

Just as Belinda had told me, Mark explains he once took Natasha to a party in Melbourne and was mortified to learn about all the stories she'd spun to his friends.

'Following the party, a number of people came up and told me about my life, and what Natasha and I had supposedly been planning. I remember thinking, "What the hell are you doing, saying we are making all these plans, when we're not?" I remember one of my friends saying, "She's mental, mate."'

Mark says their relationship began at the end of 2002 and ended at some point in 2004. When they met, Natasha told him she was separated. 'I was told that Chris was no longer around. I was supposedly post-him but, who knows? She seemed capable of running several stories and relationships at once.'

Mark remembers meeting Chris a number of times because he would drop past their house to collect his daughter for visitations. 'Chris and her were doing part-time caring for her, that was a regular thing.'

During their relationship, Mark met Natasha's immediate family. He remembers having dinner with them in the Windsor area where she had grown up. 'It was a very religious family, deeply religious.' He explains her stepfather had been a bishop.

My mind quickly rewinds to a police interview, in which Natasha had mentioned her father was a pastor who had married her and Colin, but I was in the dark about the specific religion.

On the subject of family, Mark says there is absolutely no way he is the father of any of her children. He says Natasha had a daughter when they met and Mark does not believe he is the father of her second child, a son.

He says a separation was already on the cards, prior to Natasha becoming pregnant. 'She certainly seemed to want to create drama whenever there was an opportunity.'

After they had parted ways, Natasha claimed she sent his DNA off for testing (without his knowledge), before producing a phoney-looking document from an American website, which claimed there was a 99 per cent match that Mark was the father of her newborn son. There was no evidence on the dodgy-looking certificate to prove the DNA she sent off was, in fact, Mark's.

'I did some investigating and found there was some bogus website in America you can get DNA documents from. It was all a forgery,' he says.

Yet Natasha went on to tell all his friends he was the father, even asking some of them for money to help support the child. Because Mark had been adopted and had 'come from an unknown background', he says he would never abandon a child.

'I didn't want to have a kid out there that's supposedly mine and not know. I actually think she believes the things she concocts. She's deluded.'

Following the certificate and after her son's birth, Mark recalls Natasha contacted him and asked him to do a DNA test, to which he agreed. He says he had his saliva tested at a lab in western Sydney but, after that, he never heard from Natasha again. 'It all disappeared after that.'

Whether the DNA results came back positive or negative, Natasha met Colin online when her son was just six weeks old. Colin would go on to raise him as his own.

Sometime after their separation, the Australian Federal Police contacted Mark about some documents, in which Natasha had listed him as the father of her son and forged his signature to give her authority to take her son overseas.

He says she used a lot of aliases, but often used Darcy, her biological father's name.

Mark confirms she grew up in a household with her stepfather Jack; her biological father was a man named Les Darcy.

He'd actually met Les once, when he and Natasha had stopped in at his property at Gundagai – a quintessential Australian country town, known for its historical monument Dog on the Tuckerbox – on a drive from Melbourne to Sydney.

Mark was staying at a hotel in Melbourne when his son rang him in 2017 to break the news of Natasha's arrest.

'He said, "Have you seen what the crazy bitch has done?" I wasn't shocked. I found it quite bizarre, the whole Colin thing and everything that eventuated, and thought that it had been weird. When this happened, I thought she had successfully killed the same guy, Colin. I hadn't connected the dots.'

Towards the end of our two-hour phone call, Mark encourages me to try and contact Chris, believing he will have a similar story to tell. After we hang up, Mark seems to reflect some more about his time with Natasha, summing his thoughts up in a text:

I certainly can confirm she was clearly heading down a rocky road during the short period we were in a relationship. Very little of what she said was at all real and she definitely had her own narrative that was far from what was factual or even close to reality. I, like others are probably very happy that we avoided harm and are alive to tell the story.

Trying to get in touch with Chris proves to be a lot more difficult. From a quick Facebook search, he lives interstate and appears to be happily married, if the photos of him and his wife are anything to go by. His Facebook profile doesn't allow me to send him a direct message, so I end up writing a long-winded message to his wife's account, explaining who I am and how I'd recently covered Natasha's NSW Supreme Court trial in Sydney. I explain there is a large period of her life – prior to 2009 – that I am largely in the dark about, and ask him if he would be willing to help me fill in some gaps.

I feel Chris is in a unique position to explain what life had been like with her – whether she had misled him and whether he'd seen any signs of what was to come.

A couple of days after making contact, his wife replies politely, saying Chris would like to know a bit more about the court case and passes on his email address.

I send him several links to articles I've written about the case and explain I learned about their relationship through court documents and interviews with friends.

Natasha told many people different things about him and their marriage, which I doubted were true. So I wanted to get his perspective and figure out if there was any truth to anything she said.

The following day, I get a text from Chris, asking me to contact him concerning any information I wish to publish about him regarding Natasha. When I ring back, Chris is driving on a long-haul trip for work; the hum of the truck makes it hard to hear.

He's direct and clear about his position. He believes Natasha has finally got what she deserves, but they have a daughter together and he doesn't want to cause her any grief by speaking ill of her mother.

He also gets on well with Colin and doesn't want to jeopardise their relationship. He takes his hat off to Colin for being the primary carer of Natasha's three children, while she spent the past decade in and out of jail.

Although hesitant to talk to me, Chris is willing to speak to clarify a few things Natasha said about their relationship. He's also eager to confirm he is the biological father of their daughter.

Chris says he met Natasha in his late 20s, after a chance encounter at his next-door neighbour's house. She was friends with the family and was over for breakfast when he popped in.

'When she first latched on to me, people said to me, "She wouldn't shut up about you." But she moves on to the next, she's never satisfied,' he says.

When they met, Natasha was living in a granny flat at the back of her parents' family home in Freemans Reach.

He understands she was raised in a happy household by her mother Maureen and stepfather Jack, a Mormon bishop. Natasha's father, Les Darcy, supposedly fought in the Vietnam war, but left her mother and two older sisters shortly after Natasha was born.

When Natasha met Chris, she claimed she had recently escaped an abusive marriage to a man named 'DJ', who worked for the military police up in Queensland. This was actually the dog handler she'd met at the Richmond RAAF base.

Natasha told Chris she was seeing a psychiatrist to work through her unresolved issues stemming from her relationship with DJ. She described him as 'super-possessive' and had allowed his mates to have sex with her against her wishes.

Chris says things had started well. Natasha seemed enthusiastic about their relationship and was keen to get married. Not long after they met, they were married at a chapel in Kurrajong, on the lower slopes of the Blue Mountains. From records I'd searched earlier, she'd lived in a house at Windsor from at least 2003. Chris confirms this was the home they had bought and renovated. Natasha was desperate to start a family.

'She had been desperate to have a baby and it wasn't happening, and I remember her stepdad saying, "Maybe it was for a reason."'

Chris said they never did IVF, and their daughter was conceived naturally.

'I've had two other kids since then, too.'

He clarifies their relationship was a sexual one, despite what she'd told others.

'That's the theme – she accused Mathew of being a homosexual, too. She would go for something she wanted but, once she had it, she didn't want it anymore.'

Natasha told several people that Chris's family were big names in the funeral industry but, in fact, Chris had been the manager of eight cemeteries.

Chris discovered Natasha was having an affair with Mark after accidentally discovering a series of emails when he was using her Provet laptop for work.

'It was like, once she got hold of you, she didn't want you anymore. When you're in, you don't see it. My family saw it and everything about her – like falling off a chair in surprise, so everyone would look at her.'

Natasha told Chris that Mark was the father of their daughter, but a DNA test proved otherwise. As he explains how Natasha tried to cut him out of his daughter's life when she was about six months old, I can hear the distress in Chris's voice.

'She tried to get me to walk away. She said, "She's not your daughter," before showing him what looked to be a falsified DNA test.

'Her whole thing was for me to disappear, to get me out of her life. I could never understand why she had such hatred towards me. He [Mark] takes off and she still maintains contact.'

Chris fought tooth and nail through the family law court to maintain visitation rights. It was draining and expensive, and things turned ugly.

He said Natasha applied to take out apprehended violence orders, which always seemed to coincide with their court dates. One weekend, when he was away with six mates (witnesses to where he was), Natasha told police he'd broken into her home and hung a noose over his daughter's cot.

'They [the police] would drop the case every time.'

He fought hard to maintain a relationship with his daughter, but didn't have enough money to keep fighting Natasha. The fight also put a strain on his relationship with his new wife – to whom he remains happily married to this day.

Chris has continued to pay child support, even when he wasn't required to after Natasha was jailed for the offences against Fred in 2015. 'I've always paid it, paid it all along.' He explains that he still sent Colin money while Natasha was in custody.

His daughter is never far from his mind. During the years, he didn't want to 'push it', but reached out to let her know she always had another home or place to go if ever she needed to get away.

'I tried, but there is only so much you can do with the court system,' he says, referring to his efforts to maintain contact.

'The only regret I have is not having a relationship with [my daughter]. I always hoped when [she] grew up, she would contact me and that's what happened in the end.'

PART FIVE

JUSTICE

43

NATASHA'S STORY

Four months after the jury's guilty verdict, Natasha has continued to deny any involvement in Mathew's murder, making it impossible for anyone to understand what motivated her to kill for money.

While awaiting her sentence, however, she gave a rare insight into her upbringing and what she thought of herself, during lengthy interviews with two forensic psychiatrists. Natasha told them her story but, as one of them pointed out, her account must be taken 'with a long grain of salt'.

As always, there were clear lies. She repeatedly refused to admit guilt to Dr Richard Furst and Dr Susan Pulman, who both interviewed her separately while she was in custody at Dillwynia Correctional Centre at Windsor – not far from where she grew up.

Natasha's defence team asked the psychiatrists to determine whether she was suffering from any mental illness, disorder or condition at the time she murdered Mathew.

But as Dr Furst pointed out, 'There are always difficulties in making a definitive psychiatric diagnosis retrospectively in individuals who are prone to dishonesty, as is the case for Ms Darcy.'

Before coming to their final diagnoses, each psychiatrist studied a mountain of documents outlining Natasha's criminal past, as well as her medical history, witness statements and her interviews with police following Mathew's death.

They also listened to Natasha, now aged 46, as she explained her life story, including her past relationships, and everything she said that led to where she is now.

Natasha, the youngest of three full-blooded sisters, said she grew up in a blended family after her father Les, a Vietnam veteran, left her mother Maureen when she was young. Her biological father 'was never really in our lives' and she considered the man who her mother remarried as her 'dad'. Jack, an electrician by trade, she said, was a bishop in the local Mormon church. During her very religious upbringing, she had the 'fear of God instilled' in her:

'It scares me. I had the fear of God put into me. I used to cry when I went to church. He ended up becoming the Bishop, I'm very proud of my stepfather. We had to pray at every meal and make sure we were covered up.'

Natasha said she continued to have a relationship with her mother but was largely estranged from her siblings. She described her childhood as being loving, happy, uneventful, strict and religious, but claimed she was bullied at home and at school, where she was picked on and called 'Scarface'. This nickname evolved, she claimed, after she had been kicked in the face by a horse, which resulted in her undergoing plastic surgery. The account of her scar aligns with the accounts of some who know her, but is at odds with the tale she once told about falling off a horse after being chased by 'guys on dirt bikes' at a skate park. It also contradicts the story she'd told Colin about being scarred when she was gang raped by three brothers who reeked of bourbon, in a western Sydney park.

On the subject of education, she reported being a 'fairly average student', who played netball, was involved in Girl Guides, liked dancing and loved animals, preferring to spend her time with horses and stray dogs she'd rescued. School was a lonely place for her.

'I never had any friends at school, I was always different. I had so much trouble. I was always bullied at school. I never had a best friend but would always be the one to try and help. I would take on any new girls under my wing,' she told Dr Pulman.

'We lived on an acreage. I just loved the animals, and I would just come out and say random things. People say I say strange things. Mum always said I was different. She used to say, "Try to be like other people."'

In one of her interviews with Dr Furst, she claimed to have suffered anxiety from childhood and reported a fear of her mother, sisters and animals dying, which caused her to cry at night. 'She also recalls crying "for days" after another child fell off the monkey bars at preschool and broke their arm.'

Her anxiety continued through to high school. She said she was 'good at science and biology', but was 'really bad at maths and chemistry'. She did poorly in her HSC exams, scoring a Tertiary Education Rank of only 19.6, 'despite being more capable/intelligent than that score would indicate', Dr Furst notes.

'Everyone expected me to do really well but I only got a low score. They [the teachers] actually went to the examiner because they couldn't work out what had happened,' she said.

Following her graduation from school, Natasha gave her account of five serious relationships with men, three of which resulted in marriage. The men she spoke about included 'DJ', her first husband; Chris, her second husband and father of her daughter; Mark, who she claims is the father of her second child; Colin, her third husband and father of her third child; and lastly, Mathew, her de facto, who helped care for her three children.

'People fall in love with me but then get sick of me,' she said, a victim as always.

Natasha said she married her first husband 'DJ' in 1996 when she was 21, under pressure from her family.

'After being together for six months we became engaged,' Natasha explained, adding, 'I'm very indecisive, they tried to marry me off, I was under a bit of pressure.'

After meeting DJ when he worked at the Royal Australian Air Force base in Richmond, they later moved to Queensland, after he asked for a transfer to the Amberley base near Ipswich. Similarly to what her second husband Chris had told me, Natasha told the psychiatrists she was sexually assaulted by two of DJ's friends after six months of marriage. She claimed he allowed it to happen, however, there is no independent evidence to verify this claim and Natasha is a known liar.

'I couldn't understand how he could do that,' she said, before elaborating on how she attended Ipswich hospital but never underwent an examination, pressed charges or spoke about the apparent assault with any counsellors.

As a direct result of the sexual assault, she told Dr Furst, she attempted suicide in 1997 by taking an overdose but, again, never saw a doctor or went to hospital. While it's difficult to confirm whether Natasha was raped, many victims of sexual assault do not seek the help they need for many different and valid reasons.

After her parents rescued her from Queensland, she said, she later confided in her GP in Sydney about the attack, leading her to be diagnosed with anxiety and post-traumatic stress disorder (PTSD).

'She said she then had nightmares, intrusive memories and flashbacks of being raped by the two men, trauma-related symptoms that lasted for several years, which is a pattern consistent with previous post-traumatic stress disorder,' Dr Furst wrote in his report.

A couple of years later, she met Chris, who lived in the same area. She described him as 'quiet, shy and I learned that he was very depressed'.

When she spoke about their relationship, she failed to mention anything about him being homosexual, as she had done with her colleagues at Provet. Contrary to her telling friends she was having an affair while married to Chris, she told psychiatrists that he 'left me for his secretary' shortly after their daughter was born. There is nothing to suggest this is true.

Following their separation in 2003, she met Mark, who was also going through a divorce. After receiving $180,000 from her divorce settlement, she claimed she loaned the full amount to Mark, to help him start a new business. She said he then 'took off with another woman [overseas] with my money and I never saw it again.'

Again, there is no evidence to suggest this is true. Mark moved overseas five years after their relationship ended, saying 'it is a complete lie and just a further fabrication.'

Natasha maintained – as she always had since her pregnancy – that Mark is the father of her second child, a son born in 2005. In her version, however, he left her midway through the pregnancy and never had anything to do with her son.

Following her heartbreak with Mark, she decided to get back on the horse again, meeting her third husband Colin online, a man 14 years her senior. Colin, she claimed, is the father of her third child.

'I was probably looking for a father figure,' she said, describing Colin as 'very good with the kids' before adding, 'I fall in love very quickly.'

Back in 2012, Natasha had told another psychiatrist, Dr Stephen Allnutt, that her marriage with Colin was 'great' and they had no financial issues to speak of. Despite claiming that their relationship was on steady ground, she conceded to having a sexual relationship with a local horse trainer, and had dreamed of buying the property next door to his.

Natasha had no criminal history prior to turning 34, when she attacked Colin with a hammer and torched their home after drugging him with prescription medication. It was an extreme turning point in her life and, from there, she spiralled.

'Her conduct towards her husband Colin Crossman and her motivations for those actions are relevant in relation to understanding her current offending actions against Mathew Dunbar,' Dr Furst found.

Natasha's account of her relationship with Mathew was largely similar to what she'd told police during her interviews and others she'd spoken to following his death: it was loving, non-sexual and she tried her hardest to prevent his suicide. She vehemently denied having anything to do with his death.

'Ms Darcy maintained Mathew had killed himself and said that she "should have done more to get him help", continuing to deny that she was ultimately responsible for his death/murder,' Dr Furst reported.

Similarly, Dr Pulman noted, 'Ms Darcy was unwilling to accept this verdict [of murder] and maintains she had no involvement in her partner's death. Therefore her motivation for having committed the offence could not be explored.'

During her interviews, Natasha alluded to an array of disorders or illnesses she thought she may have, then outlined other apparent diagnoses she'd received in the past.

Aside from suffering anxiety for most of her life, she claimed her mother 'has obsessive compulsive disorder' while her 'Aunt Flo' had bipolar disorder. Her GP also apparently thought she could be on the autism spectrum. Following her alleged sexual assault in her early 20s, she described having panic attacks and anxiety, was hyper-vigilant about people being behind her, and was often unable to sleep due to worry. She reported suffering nightmares; feeling anxious about going to the shops; and experiencing dizziness, sweatiness and shaking for periods of up to 15 minutes, consistent with a diagnosis of PTSD.

Natasha appeared to be fixated with having PTSD, harping on about it repeatedly during her interviews with police after Mathew's murder. One of the first things Natasha ever told me, as we stood on opposite sides of the farmgate at Pandora, was that she had been diagnosed with PTSD and suffered from flashbacks, after claiming she found Mathew dead following his suicide.

Natasha's lies made it hard for any psychiatrist to diagnose her properly but, following her attack on Colin, Dr Allnutt concluded in 2012 that Natasha had 'some significant underlying psychological and personality issues that needed to be explored with her' and suggested that her psychological makeup was unstable.

A decade later, Dr Furst said that the fact she went on to kill Mathew 'suggests the suspicions of Dr Allnutt in that respect were well founded'.

Dr Furst found she had no major mental illness, mood disorders, or any symptoms of psychosis or cognitive impairment, including schizophrenia or bipolar. She appeared to be a person with average intelligence and spoke logically throughout their interview.

'The main symptoms that she described to me relate to anxiety, a tendency to rely on others to make decisions for her and stress,' he said, concluding:

'Overall, and having regard to her pattern of offending dating back to 2009, Ms Darcy meets criteria for the diagnosis of a personality disorder as her primary psychological and psychiatric problem, with clear tendencies towards dishonesty and manipulation of other people, particularly those close to her but also authorities investigating her offences, past and recent.'

He went on to state that the prognosis of people with personality disorders was not 'encouraging' because these were 'entrenched and enduring' conditions.

Because of her tendency to target intimate partners, he found her risk of reoffending would only relate to people she formed relationships with, not the wider community.

'Ms Darcy will likely have many years ahead of her to reflect on her offending and will hopefully come to provide a more honest version of her murderous actions. In the event that she continues to deny her offending and denies responsibility for killing Mathew Dunbar, the prospects of her being successfully rehabilitated would be much more limited.'

In reaching her conclusion, Dr Pulman concentrated heavily on Natasha's history with men.

'Ms Darcy has a history of unstable relationships most likely characterised by conflict due [to] her traits of a dependent personality structure. She relies on others to care for her emotionally, psychologically and financially. Ms Darcy has a preoccupation with being abandoned and left to fend for herself,' she wrote, adding that Natasha harboured a strong urge to seek a new relationship for support as soon as her previous one had ended.

People like Natasha, she said, with 'dependent personality structures', have trouble with making everyday decisions, avoid personal responsibility, demonstrate helplessness when a relationship ends and can be oversensitive to criticism.

Dr Pulman considered Natasha's admission of being terrible with managing money and having spent large portions of her life unemployed. She often depended on her partners financially.

'Her dependency has acted as a distorting influence in her interactions with others with her being desperate to persuade partners into taking care of her which at times may have left partners feeling overwhelmed,' Dr Pulman wrote.

'When feeling potential abandonment or loss of a partner, she may appear helpless and act irrationally in an attempt to persuade partners to take care of her,' she said.

I wonder whether Mathew had ever threatened to leave Natasha, like when he'd mentioned this to Sally Heazlett at Walcha hospital, which caused her to act 'irrationally'. Or whether Natasha had felt any sense of abandonment when Mathew told her she needed to rein in her spending or he'd cut her off financially.

In the end, Dr Pulman found Natasha had 'a complex personality structure together with a generalised anxiety disorder . . . It is likely however that her complex personality structure and history of unstable relationships contributed to her dysfunctional behaviour around the time of Mr Dunbar's death.'

At Natasha's sentencing hearing in October 2021, the trial judge, Justice Julia Lonergan, finds that the reports of the forensic psychiatrists did little to assist Natasha. A sentence hearing is where the prosecution and defence put forth arguments and present evidence about what sentence an offender should receive. The defence had arranged for Natasha to be assessed in jail, but Justice Lonergan points out the difficulty of any psychiatrist being able to diagnose her 'when they really don't know what they can believe'. She also questions whether rehabilitation will ever be an option for Natasha, when she refuses to accept what she's done on any level and shows no remorse.

During the hearing in Sydney's NSW Supreme Court, Crown prosecutor Brett Hatfield argues that Natasha should be given a life sentence.

'Her culpability is so extreme, because of the degree of planning and persistence, the calculated and cold-blooded nature of the killing, the callous disregard for the deceased, and the purely financial motive is such that the community interest in retribution, punishment, community protection and deterrence can only be met through the imposition of a life sentence.'

Defence barrister Janet Manuell concedes there was no doubt her client will receive a lengthy sentence but that, during the many years Natasha will likely spend in jail, she will have the opportunity to seek treatment and change. She also highlights that, in the only other two cases in NSW in which women had killed their partners for financial gain and continued to deny guilt, they had not been given life sentences.

'She will be a completely different person by the time of her release,' Manuell tells the court.

The maximum sentence for murder is life imprisonment with a standard non-parole period of 20 years.

Did Natasha's offending warrant a life sentence? It is up to Justice Lonergan to decide, and it will take her another four months to make up her mind.

44

SENTENCE

It is February 2022 and the small group who brought down Natasha chat quietly in a semi-circle outside the NSW Supreme Court's towering Law Courts building in the heart of Sydney's CBD. They are minutes away from learning Natasha's fate, eight months after the jury's guilty verdict. Detective Senior Constables Graham Goodwin and Craig Dunn were never going to miss it; the five-hour drive from Tamworth is a small price to pay to see this case through to the end. It's been 13 years since they first crossed paths with Natasha and, together, charged her with Colin's attempted murder.

They stand with Crown prosecutor Brett Hatfield and solicitor Hugh Buddin, talking about what is about to happen and the fact that Natasha has refused to come in person to her own sentencing. 'It's a bit like missing your own wedding,' quips one of them.

The question on everyone's lips: will she get life?

After checking in with the court's QR code, and showing proof of vaccinations at the security checkpoint, the group file into the lift, catching it up to Courtroom 11D. Due to COVID-19 restrictions, no media are allowed in the court, so I make my way to the courtroom bunker on the ground floor, the place where I made my first calls about the suspicious death of a farmer at Walcha and the potential

358

involvement of his widow more than four years ago. Here, I'll watch Natasha's sentencing on my laptop, having been granted access to watch online, along with more than 25 other people, including many from Walcha.

Natasha is also absent from the courtroom, having requested to learn her fate from Dillwynia Correctional Centre. She pops up on a video screen a few minutes before the proceedings begin, her long hair pinned half-up. Wearing a dark green T-shirt and trackpants, her face is vacant as she stares at the screen. The court officer asks her to confirm she is Natasha Darcy.

'Yes,' she says quietly, nodding.

At 10.17 am, Justice Julia Lonergan strides into the room in her red judicial robes. A few seconds after sitting down, she begins to speak. It will be about an hour before the court hears her final decision. First, she will read her sentencing remarks.

'Natasha Darcy met Mathew John Dunbar in 2014,' Justice Lonergan begins, reading from her typed judgement in her hands.

'A kind man, generous to a fault, he wanted to share his love and good fortune with a partner whom he could provide for, care for and cherish. He wanted that person to be Natasha Darcy. He provided a home for her and her three children, money for what they needed, generous gifts and his attention, his time, his love and support,' she says, glancing up occasionally from her notes.

While the jury handed down a guilty verdict, it's the role of the trial judge to decide the facts of the case, established by the evidence presented. While Justice Lonergan outlines the entire case – starting from Natasha's Google searches three months before the murder – there are two key facts she finds have been proven beyond reasonable doubt. They are what the Crown described as 'two dry runs' in the lead-up to Mathew's death and prove Natasha's 'ugly' persistence and planning of his murder.

Justice Lonergan finds that a week after Mathew's suicide threat in June 2017, Natasha drugged him, possibly with sertraline, Mathew's antidepressants and/or with clonidine. She reached this conclusion based on several facts, first noting that, while Mathew was still in hospital, Natasha had googled:

- antidepressant types
- sertraline
- sertraline overdose

Adding weight to the fact that Natasha had given Mathew an overdose was the evidence of the police, who came to Pandora to check on his welfare, following his admission to Banksia.

'Police observed Mathew to be extremely pale, unsteady on his feet, and very dry around his mouth. He was unable to speak intelligibly, slurring his words. The evidence of Mr Farrar, pharmacologist, was that this presentation was consistent with a clonidine or sertraline overdose.'

In reaching her conclusion, Justice Lonergan was also assisted by the evidence of a text message Natasha had sent Colin Crossman, stating:

'I think that Mat took his whole month of antidepressants, that's why he's so sick. Will it do permanent damage? Don't tell anyone. I don't want to have him committed again.'

Colin replied, 'I don't know. Ring the doctor' before Natasha texted back: 'Ok, I'll call Banksia.' However, she didn't call Banksia or seek any medical help.

'I accept that the offender drugged Mathew sometime between his return home (after he had attended the vet and the pharmacy in Walcha on the afternoon of June 20) and when the police visited Pandora on the afternoon of June 21.'

Justice Lonergan also found beyond reasonable doubt that Natasha had poisoned Mathew with ram sedatives, causing the leg injury that caused him so much anguish in the final days of his life. Natasha had also used this injury to lay a false trail, telling anyone she could that Mathew was deeply depressed and suicidal because of the troubles he was having with his leg.

'I have concluded that the offender, without Mathew's knowledge, sedated him and injected acepromazine into his calf. When he regained consciousness, over a day later, the offender told Mathew that he had "passed out whilst out on a walk". This history was repeated to the doctors who investigated and treated him. Mathew's calf was swollen and infected. I am satisfied that an injection of acepromazine was administered by the offender into Mathew's calf and caused Mathew's calf condition.'

The judge doesn't say one way or another if she found the overdose and poisoning were two attempts to kill Mathew, or 'dry runs', but said the actions showed the level of planning and persistence Natasha had in the lead-up to the murder she later carried out.

As she nears the end of her judgement, Justice Lonergan finds Mathew's death was 'a murder of high objective seriousness' aggravated by the fact that Natasha:

1) drugged Mathew with Seroquel, acepromazine, temazepam and clonidine (a medication prescribed to her son)
2) killed him in his own home, a place where he should be safe
3) committed the crime while on parole for perverting the course of justice
4) murdered Mathew motivated by greed and to gain a financial benefit, having manipulated him into changing his will
5) took Mathew's life after 'a very high degree of planning for well over three months'.

'Searches conducted by the offender on her iPhone from April 2017 to the night of the murder indicate [a] perseverant focus on ways to kill. As time passed, the searches became centred around drugs, concepts and ideas that could be manipulated into the appearance of suicide. Emotional abuse and sneaky physical attacks escalated into a more focused and fool-proof method to achieve the outcome she desired. The offender was callous, relentless and heartless in her pursuit to get rid of Mathew who stood between her and the valuable, almost entirely unencumbered property, "Pandora". Greed was her motive. Deception, lies and manipulation were glibly applied before and after she killed him. Her lies and methods were stupid, clumsy and ugly but were sadly successful in achieving Mathew's death. They were not, however, good enough to evade detection,' she says, raising her eyebrows ever so slightly as she glances in Natasha's direction.

Moments before voicing Natasha's ultimate punishment, Justice Lonergan looks up from her notes to acknowledge the deep loss felt by Mathew's mother Janet and the people of Walcha, who had all described him as a generous and kind soul.

'That was a common theme from his friends and others who gave evidence at the trial. His loss is a significant one to the Walcha community where he was well liked, respected and admired. I convey the Court's sincere condolences to his mother and his many friends,' she says.

The court hears that Natasha has shown 'nothing remotely resembling remorse or contrition' and that her chances of ever rehabilitating were 'guarded' given her underlying personality disorder but, most significantly, because she refuses to accept the verdict or acknowledge she killed Mathew.

'It is difficult to predict how, when and if that situation will change.'

Despite all this, however, Justice Lonergan tells the court she is not persuaded that Natasha's level of culpability was so extreme as to warrant a life sentence, and that the punishment and community's protection could be met through the imposition of a very lengthy sentence.

'Please stand up,' she asks Natasha, who scrunches her face in confusion and doesn't move. She orders her again. 'Stand up.'

Natasha clumsily stands with her hands clasped in front of her, staring blankly ahead, as Justice Lonergan reads her sentence.

'Natasha Darcy, for the offence of the murder of Mathew John Dunbar, I sentence you to a term of imprisonment of 40 years.'

Natasha is frozen. Her face doesn't move. She continues to stare vacantly, as Justice Lonergan informs her she will serve a minimum of 30 years in jail before she is eligible for parole, with her sentence dating back to the time she was arrested in November 2017.

This means she will be in her early 70s before she gets out, but could quite possibly be in her 80s if she serves her full sentence, which is possible if she continues to deny her guilt. Statistically, her life expectancy is 86 years.

Natasha maintains a trance-like state as she learns she will be eligible for release on parole on 17 November 2047.

Justice Lonergan stands to exit the courtroom. The video screen connection is cut dead.

EPILOGUE

The proceedings relating to Mathew's estate were halted pending the outcome of Natasha's trial but in March 2020, his property Pandora sold for $4.65 million. All of the parties who went for a slice of his estate eventually settled at mediation in the NSW Supreme Court in April 2023.

In NSW, the forfeiture rule is a legal principle which prevents someone who is criminally responsible for the death of another from inheriting or obtaining any benefit from their victim's death. This means that as it stands, Natasha cannot benefit from Mathew's will.

However, at mediation, it was agreed that $500,000 from Mathew's estate would be set aside for Natasha pending any successful appeal against her conviction. While she flagged her intention to appeal shortly after she was sentenced, the period of time for her to do so expired in March 2023. At the time of publication she was yet to lodge an appeal.

The forfeiture rule may also extend to the children of a perpetrator; however, it is a grey area of the law. In his final will, Mathew named Natasha's children as beneficiaries in the event of her death. His desire for Natasha or her children to inherit his estate was so strong, he asked his solicitor to attach a note to the will which states,

'Mathew instructed me that he would like his estate to be given to Natasha, then her daughter and then to Natasha's two other children.'

It is understood $1 million was awarded to Natasha's three children following mediation and if she loses any appeal, the money set aside for her will go to them.

The remainder of Mathew's estate was divided between family and The Armidale School (TAS), which Mathew named as a beneficiary in the will he made before meeting Natasha.

'I express the wish that if possible, the School use the funds to establish or assist in the establishment or operation of a school farm to assist students of the school in their agricultural studies,' Mathew said.

In 2019 TAS established the Mathew Dunbar Memorial Award recognising an outstanding Army cadet.

ACKNOWLEDGEMENTS

It's impossible to express the gratitude I have for Mathew's friends and family, who shared memories of happier times, filled in many gaps and helped me understand who he was. I'm sorry he was taken from you.

A warm thanks to Lance Partridge, for trusting me from the beginning and for not mincing words. Everything you said was true. Trish, I'll never forget your hospitality and appreciate you staying in touch and letting me devour your divine caramel slices and pavlova. Thank you to Di and Bill Heazlett, for inviting me into your home and sharing stories about your time with Mathew. Your gut feelings were right all along.

To Ross King, thank you for not booting me off your property and inviting me in for tea. Your insight was invaluable.

We met later down the track, but I'm glad we did. Thanks for everything, Fred.

To Mandy, thank you for trusting me with your story. You are a brave woman.

I will always appreciate the warmth and kindness of those who knew Mathew and those who helped me along the way including Belinder Wauch, Chloe Hoy, Mark Doran and Dave Lucietto.

Thank you to Janet Dunbar, for sharing your memories of Mathew's childhood. I'm sorry for the pain you continue to endure.

A sincere thank you to everyone from Walcha, for your insights, information, stories and trust. I haven't thanked you all personally because I think you'd prefer it that way.

Cheers to photographer Nathan Edwards, for accompanying me on a few wild days in Walcha.

I can't express enough gratitude to the police who helped bring Natasha down and investigated her prior crimes, especially Detective Senior Constable Graham Goodwin, Detective Senior Constable Craig Dunn and Sergeant Anthony Smith. Thank you so much for speaking to me, fact checking and providing me with invaluable background. Thank you to Ainslie Blackstone and Michelle Minehan, too, for your help since day dot.

Well done and a big thank you to the prosecution team – Crown prosecutor Brett Hatfield, Andrew Baker and Hugh Buddin – for fighting a good fight, helping to clarify my notes and for the entertaining chats in the court breaks.

To Elaine and John Schell, thank you for your company throughout the trial and for the thoughtful travel coffee mug.

A third of this book would never have seen the light of day if it weren't for the efforts of legend Tim Henderson at the NSW District Court registry, who helped me to locate all Natasha's court files. You went above and beyond, and I appreciate you photocopying a tree's worth of material for me. Thank you to Angus Huntsdale, for looking up matters for me when it wasn't your job anymore, and to Sonya Zadel, Geraldine Nordfelt and Suzie Smith in the NSW Supreme Court media team, for dealing with my hundreds of requests for exhibits, questions, and too many emotional and exasperated phone calls.

Thanks to my fun agent Fiona Inglis, for your energy and guidance in pitching this book, your constructive criticism on the first chapter and for locking in my first book deal.

Thank you to Simon & Schuster's publisher Emma Nolan, for taking the book on, as well as editor Bronwyn O'Reilly and inhouse editor Rosie McDonald, for taking my panicked phone calls and getting it all together. A big thanks to Jess Cox, for making the final edit a fun and easy process. It's a breeze to work with like-minded people.

I couldn't have written this book without the support of Channel Nine. Thank you to Darren Wick and Simon Hobbs, for giving me the time, and to Fiona Dear, Mathew Woolfrey, Ollie Clarke, Scott Pritchard and Ben Lynch for doing the story justice on the telly. I especially appreciate all the chiefs of staff, for your patience and listening to me rabbit on about this case the past three years.

To all my friends and fellow journos who listened to the tale a thousand times over and somehow still feigned interest until the end – especially my close friend and crime buddy Ava for advice and being the one to hear my screams and frustrations. Tiffy and Matty, thanks for your support and always asking me how it was going.

Luke, I love you and feel lucky to have you in my corner. Thank you for listening to every update, enduring every tantrum and toasting every success, and for all the knocks on the study door to tell me you were proud.

To my beautiful and selfless Mum – thank you for somehow keeping me alive until my mid-thirties, so I could write a book. And for believing this was a book before I'd written the first article. And for annoying me to keep a diary.

Thank you to the great influences in my life, my Nanna and Da, hopefully you'll read this wherever you are, and to Lily, for being my sister.

My last and biggest thank you to my sister Tess, who brought the case to my attention and kept bugging me about it when I didn't believe it could be true. I still can't.

ABOUT THE AUTHOR

Emma Partridge is an award-winning journalist who has covered crime in Australia for more than a decade. After working for regional and local newspapers across NSW, in 2013 she joined *The Sydney Morning Herald*. In 2017, she became chief court reporter for *The Daily Telegraph*, where she covered court cases and crime investigations. It was here she first reported on the death of farmer Mathew Dunbar, publishing the front-page article, 'The grazier and the widow of Walcha', on 17 November 2017.

Emma moved from print to television journalism in 2019, taking the role of senior crime editor for Nine News Sydney, where she works today.

She lives in Sydney with her partner Luke. This is her first book.